Eh, Paesan!
Being Italian in Toronto

Shouts of 'Forza Italia!' rang out along St Clair Avenue West each time Italy won a game in World Cup 1994. But is a soccer tournament all that almost a half-million Toronto Italians have in common? What does it mean to be Italian in Toronto? In this book Nicholas DeMaria Harney invites us to explore with him the symbols and sites of Italian culture in Canada's largest city. Ethnic identity, we discover, is a process – it is constantly being remade and reproduced. Do Canadians look beyond the stereotypes that picture Italians as peasant construction workers, members of organized crime, and soccer fanatics to see the diversity of Italian life in Toronto? Second-generation Italian Canadians, exposed to Italy's fashion, sports, and design worlds, have new images to confront. In today's global economy, ideas and products arrive rapidly from Italy, targeted at people of Italian heritage and nourishing *Italianità*, spaces of Italian cultural life.

While the familiar greeting 'Eh, paesan!' is commonly used by young Italian Canadians, Harney leaves no doubt that their Italianness and that of their parents is rooted in Toronto.

NICHOLAS DEMARIA HARNEY is a recent graduate of the doctoral program in anthropology at the University of Toronto. He is currently a lecturer at the University of Toronto at Scarborough.

ANTHROPOLOGICAL HORIZONS
Editor: Michael Lambek, University of Toronto

This series, begun in 1991, focuses on theoretically informed ethnographic works addressing issues of mind and body, knowledge and power, equality and inequality, the individual and the collective. Interdisciplinary in its perspective, the series makes a unique contribution in several other academic disciplines: women's studies, history, philosophy, psychology, political science, and sociology.

Published to date:

1 *The Varieties of Sensory Experience: A Sourcebook in the Anthropology of the Senses.* Edited by David Howes
2 *Arctic Homeland: Kinship, Community, and Development in Northwest Greenland.* Mark Nuttall
3 *Knowledge and Practice in Mayotte: Local Discourses of Islam, Sorcery, and Spirit Possession.* Michael Lambek
4 *Deathly Waters and Hungry Mountains: Agrarian Ritual and Class Formation in an Andean Town.* Peter Gose
5 *Paradise: Class, Commuters, and Ethnicity in Rural Ontario.* Stanley R. Barrett
6 *The Cultural World in Beowulf.* John M. Hill
7 *Making It Their Own: Severn Ojibwe Communicative Practices.* Lisa Valentine
8 *Merchants and Shopkeepers: A Historical Anthropology of an Irish Market Town, 1200–1986.* Philip Gulliver and Marilyn Silverman
9 *Tournaments of Value: Sociability and Hierarchy in a Yemeni Town.* Ann Meneley
10 *Mal'uocchiu: Ambiguity, Evil Eye, and the Language of Distress.* Sam Migliore
11 *Between History and Histories: The Making of Silences and Commemorations.* Edited by Gerald Sider and Gavin Smith
12 *Eh, Paesan! Being Italian in Toronto.* Nicholas DeMaria Harney

Eh, Paesan!

Being Italian in Toronto

Nicholas DeMaria Harney

UNIVERSITY OF TORONTO PRESS
Toronto Buffalo London

© University of Toronto Press Incorporated 1998
Toronto   Buffalo   London
Printed in Canada

ISBN 0-8020-4259-7 (cloth)
ISBN 0-8020-8099-5 (paper)

Printed on acid-free paper

Canadian Cataloguing in Publication Data

Harney, Nicholas DeMaria, 1966–
    Eh, paesan! : being Italian in Toronto

    Includes index.
    ISBN 0-8020-4259-7 (bound)   ISBN 0-8020-8099-5 (pbk.)

    1. Italian Canadians – Ontario – Toronto.*   2. Italian Canadians –
    Ontario – Toronto – Ethnic identity.   3. Italians – Ontario –
    Toronto.   I. Title.

    FC3097.9.I8H37 1998   305.85′010713541   C97-932540-4
    F1059.5.T689I84 1998

University of Toronto Press acknowledges the financial assistance to its publishing program of the Canada Council for the Arts and the Ontario Arts Council.

Contents

Preface vii

Acknowledgments xi

1 Entering the Field: Ethnicity, Space, and Transnationalism   3
2 Italy, Migration, and Settlement in Canada   12
3 Gifts and Ethnicity   39
4 The Piazza of Corporate Unity   52
5 Remembering the Apennines and Building the Centres: Italian Regionalism in Canada   80
6 Culture, Calcio, and Centro Scuola: Italian-Canadian Collective Pedagogy   102
7 Locals in a Global Village   124
8 The Journey of the Saints and Madonnas   143
9 Italianità for the Canadian-Born   157
   Afterword   174

Appendix   177

Notes   181

Glossary   187

References   191

Index   203

Preface

This is the study of ethnicity, community, and transnationalism, based on fieldwork among people of Italian heritage in Toronto between 1992 and 1995. I had been interested in how ethnicity manifested itself in a city. I wanted to do urban fieldwork, but not in its most traditional form – the neighbourhood study in which everyone living in one particular area becomes part of a research project. That approach did not seem appropriate to the way I saw people actively assembling ideas of community. To understand how an imagined community of Italians manifests itself in Toronto, I felt the need to stretch beyond the traditional territorial field of neighbourhood life and its daily face-to-face interactions and to understand what other forms of community neighbourhoods existed in the city. For this reason I chose several different forms of associations and institutions as nodal points from which to develop contacts that would allow me to radiate out to more complex networks of people.

A second issue I wanted to understand was the relationship between the transnational movement of people, ideas, products, videotapes, technology, and letters, and the creation of ethnic identity and ethnic community. Although studies in transnationalism have been in vogue for the last several years, Toronto's ambience, its streets, shops, and schools, have shown signs of this dimension since the massive post-1950 migration to Canada of hundreds of thousands of people from many parts of the world. In a city as heavily polyethnic and immigrant-based as Toronto, one could sense Bhabha's (1990) notion of the nation-space being expanded as a result of the plurality of identities and communities present in civic and commercial discourse. For example, Sunday morning ethnocultural television programs consist of hours of local community events coupled with news from the homeland or other diaspora targets. The abundance of cultural events, consumer goods, and foods in local markets also indicates that a plethora of different tastes is transforming the way 'Canadianness' is being constructed.

My fieldwork was conducted predominantly in the greater Toronto area. Although I did intermittent work in the fall of 1992, the main portion of the research formally began in February 1993 and continued until the spring of 1995. I am still in contact with many informants who have become friends, and I continue to frequent the social spaces of Italianness in the city today.

My familiarity at the outset with several key informants at Italian-Canadian institutions made it easier to participate, observe, and gradually expand my network of contacts through repeated encounters at events and in restaurants, homes, and clubhouses. At times I faced the classic research dilemma of having ambiguous status within the community under study, and was concerned that my anthropological affiliation was unclear; most knew I was not a journalist, and ultimately I was most often assumed to be writing a contemporary history of the community. Several witty informants helped include me in a community that prides itself on its practical work experience, by explaining to friends that I was doing a PhD: a degree in Plumbing, heating, and Drainage. Furthermore, my muted Italian heritage – I have ancestors who emigrated from Italy before the turn of the century – helped relieve awkward moments when new acquaintances were uncertain where to place me. By the end of the research, informants from four different Italian regions placed some kinship claim on me. I have used the actual names of prominent public figures; others, who requested anonymity, have been given pseudonyms to protect their privacy.

Urban anthropology requires a fair amount of perseverance in order to develop both networks of informants and opportunities for field observation. The limitations placed upon the researcher by the busy city schedules of informants, the infrequency of contact with them, and the spatial complexity of research sites require flexibility concerning when and where fieldwork is pursued. I conducted extensive field observations at activities organized by several Italian heritage associations and institutions, whether they were held at banquet halls and parks or in home basements. These research sites were rich sources of ideas, questions, and ever-widening networks of people. Gradually, instead of merely appearing 'on site' unannounced, I received invitations to all manner of communal meetings and gatherings. To supplement the informal conversations at ethnocultural centres and community events and in casual settings, I conducted more than 100 formal interviews, for example, with community activists, politicians, priests, school teachers, labourers, waiters, business people, and cultural activists. An open-ended interview technique lessened the often intrusive and formal nature of such questioning, and elicited more detailed and complex responses than too strictly followed, structured sessions could have done. This method also permitted me to follow interesting issues raised during the course of each interview. I also conducted archival work in Italian-Canadian community collections and at the Multicultural History Society of Ontario and the Ontario Archives.

Finally, I travelled the migration links back to Italy to uncover the transnational networks facilitating the 'imagining of Italian-ness' in Toronto. For eight months, during the winters of 1993 and 1994 and in March and April of 1995, I followed these transnational linkages from the Italian peninsula, and in Abruzzo and Calabria pursued the Italian sources of activities I had observed in Toronto. Interviews in Italy included government officials in Abruzzo, Calabria, and Campania, and people with ties to Canada via informal, commercial, and familial networks. I also had the opportunity to travel with several Italian-Canadian youth sports teams as they experienced the cultural and social life of Italy.

I hope this book will return at least in part the many gifts of generosity, time, patience, pasta, and *espressi* so many people offered during the course of my research. I can never completely return all they have given.

Acknowledgments

Many people have provided assistance, guidance, and support during the research and writing of this book. First of all I am greatly indebted to the people I interviewed and to the many who offered helpful insights in less structured settings. I thank them all for putting up with my sometimes repetitive and intrusive questions. The patience and generosity of spirit of the people associated with Villa Charities, Centro Scuola, the *Eyetalian*, the Calabro-Canadian Confederation, Casa D'Abruzzo, the Veneto Centre, Circolo Morgeto, and the Canneto Society have been a source of great comfort. I particularly want to thank my two *compari* Palmacchio Di Iulio, whose astute ethnographic sense eased my navigation of the channels in the community and in polyethnic Toronto, and Alberto Di Giovanni, who gave me a more sophisticated appreciation of culture and *Italianità*. Eh! I also am grateful to my *paesani* Nick Bianchi, John Montesano, Teresa Tiano, and Joe Barbieri for easing the fieldwork by welcoming me so freely into their world, and for helping me with the book's title.

Peter Carstens gave me the freedom to pursue my research ideas, and then with his steady insistence and sage advice encouraged me to focus and to finish. Robert Shirley, Janice Boddy, and Michael Lambek offered perceptive comments throughout. Thanks also go to Richard Lee, Michael Levin, John Jackson, and Franca Iacovetta, and to William Callahan and Stefano, Kate, and Elizabeth Harney, who provided helpful editorial comments. George Pozzetta encouraged me at an early stage in my fieldwork when I was also struggling with the death of my father, Robert F. Harney. George's subsequent death has left more than an immense hole in Italian migration history. His good spirits and sound advice are sorely missed.

In Italy, Cesare Pitto of the University of Calabria was a wonderful friend and mentor. Sicily under the guidance of Mario Bolognari was an adventure I will never forget. Gianfausto Rosoli and Mike and June Hager made me grateful that all roads lead to Rome. *Il mio fratello maggiore*, Mario Motti, survived my tortured Italian and linked me in turn with Rodolfo Figari, Antonella Perito, and Paolo Scudellaro, who showed me *la dolce vita* in Naples on vico pazzariello. The late Lorenzo Petricone, *consultore* of Abruzzo in Toronto, generously hosted me in Montesilvano (Abruzzo) in December 1993.

My research was supported by the Social Sciences and Humanities Research Council of Canada, whose two-year doctoral fellowship allowed me to conduct fieldwork from 1993 to 1995. I also want to acknowledge the early support of the Fondazione Giovanni Agnelli of Turin, Italy, which awarded me a fellowship for beginning graduate work in Italian American Studies in 1992. The Benedykt Heydenkorn Fellowship of the Multicultural History Society of Ontario (1996–7) provided the perfect setting in which to rewrite portions of the manuscript.

Numerous people helped with various portions of this book. I am grateful to Vince Pietropaolo for allowing me to use his wonderful photographs on the cover. I would like to thank Laine Ruus and Cristina Sewerin of Data Services at Robarts Library and Marcia Ferreira of St Anthony's church in Toronto for helping tie up loose ends. Siegfried Schulte of the Department of Geography at the University of Toronto and Bennie Seliger of DCS Graphics ably prepared several of the maps. Virgil Duff, Patricia Thorvaldson, Margaret Williams, and the anonymous readers from University of Toronto Press also encouraged me throughout the preparation of the manuscript.

Finally, I wish to thank Diana Harney and Lalita Sood for their love and patience. All shortcomings in this book are mine alone.

Eh, Paesan!
Being Italian in Toronto

1. Entering the Field: Ethnicity, Space, and Transnationalism

Eh, Paesan! explores the ambiguities and tonalities of ethnicity in a North American city. More specifically it situates contemporary concerns in anthropology regarding transnationalism and diaspora communities within the lived experiences of men and women of Italian heritage in Toronto, Canada. Viewing ethnicity as a social construction, I investigate how it is constituted both within the social and physical space of this polyethnic city and within the transnational and diaspora circuits of Italian migration.[1] Italian immigrants and their children make choices within the social, political, and economic structures that shape, deny, and offer opportunities for them to create meaningful worlds.

This book, then, examines the concepts of ethnicity and ethnic community[2] in a polyethnic state and in an increasingly global system of cultural, economic, and technological exchange. To better understand the intricacies and indeterminacies of these concepts I have studied a number of Italian-Canadian voluntary associations and institutions in Toronto, concerning their role as local sites of cultural production and exchange. Through these sites I interpret the constant refashioning of 'Italianness' and examine the social construction of an ethnic community. These local foci of identity construction act as generative structures in the production of Italian-Canadian identity.[3] Ethnic identity does not emerge from a monolithic, shared culture but through a complex, diverse social field that forms a social space within which numerous interests compete and conflict for expression and distribution of meaning within the community, and articulation to the greater public culture.

People of Italian heritage constitute approximately ten per cent of greater Toronto's population. The Italian-Canadian voluntary associations and organizations that have proliferated since the arrival of large numbers of Italian immigrants in Canada in the early postwar period are sites whereby persons of Italian heritage can construct, imagine (Anderson 1983), and manage multiple identities within the boundary-expressing symbol (Cohen 1985:15) of Italianness in Toronto. In the postwar period Italian immigrants found a Canadian political culture that was engulfed in debates about national identity, regional distinctions, and linguistic tensions. This fractured political culture suited the ambiguity within the immigrant Italian identity itself. Like Canada, Italy is a fragmented nation, a state composed of varied identities, each at times internally in conflict. Multiple forms of Italian identity based on local sites of cultural production, either a single town or a cluster of towns or regions within Italy, were maintained and reconstructed in Canada. The nation-space that the discourse of multiculturalism opened in the 1970s added to the opportunities available to Italian immigrants wishing to express their multiple identities and to legitimate these sentiments through the sanction of the Canadian state. By means of its public policy and legal frameworks the state's role is critical for the definition and negotiation of pluralism (Levin 1993:172–8). This book thus examines the different social fields forged from the immigrant experience and the hegemonic interests of various states (Canadian and Italian), both local and national, that seek to stir national or ethnoregional imaginings and sentiment in the immigrant and ethnic settlement in Canada.

The class distinctions within 'Toronto Italia' reveal the complicated temporal and spatial realities of migration and generational change. Old-world status and class positions can change in the face of new opportunities available in Canada for social/class mobility. For example, someone with Italian- and English-language skills and specific knowledge can become an ethnic broker offering services to immigrants unfamiliar with Canada's formal systems. Professionals, semi-professionals, notaries, lawyers, travel agents, and coethnic civil servants can act as intermediaries between immigrants and government bureaucracies, answer legal questions, assist with unemployment forms, handle the paperwork required to secure Italian pensions for work done before migrants left Italy, or help resolve other issues back in the home town.

The vast majority of Italian Canadians arrived here as semi-skilled or unskilled workers and peasants, and entered factory work and the construction trades. Some became wealthy as developers and contractors building Toronto's infrastructure and outlying bedroom communities. Many, raised with the peasant preoccupation for economic security for family, bought homes and land. This attachment to land served them well as the postwar economy in Toronto boomed, increasing the value of both homes and lands. The children of these immigrants, raised and educated in a consumer society, now combine the values of their parents with the tastes and consumption patterns of North America. Although the primary category of social differentiation explored here is ethnicity, class differences are embedded in the ethnography throughout.

Understanding ethnicity as a key category of social life and action has become central to social studies in the last thirty years. Generally, two positions are contrasted: that of primordialists and that of circumstantialists. The first position takes as its starting point the subjective, affective assertions of identity (Geertz 1963; Isaacs 1975). In contrast, circumstantialists view ethnicity as a device manipulated by actors to achieve political and economic interests reflecting changes in circumstance and opportunity (Despres 1967; Cohen 1969; Levin 1995). Neither approach is sufficient on its own, because the former overemphasizes the emotional and personal aspects of ethnicity and the latter gives too little weight to experience and the ambiguities of culture. Recent work has argued for viewing ethnicity as a social construction (Conzen et al. 1990; Bentley 1987; Eriksen 1991). Bentley employs Bourdieu's (1977) concept of habitus to suggest how ethnicity and ethnic identity operate within structured patterns of experience that can be comprehended and altered by social action. Anderson's definition of the imagined nation also looks at the construction of a community. In his view a nation is an 'imagined political community' whose members 'will never know most of their fellow members, meet them, or even hear of them, yet in the minds of each lives the image of their communion' (1983:15). This perspective suggests a way of understanding the endurance and vigour of national identity and feeling. Ethnic communities are different, but Anderson's position can be usefully applied to them.

Ethnicity, then, needs to be seen as process. Ethnic groups are constantly being remade and reproduced (Keyes 1976; Werbner 1990; Eriksen 1993). An important feature of this reproduction and construction of ethnicity today is the increased intensity of transnational networks and the globalization of culture. Air travel, electronic media, telephones, video and audio cassettes, multiple citizenships, and a mobile employment market serve to enhance connections and diminish distances between people in the same diaspora (Appadurai 1990, 1996; Hannerz 1989, 1992). The time-space compression that Harvey (1989:240) argues occurs in this postmodern epoch of capitalism manifests itself in the cultural practices of Italians in Toronto. In an accelerated fashion Italian immigrants and their children can interact with and expend emotional energy on ties with their 'homeland' in every sphere of social life they choose, from following the Juventus and Milan teams in Italian professional soccer, to watching RAI TV personalities, to buying Armani, Gucci, and Hugo Boss.

Despite living overseas, as a diasporic community Italians in Toronto maintain a sense of belonging and loyalty to their natal or ancestral homeland. This is true for reasons of language, religion, kinship, work, and commerce, as well as of cultural practices and expectations. Even if the degree of affinity Italian Canadians feel for Italy varies in time and according to conditions, the diaspora survives if individuals imagine a common migration experience and a feeling of coethnicity with others of Italian heritage (Cohen 1997:ix). This diasporic identity is bolstered by the changes in world capitalism mentioned earlier – a transnationalism that includes the movement of labour, capital, consumer items, and information across nation-state borders. Consumption is a central

component of transnationalism, especially in industrial economies. In the summer of 1997 at the Canadian National Exhibition,
the exhibit 'Welcome Italia' peddled products from many of Italy's
regions, testifying to the commercial and marketing possibilities
Italian national and regional governments see for Italian businesses in a city such as Toronto.

However, transnational connections are even more varied. They
also include the personal travels of Italian Canadians to visit kin
or to explore Italy with Italian-Canadian tour groups, sports
teams, and student exchange programs sponsored by ethnic voluntary organizations. Some hard-working Italian Canadians who
laboured, for example, in construction in Canada for thirty years,
invest in land and build new homes in their village of birth. This
investment is made with the intention either to return perma-
nently upon retirement, or to return intermittently as seasonal
labour if the Canadian construction and building trades demand
it, or depending upon the needs of children and grandchildren
who have remained in Italy. To understand transnationalism we
also need to consider how different governments insert themselves
outside their territorial boundaries to influence and sustain
diasporic communities.

The children of Italian immigrants juggle the many worlds of
Italianità: the new consumer and marketing realities of modern
Italy, the different generational and cultural gender expectations,
their parents home-town–centred loyalties and cultural traditions,
and the pressures arising from the spatial transformation of urban
ethnic neighbourhoods to suburban settlements. The movement
of Italian olive oil, pasta, ceramics, fashion, services, technology,
and entertainment crosses national boundaries to create contradictions, confluences, and new meanings for people as they con-
sume items that take on ethnocultural, symbolic significance.
Italianness, therefore, is continually remade and reinterpreted as a
result of the movement of migrants, media images, and cultural
objects.

It is not only kinship, economic, and political ties that construct
the ethnic community, but also the images of the country of emigration that influence transnational projects (Gold 1984) and the

development of a diaspora community. Italy's booming fashion industry, successful soccer team, and talented intellectuals influence the imaginings of Italians here in Toronto. Anderson's (1983) concept of an 'imagined community' features human agency as integral to the construction of community. He argues that Gellner's suggestion that people fabricate or invent nations (Gellner 1964:169; 1983) is too cynical, and discounts the imaginative and creative quality of nationalism. 'Communities are to be distinguished, not by their falsity/genuineness, but by the style in which they are imagined' (Anderson 1983:15). This notion of imagining corresponds well with the new spatial realities of transnational ethnic communities. It permits us to see how people who have emigrated from the same village to different migration targets around the globe can see themselves as part of one community.

Space is central to the construction of identity and culture in the postcolonial world (Gupta and Ferguson 1992). The presence, in polyethnic states, of diverse immigrant communities that maintain ties across state borders requires that we rethink the connections between how spatial arrangements influence the imagining of complex forms of identity and culture. Italian immigrants in Toronto reterritorialize their Italian identity by creating associations and institutions within the city's topography. This remapping of identity onto new spaces is integrated into the global imagining of Italianness by those in the transnational networks. Reterritorialized communities actively create sites for the elaboration of cultural practices. By doing so they force the anthropologist to observe the socio-spatial arrangements of the urban environment.

As an anthropologist I recorded, in the form of fieldnotes, both my movements across the spaces of Toronto Italia and my experiences with Italians there. All were written at or near the time of an event observed or an interview conducted. The following fieldnote illustrates several themes that run throughout this book.

Fieldnote, 20 February 1993
It is a cold winter evening and I am parked in a driveway in Downsview, a suburb in the northwest part of Toronto. Tony is active in the organiza-

tion of an Italian regional association and his name keeps surfacing in conversations and in the press. I have been told that regional governments in Italy are trying to encourage a strong sense of identity in order to encourage people who have emigrated to invest in their home towns. This is our second arranged meeting following many missed phone calls. We have scheduled a meeting for 7:30 p.m. but his place looks deserted. The lights are out except for the outdoor lamp above the double-car garage that illuminates the interlocked brick driveway. I knock once, then again. Receiving no response I decide to wait until 8:30, thinking we must have gotten our times confused. It is several months into my fieldwork and I am seriously considering renting a cellular phone. A car has been indispensable for meeting informants and for travelling to homes, clubs, and events. This night it is even more important because it is sheltering me from the frigid February winds.

A few cars edge towards the house but ultimately turn into other driveways. Maybe I should interview these people instead? I look for signs of Italianità at neighbouring houses: a metal grape arbour barren in the cold, awaiting the spring vine; a metal square patch of the *tricolore* (Italian flag) on the back of a car. I could just knock on one of these doors and say, 'Hi, I am an anthropologist interested in Italians in Toronto. Can I ask you a few questions?' I also dream of being offered a hot espresso and some almond *biscotti* (cookies), or better yet, some homemade wine and aged cheese.

Gusting winds force me to face reality. My informant is not coming. It is now 9 p.m. and I cannot decide what to do. I think about heading home. Instead I go to a local bakery for an espresso, where I pick up the most recent issue of the *Corriere Canadese*. Then I head home. I hear the next day that Tony was at a meeting (with other community activists whom I've also interviewed) to plan an ethnoregional centre. I am frustrated that I did not hear about it. Just last night I was speaking to him about regional clubs. I guess he forgot to tell me.

The fieldnote suggests the importance of the relationship between ethnicity and space, both locally and globally. Ethnic communities need to be both imagined and creatively constructed in city spaces. City life permits little of the everyday, repetitive, face-to-face interpersonal encounters found in small-town or village life. Actors need to claim civic space, to create new *piazze* (neighbourhoods, town squares, street corners), to express ethnic solidarities, and to create a sense of community. In many ways an urban ethnographer's struggle to explore the construction of communities in cities is akin to attempts by the actors themselves to find creative ways to maintain and develop networks in the fragmented structure of city life.

The fieldnote also hints at the existence of multiple layers of ethnic identity in Canada. Italian immigrants and their children must navigate the hegemonic goals of various states, in Italy and Canada, that wish to mould and shape their loyalties and sense of peoplehood. Diaspora circuits and transnational networks are constituted in locally specific circumstances. The circulation of people in a system of global capitalism has stretched the borders of homelands in the imaginations of those who travel the chain migration networks to different destinations around the world. States, subnational state structures, and commercial interests seek to harness these dispersed people by rousing sentiments about belonging that surface in immigrant communities out of memory and nostalgia for place. In Canada these global processes become domesticated and are intertwined with experiences of civic pluralism. Ethnic brokers and leadership located at the interstices of transnational networks mediate this process of domestication and manipulate international linkages.

Within this context I explore the complex intersection of local, national, and transnational dimensions by examining key institutions within Toronto's Italian settlement. Specifically, Chapter 2 looks at the historical context of Italian migration and the general contours of the Italian settlement in the greater Toronto area. Chapter 3 examines the role of gift-giving in the construction of community solidarity and the competition between community members for status and prestige. Chapters 4 through 9 each select an institution or association within the Italian settlement in order to examine the production of multi-stranded forms of identity.

To understand the process of imagining the heterogeneity of

Italian-Canadian identity, it is necessary to discuss the historical conditions that brought several hundred thousand Italian migrants to the urban streets of Canada's largest city.

2. Italy, Migration, and Settlement in Canada

The history of emigration from southern Italy and the impoverished northern areas beyond the economic Milan-Genoa-Turin triangle reflects the economic deprivation of these regions and the movement of talent to opportunity. In the south, intensive cultivation, dry summers, mountainous topography, and poor soil produced deforestation and erosion, and prevented the use of mechanized farming techniques (Schachter 1965). Centuries of exploitation for the benefit of central and northern governments limited southern economic development (Fortunato 1911; Nitti 1958; Gramsci 1966). Semi-feudal land tenure arrangements and the constant subdivision of land to accommodate inheritances for sons and dowries for daughters produced an ever-decreasing source of income and subsistence. Industrialization in the post-unification period (after 1861) in the south emerged from three social and political conditions linked to the development of a unified Italian state (Tarrow 1967). First, the inclusion of the *Mezzogiorno* (the south) in modern Italy resulted from conquest by northern royalist troops, not from a revolutionary movement. Second, the pro-conquest southern bourgeoisie was conservative in its economic and political views as it sought power and status. In contrast, the northern bourgeoisie developed strong industrial and commercial activities and saw independence as a means of advancing economic expansion. The southern bourgeoisie was closely tied to the land and used the Risorgimento (movement to reunite Italy) to consolidate its land ownership. In the south the new Italian state sold church and public lands at low prices after unification. Speculators and bourgeoisie landowners seized the opportunity to consolidate their hold on most of the land. Third, the post-Risorgimento national government exacerbated regional disparities when it lowered internal tariffs that had protected some small southern cottage industries from more efficiently produced northern competition. A similar reduction in tariffs imposed on imports deprived the weak southern agricultural economy of protection against cheaper foreign grain. The national government also invested more in the north's commercial infrastructure.

Southern peasants rented and sharecropped land, paying exorbitant prices to absentee landlords. Although some peasants owned small plots, in most cases such parcels were located on hilly and inhospitable terrain offering a meagre return from exhausted soil. Wealthy commercial farmers and the urban bourgeoisie, who often knew little about farming, owned the most fertile valley land (MacDonald 1963–1964; Bell 1979). As a result, beginning in the 1880s poor Italians from the countryside began to emigrate, a process that continued until 1924 when laws on both sides of the Atlantic restricted labour flows. Remittances from workers in northern Europe and North and South America allowed some peasants to improve their economic situation during the early twentieth century. But because of the limited commercial infrastructure and agrarian-based economy of southern Italy, the new wealth of returned southerners was channelled into increasing their land ownership rather than innovative commercial or industrial activity.

American and Canadian immigration quota laws in 1921 and 1924, introduced because of economic difficulties and nativist hostility to immigrants, reduced immigration considerably. In Italy after 1924 Mussolini's government limited external and internal migration. In 1928 emigration was made illegal (Cannistraro and Rosoli 1979). As a result Italians remained at home, thereby increasing pressure on a weak agrarian economy. By the end of Second World War southern Italy, devastated by the Allied military campaigns, neglected in the Marshall Plan, and troubled by a high birth rate and an exhausted agrarian system, had a surplus population ready to migrate. Of course the poorest southern peasants, agricultural labourers on large commercial farms, did not migrate; those who did were those who could afford the cost of transatlantic travel: small landholders, tenant farmers, sharecroppers and artisans (Sturino 1978).

Italians emigrated primarily from agro-towns rather than from areas of isolated and scattered farmhouses. Often located in hilly country, agro-towns formed part of a peasant agricultural community in which peasants departed each morning to work in the surrounding fields. The centre of town was the piazza (town square) surrounded by a church, a café, municipal offices, small shops, and artisan workplaces. Social life revolved around the town, producing *campanilismo* (strong loyalty to one's village).

For southern peasants the household formed an economic unit wherein all family members contributed to the labour and subsistence of the family. An immense literature exists on the social relations prevailing among the southern Italian peasantry. Edward C. Banfield (1958), who coined the term *amoral familism*, argues that these relations were competitive, often in a malevolent way. Southern Italians distrusted others and acted selfishly while seeking, he said, 'to optimise the material, short-run advantage of the nuclear family.' Since Banfield's analysis other anthropologists have taken issue with this interpretation, arguing that kin cohesion and cooperation were central to obligations, rights, and work practices in southern Italian towns (Brogger 1971; Davis 1973). The work of anthropologists (Cronin 1970; Boissevain 1970) and social historians (Sturino 1990) on immigrant communities and chain migration has stressed the elasticity of kin relations and the cooperative tendencies of Italian immigrants in the migration process. This cooperative interpretation does not deny that conflict and competitiveness existed among Italian peasants and immigrants.

But instead of viewing discord as a reflection of an innate moral system, scholars opposed to Banfield interpret it in the context of sociohistorical conditions dependent on limited economic resources and exploitative elites and middle classes that compelled peasants to concentrate their energies on caring for their families. Alongside these kin dynamics there existed patron-client relationships between the farming and labouring classes on one side and the middle classes and professional elite, including government workers, on the other. Despite the resentment peasants felt towards elites, absentee landlords, and government officials, they could not alienate local dignitaries. They needed them to help navigate a complex Italian bureaucracy, since few peasants could read or write (Lopreato 1967). Peasants also nurtured local elites with gifts and praise, for they needed their services as notaries, doctors, and advocates.

A family culture of work, responsibilities, and obligations permitted, however, a measure of collective activity in the form of mutual benefit societies. By the 1870s, in response to economic transformations that disrupted agrarian society, peasants formed societies that responded to the needs of artisans and labourers and extended beyond family ideas about kinship, neighbourliness, and mutual cooperation. In Fascist Italy trade unions and peasant leagues were declared illegal. Further, Fascist organizations took control of key positions in peasant mutual-aid societies that offered farm and credit services. Voluntary associations based on collective action were also discouraged. In their place patron-client relations became more important for survival. As a result few Italian peasants formed self-help groups, during the 1920s and 1930s, and their experience with voluntary collective activity was largely limited to religious societies promoting devotion to patron saints. Southern Italian Catholicism focused on the communal ritual celebrations of local saints. In like manner, an active form of association among Toronto's Italian population in the postwar period was the celebration of the Madonna, or of local saints from the immigrants' village of origin.

The Migration to 'America' and the Early Italian Settlements

Italians have migrated to America *en masse* since the turn of the century. Since the days of Giovanni Caboto's voyage in 1497, they journeyed to America as individuals in the service of foreign monarchs (English, French, or Spanish). Whatever the century of migration, Italians arrived on the shores and frontiers of Canada as individuals of talent seeking opportunity, whether as musicians, language teachers, itinerant artisans, or labourers. Many early migrants were cosmopolitan or European in outlook. To speak of them strictly as Italians in sentiment fails to do justice to the historical reality of their times.

The history of significant Italian migration began about twenty years after the formation of the Italian State in 1861 (Foerster 1919; Ramirez 1989; Harney 1989). After this period, until the massive migration of the 1950s and 1960s, men and women who migrated based their identity on their *paese* (home town) of origin, or their province or region. Economic changes in mid-nineteenth-century Europe forced many peasants to seek opportunities in the industrializing cities of Europe and North America.

Since Elizabethan times the English-speaking world has created stereotypes about Italians that have influenced the way Italian Canadians today have constructed their ideas of Italianness in North American society (R.F. Harney 1985). An early generation of educated artisans and teachers from Italy confirmed a first opinion of Italians as artistic geniuses. Italy was a land of high culture, opera, sculpture and art, of medieval and Renaissance glories. A second image developed when English-speaking people saw the workers arrive who were to provide labour in factories and work gangs. These Italians were perceived as backward peasants who were clannish, Roman Catholic (in Protestant Ontario), superstitious people with a propensity for crime. As the stereotype went, Italians could be emotional, dangerous, and quick to pull a knife or steal your woman.[1]

Between 1876 and 1915 more than seven million Italians immigrated to the Americas. The United States received the largest share – more than four million arrivals – Argentina less than two million, and Brazil about one million. A smaller but significant migration pattern affected Canada (Favero and Tassello 1978). Italian migrants choosing Canada may have had brothers or cousins who sought work in target areas in northern industrial Italian cities such as Turin, Milan, and Genoa, as well as in parts of northern and western Europe. Despite the Canadian government's preference for immigrants from northern Europe to settle and farm the prairies, Italians laboured throughout the country in back-breaking seasonal work. Recruitment programs established by major Canadian companies such as the Canadian Pacific Railway, the Canadian National Railway, and the Dominion Coal Company used *padroni* (labour agents) to engage workers virtually as chattel for railway construction, clearing brush in Canada's hinterland, or other forms of manual labour.

Between 1901 and 1911 almost two million Italians arrived in the United States, while only 60,000 came to Canada. Italian migrants saw the boundary between the two countries as irrelevant. Many may have crossed into Canada following work opportunities and kinship chains. They were going to *fare l'America* (journey to America) in order to make a better life for themselves and their families. During these first years migration chains were established that would continue throughout the next century, pausing only when world political and economic crises occurred. Franc Sturino (1990) has studied, for example, the kinship networks of people from the Rende area in Calabria, which provided information about work and housing. These networks also created an *ambiente* (ambience) and sense of community in a foreign land. He established that these ties in fact stretched throughout North America. Similarly, John Zucchi (1988) stressed the importance of paese networks in early Toronto for immigrants from several towns in Puglia and Basilicata.

At first male seasonal workers predominated in these settlements, returning to the cities after clearing brush, setting rails, mining in northern Ontario, or labouring on the farms of the Niagara peninsula. Gradually, as Toronto and other cities needed labour to build an urban infrastructure of sewers and trolley lines, the Italian population grew and became more permanent. By 1910 former sojourners were settlers working as stonemasons, tailors, bricklayers, and cobblers, and during this early period Toronto contained several neighbourhoods known as 'Little Italies.' The most important were, first, the area around College and Grace Streets, second, Davenport Avenue and Dufferin Street, and third, an area known as the Ward in the downtown, bounded to the south by Queen Street (see Map 2.1), where today Toronto's city hall and

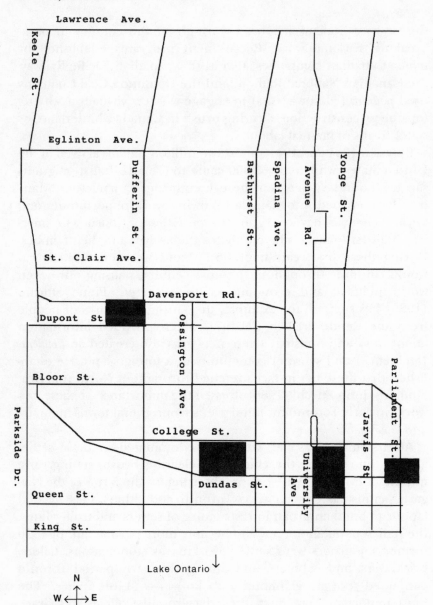

Map 2.1: Concentration of Italians in Toronto, 1890–1940
(Source: Sturino 1990:169)

the hospitals on University Avenue are located. Although the term *Little Italy* was often intended to demean Italians, it also indicated a more permanent presence in the city. During these years, as manufacturing expanded around Toronto, Italians secured jobs in foundries and the new automobile factories. Commercial opportunities also increased for small tradesmen. Enterprising Sicilian immigrants from Termini used their peasant agricultural skills, knowledge of fruits and vegetables, and access to produce shipped by railway to establish a niche as food wholesalers and retailers. As these sojourners became more settled they sent for wives from Italy. By 1921 the female population in Toronto was only slightly less than that of the male.

Since the first appearance of a small Italian settlement in Toronto before the turn of the century, immigrants from the same home towns, provinces, or regions felt the need to associate with kin, both real and fictive, to ease the burdens of life in a new, foreign, and often hostile English-speaking environment. Pre–First World War mutual-aid societies and voluntary associations promoted a sense of an immigrant and ethnic collectivity. Organizations such as Umberto Primo, Vittorio Emanuele, and Operaia Ontario (in 1919 these combined into the Società di Mutuo Soccorso Italo-Canadese), and Famee Furlane attempted to ease the stress of immigrant life through a variety of services. They provided illness and death benefits, social and cultural activities, language classes, and information concerning jobs. Many societies, although pan-Italian in name, possessed memberships based on paesi linkages and networks of mutual support (R.F. Harney 1981). By the 1930s the Italian population of Toronto numbered no more than 20,000 individuals, from a number of different Italian regions: Calabria, Sicily, Basilicata, Abruzzo, Molise, Puglia, Lazio, and Friuli.

During the 1920s and 1930s immigration restrictions and regulations, encouraged by racialist and xenophobic notions in Canadian public opinion and politics, limited Southern European, hence Italian, immigration. At the same time Fascist government policy in Italy viewed the continuing, large-scale emigration as a national embarrassment. In 1924 and 1929 the Italian authorities enacted laws to impede Italian emigration. These legal changes and the effects of the Depression halted Italian immigration to Canada until after the Second World War.

Between 1920 and 1938 the Italian-Canadian community established a number of associations and mutual benefit societies: Circolo Colombo, Società Italo-Canadese, lodges of the Sons of Italy (Scardellato 1995), and the Comitato Intersociale, an umbrella group of Italian organizations in Toronto. Aggressive Fascist intervention by the consular authorities produced new clubs after 1927. With the aid of an active and intrusive Fascist vice-consul, Italian-language teaching and communal activities flourished (Zucchi 1988; Pennacchio 1993). The British and Canadian press, governments, and much of public opinion at first looked favourably upon Mussolini's regime. While some members of Canada's Italian population opposed the Mussolini regime, others joined in patriotic events, clubs, and associations because it appeared that Mussolini might bring stability and prosperity to Italy, as well as international recognition and respect.

But Mussolini's aggression in Ethiopia in 1935 and other bellicose actions turned public opinion in Britain, Canada, and the United States against him. Italian Canadians also discovered that loyalty to two nations left them in an uncomfortable position when war developed. In fact Canadian authorities rounded up many prominent leaders and sent them to internment camps, while others were forced to register with local police. As a result the tense war years encouraged many Italian Canadians to muffle cultural expression and become more Anglicized as a means of reducing the hostility shown them by other Canadians and the government. Many changed their last names. Associations and clubs closed if they were receiving support, funds, school books, and symbolic imagery from Italian consular officials. Finally, removal of the Enemy Alien Act in 1947 allowed Italians to migrate to Canada once again.[2]

Post-1945 Migration from Italy

Following the war, circumstances converged to reopen the Italian migration flow to Canada. Italy was devastated by war and it faced

political instability. Communist party popularity also worried
Allied governments. Possessed of a young population needing
work and with limited economic prospects at home, Italy, or more
precisely the ruling Christian Democrats, needed to allow many to
emigrate. After 1945, when Canada's heavy industry, construction,
and manufacturing sectors required labour, Canadian authorities
continued the traditional ethnic preference for northern European immigrants to meet the country's demands. But it soon
became evident that southern Europeans were more likely to wish
to immigrate to Canada. As a result old chain migration networks
to Canada reopened while new ones began. To emphasize the relevance of chain migration for Italians coming to Canada, between
1946 and 1967 nearly 90 per cent of all Italian arrivals were sponsored by Canadian family members. This high percentage underscores the importance of kin networks for securing assistance with
employment and housing, as well as with social activities. During
many of these years arriving dependents formed nearly 50 per cent
of the total, numbers that suggest a far more permanent migration
than at the turn of the century. Immigrants from the northern
regions of Friuli and Veneto arrived first, in the late 1940s; by 1949
southern Italians began to enter the country.

According to official statistics, between 1951 and 1961, Canada's
Italian population increased fourfold, from 150,000 to 450,000.
Older Italian settlements were quickly overwhelmed by the new
arrivals. Throughout the 1950s more than 20,000 Italian immigrants entered Canada annually. After a brief drop to around
14,000 at the beginning of the 1960s, because of recession in Canada, emigration from Italy reached a peak of more than 31,000 in
1966. These numbers began to drop sharply by the early 1970s (see
Appendix, Table 1). Between 1946 and 1983 it is estimated that
between 433,159 and 507,057 Italians came to Canada. The lower
number arises from Italian sources, which according to Jansen
(1987) tend to underestimate the number of emigrants. The
higher number is from Statistics Canada.

Of these emigrants almost 70 per cent came from the south, 12
per cent from central Italy, and 18 per cent from the north. Heavy
migration occurred from several specific areas: the provinces of

Cosenza and Catanzaro in Calabria, L'Aquila in Abruzzo, Campobasso in Molise, and smaller but significant numbers from Sicily, Lazio, Puglia, Veneto, and Friuli (see Map 2.2). In 1981 46 per cent of the Italian-Canadian population was foreign-born, of which 99 per cent were born in Europe. To underscore the relative newness of this immigration cohort as compared with the United States, one can note the median year of Italian immigration. Of officially counted Italian immigrants arriving in the United States over the last century (1876–1983) one-half immigrated before 1910; for Canada the year was 1955.

Canada is primarily an urban country. Sixty-one per cent of the population lives in cities of over 100,000 inhabitants (Artibise 1988:237). Following this pattern, as shown in Table 2 (see Appendix), Italian immigrants chose to settle in urban centres. Seventy-four per cent of Italians in Canada now reside in urban centres of more than 500,000 people. Before the postwar influx of new immigrants, Montreal was the Canadian city with the highest number of Italian Canadians, nearly twice the figure for Toronto in pre–Second World War days. Not until the mass migration of the 1950s and 1960s did Toronto become the dominant city for Canada's Italian-Canadian population. As shown in Table 3 (see Appendix) almost 40 per cent of Italian Canadians of single and multiple origin now live in the greater Toronto area; a significant majority of that number are of single Italian ancestry.

In 1971 56 per cent of Italians in Canada had received less than a ninth-grade education; only 5 per cent had studied in secondary school. By 1981 these proportions changed to 38 per cent and 25 per cent respectively. Of Italians between the ages of 15 and 24, more than 56 per cent were still in school; the Canadian-born children of Italian immigrants neared the Canadian average in university education. Moreover, the rate of increase in education levels accelerated more rapidly than in the Canadian population as a whole (Sturino 1985; Jansen 1988,1991). While more than 70 per cent of Italian immigrants arrived with less than a ninth-grade education, in the last twenty years the children of this migration cohort who had been educated in Canada showed considerable movement towards attaining or surpassing national educational

Map 2.2: Italy's regions as sources of migration
(Adapted from Jansen 1987: 9–10)

levels. This dynamic emphasizes the value immigrant parents have placed on education for their children. It also indicates conditions that could lead to conflict and misunderstanding between the migration cohort and their children because of linguistic, cultural, and aspirational differences.

Between 1962 and 1977 Canadian immigration statistics show that on average 76 per cent of Italian immigrants intended to enter low-status manual jobs upon entry to Canada (see Appendix, Table 4). In contrast, European immigrants from Greece and Portugal indicated percentages of 58 per cent and 54 per cent, respectively; for Indian and Chinese immigrants the proportion was 33 per cent or lower.

Liviana Calzavara's study (1982:251–67) of the relevance and use of social networks by five different ethnic groups in Metropolitan Toronto underscored the centrality of intra-ethnic group contacts for Italians in finding employment. Even when their network of interpersonal contacts was not ethnically homogeneous, Calzavara found that Italians relied heavily on kin and coethnics to find employment. The author speculated in her sample that this exten-sive use of kin and coethnics by Italians could be a result of the high degree of group segregation (59 per cent) in specific occupa-tions, the presence of many kin because of sponsorship in migra-tion, and low geographic dispersion of the group.

According to Jansen (1991), for male Italians of different census categories (single-origin, multiple-origin, and Canadian-educated)[3] construction was the number one occupation, followed by machining/assembly/repair. In Toronto the top category of occupation for the entire male workforce was managerial/adminis-trative. For single-origin Italian males, construction predominated. Canadian-educated Italian males and multiple-origin Italian males tended to have a higher percentage of work in clerical and sales positions than did single-origin Italians. Italian females in the Tor-onto labour force worked in predominantly clerical and service positions. Forty-two per cent (41.9) of Canadian-educated Italian females were employed in clerical positions, almost 10 per cent more than for the total Canadian female workforce. Single-origin

Italian females took as their second occupational choice machining/assembly/repair, in contrast to the total female labour force, multiple-origin, and Canadian-educated Italian females who worked in service positions. As Jansen (ibid., 159–79) has argued, these statistics reveal that in spite of the low-entry-level positions of Italian immigrants, later generations of Italian Canadians improved their occupational position rapidly and soon approximated the Canadian average.

By the late 1980s in greater Toronto, several generations of Italians in Canada since the postwar boom (immigrants, their Canadian-educated children, Canadian-born children, and some grandchildren) formed a population of between 350,000 and 500,000 people (see Map 2.3). Their settlement areas followed the historic Toronto pattern of high density in the southwest near Kensington Market, Dundas, College, and Grace Streets, to the north/south feeder streets of Dufferin and Ossington, and further west to Islington. Over time Italian Canadians gradually moved north and west, changing the community's centre from College and Grace Streets in the 1950s and early 1960s, to St Clair Avenue (Corso Italia) and Dufferin Street in the late 1960s and 1970s, and to Lawrence Avenue and Dufferin Street, and Keele and Finch Streets, in the 1970s and 1980s. By 1991, the process of suburbanization could be observed among Italians in Toronto.

Early in my fieldwork I realized that without a car to follow the migration routes Italian Canadians have taken throughout greater Toronto to find new homes and establish new businesses, I would be lost. The following fieldnote describes one such foray to look for twenty-five-year-old Dominic, whom I had arranged to meet to discuss Italian regional government activities in Canada.

Fieldnote, 16 March 1993
Driving up fast-paced Highway 400, I passed the small factories and warehouses that line this major artery and offer work to many Italian Canadians. A little later in the afternoon I was supposed to meet a young man

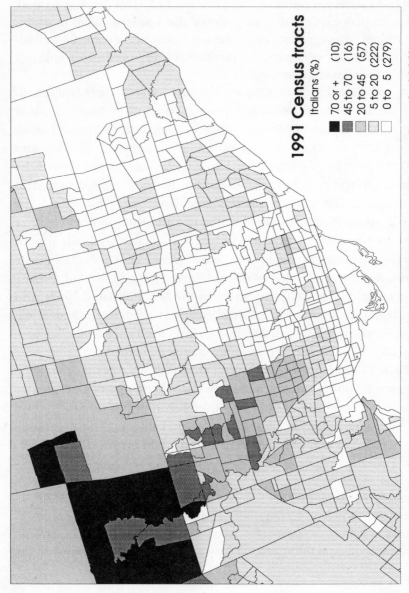

1991 Census tracts
Italians (%)

■ 70 or + (10)
▨ 45 to 70 (16)
▨ 20 to 45 (57)
□ 5 to 20 (222)
□ 0 to 5 (279)

Map 2.3: Concentration of Italians in Toronto, 1991 (Source: Census Canada 1991)

who was involved with one of the Italian regional associations. He had said there was a Nino D'Aversa Bakery up north near Kipling Avenue and Highway 7, and I had assured him I would find it. When I reached the intersection of Highways 7 and 400 I was struck by the patches of low-rise commercial developments and residential settlements in the distance, and a lone glass office tower immediately to my right. Real estate signs of companies such as Pine-West, Nardi, and Pantalone offering to lease or sell the land to build a custom business complex abounded between areas that already have low-rise manufacturing and commercial buildings. I had turned west onto Highway 7 and passed the flashy signage of Al Palladini's Pine Tree Lincoln-Mercury dealership at Weston Road.[4] As I drove these first tentative kilometres, I was struck by the walled housing tracts to the north, interspersed with the occasional business, and the low sprawling malls on the streets just to the south. The architectural style of the homes, with their marble, brick or stone patios, and stretches of wood-beamed arbours hinted at the ethnocultural make-up of the neighbourhood. The relationship between Italian immigrants and nature became a shorthand for me as I navigated settlements in the city. Backyards flush against the formed-stone walls revealed the tops of fruit trees and the weathered wood of shacks for storing equipment and tomato stakes and bean poles. I learned later that there is one practical reason, aside from the political, why many Italian-Canadian front lawns are dotted with the signs of several political parties during election campaigns: the wooden stakes are handy, sturdy, and free support for the summer's harvest.

An exciting part of fieldwork is the constant changes revealed as one wanders in various new landscapes. Gradually, I began to see more, and differently as well. The developments in and around the strip malls of Steeles Avenue and Highway 7 that once seemed barren and sterile were becoming steadily more complex, here revealing the small winery of someone I had met at the Veneto Centre; there the Tavola Calda, smelling of warm lasagna, grilled sausage, peppers, and the espresso coffee I had shared with a few informants who had now become friends. These signposts became more numerous when I discovered the many social clubs that dotted the second floors and storefronts of these commercial centres. I discovered that once you entered one of these places, so anonymous and dull from the outside, there was often a *gettone* (table soccer) table,[5] a large-screen television, a bocce court, and an espresso bar, all of

which created an internal piazza where people could hang out. Each time
I went for the requisite espresso at the Molisana or Nino D'Aversa Baker-
ies with someone I was interviewing, I noted it down, so that at some
opportune time I could relax and write up my fieldnotes between meetings or after a saint's *festa* (holiday celebration).

According to the 1991 census, in five Toronto-area census-tract
divisions, all of them north of Lawrence Avenue West, Italians comprised more than 50 per cent of the population (Census 1991).[6]
The highest concentration (79 per cent) lived in the tract
bounded by Steeles Avenue West on the north, the Humber River
on the east, and Islington Avenue on the west. Settlements had
developed as well in Mississauga and Scarborough, and large numbers had moved north of Steeles Avenue into the newer residential
developments in Vaughan, where Italians constituted 37.3 per cent
of the population. In four census-tract divisions in Woodbridge, a
former township incorporated into Vaughan, they constituted over
80 per cent of the population. If home ownership is an indication
of immigrant mobility, by 1971 Italian-Canadians were doing well,
with the highest percentage of any group owning a home, at 83 per
cent (Richmond and Kalbach 1980:404,407; Sturino 1985). By
1986 that proportion had reached 86 per cent.

Today geographic density and numerical strength enable some
immigrants to conduct their daily lives in the Italian language or in
a dialect (Tosi 1991). The proliferation of ethnic organizations
and businesses and the intensity of interpersonal contacts between
people of Italian heritage in Toronto has created the conditions
for what Breton (1964) has called 'institutional completeness.'

Many immigrants of the 1950s and 1960s are able to converse
predominantly in dialect or Italian throughout the day. They work
on construction sites or in factories with other Italians, listen to
Italian radio, watch Italian-language television, and frequent stores
and social events at which Italian is the language of interaction.
Many speak to their Canadian-born-and-raised children in dialect
or Italian, although the children tend to respond in a mix of
English, Italian, or dialect. Franca Iacovetta (1992) noted that in
the postwar period immigrant Italian women began to play a

changing role in family economies. New opportunities developed from urban economic expansion. Women found work in food processing factories, light manufacturing, and clothing companies with fellow paesani. This allowed them to live within the circumscribed world of Italianità, communicate in Italian, and avoid the usual conflict with traditional beliefs about women's roles.

The Contours of Italian-Canadian Associational Life

In 1954 the Italian-language newspaper *Corriere Canadese* noted that there were thirty-eight Italian community organizations servicing some of the estimated 50,000 Italians living in Toronto (Iacovetta 1992:142). By 1984 that number had reached 240 organizations (Ministero degli Affari Esteri 1984), and by the 1990s over 400 organizations (Buranello and Lettieri 1993). These official numbers represent only groups that affiliated with umbrella Italian-Canadian organizations or secured recognition by the Italian consular authorities. There are both omissions and some duplication in the official lists. Several types of associations and organizations provide social, cultural, political, and welfare services (see Map 2.4). Some, such as the National Congress of Italian Canadians (NCIC) or the Canadian Italian Business and Professional Association (CIPBA), seek to represent a broad segment of the Italian-Canadian population. Others recruit their membership from people with specific locally based identities constructed from experiences either in Toronto or Italy. For example, the Circolo Morgeto Social Club is composed mainly of people who emigrated from the town of San Giorgio Morgeto in Reggio Calabria. The Roding Park Social Club draws its membership from the many Italians who live near this North York park. Many of these clubs have small storefronts in strip malls in northwest Toronto or hold meetings in members' basements.

In a recent study Buranello and Lettieri (1993:150) differentiate between each of the Italian-Canadian regional associations that use geography, both Italian and Canadian, as the primary category of distinction; for example, home-town clubs, area clubs, city clubs, regional clubs, ethnic clubs, provincial federations, and regional

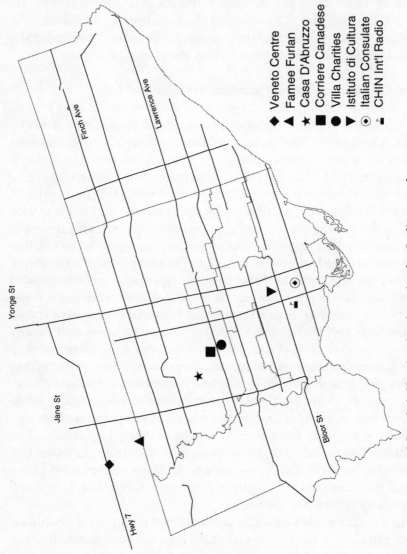

Map 2.4: Key institutions in the Italian settlement

◆	Veneto Centre
◀	Famee Furlan
★	Casa D'Abruzzo
■	Corriere Canadese
●	Villa Charities
▶	Istituto di Cultura
◉	Italian Consulate
▲■	CHIN Int'l Radio

federations. Although this classification is useful in differentiating the various associations present in Ontario, a more analytically promising direction is yielded by the classic study of Polish-American associations in Chicago by Thomas and Znaniecki (1958). These authors see three levels of associations intermeshed: (1) 'local' associations which are composed of kin, friends, and associates and are segments of a greater urban ethnocommunity, (2) 'territorial' associations which are focal points for an urban ethnocommunity such as a community centre or church, and (3) 'superterritorial,' federated associations which unite local associations from different ethnocommunities. This model enables us to see the relationship between social scale and association type, thereby offering insight into the way in which elites are able to claim to represent the interests of the hundreds of members of local clubs. Among Italian Canadians in Toronto today, all three forms of association exist.

At the superterritorial level, a national lobby group, the National Congress of Italian Canadians (NCIC), claims to represent the interests of all Italian Canadians. The NCIC attempts to assert its legitimacy through reference to its constitution as a group. If one were to view Italian-Canadian institutions in a pyramidal structure, the National Congress is nominally at the top, and it is linked with regional and local districts of the National Congress, which have as their constituents the presidents and delegates from local clubs, associations, churches, and the public. The cultural and political orientation of the National Congress is towards integration into Canadian society while at the same time encouraging the retention of Italian cultural traditions.

A sketch of the associational life of Italian Canadians must be seen also in the context of some other relevant factors. Already in the late 1970s, and later in the 1980s and 1990s, both print and electronic Italian-language media were prevalent in Toronto. In the 1970s seven Italian-language newspapers existed at various times. By the 1990s only three newspapers have appeared regularly, but the Italian-language electronic media have been strongly evident: two radio stations and several television channels, including a cable network, Telelatino, which provides direct service from the RAI Network in Italy. Furthermore, the presence of Italian-Canadian food-service stores, restaurants, travel agencies, businesses, and construction firms creates an Italian-Canadian ambience in several areas of the city.

One method of mapping the contours of the Italian-Canadian community in the postwar period is to discuss the institutions that emerged from within the Italian-Canadian settlement. Because of the prewar Fascist involvement in many clubs and associations, the institutional structures in place before the war were either disbanded or discredited. The overwhelming sheer numbers of new Italian immigrants in Canada in the postwar period, coupled with their socially different ways as distinct from the prewar Italians, were perhaps the more decisive factors that led to the indifference shown towards the older Italian institutions by the newer Italian immigrants. The war, twenty years of living under Fascism, the rise of mass political parties in Italy, and universal basic education had created immigrants who were far different from those who left Italy for Canada under the constitutional monarchy. At an early meeting of prewar and postwar community members, the difficulty of choosing a language of business – English or Italian – emphasized the difference in identity between the two migration cohorts.

The first attempt by the largely prewar Italian-Canadian leadership to rally Italians around a common cause – the return of the former Italian Consulate at the corner of Dundas and Beverley Streets (Casa D'Italia, which had been confiscated during the war by the RCMP) – reflected the interests of those who came to Canada before 1945. But the campaign was significant because it was the first attempt to create a pan-Italian sense of community, and it relieved some of the humiliation and fear that befell Italian Canadians, especially their leaders, who had been denied their rights as citizens and forced to mask their cultural heritage in Canada during the Second World War.

Several early institutions provided welfare support to Italian immigrants arriving in Toronto. The Italian Immigrant Aid Society, founded in 1952 with the assistance of the clergy and the Canadian Italian Professional and Business Association, provided shelter, information, food, interpreters, and referral services.

Centro Organizativo Scuole Tecniche Italiane (COSTI), an organization formed in 1963 by several immigrants, one of whom was an Italian immigrant priest, taught English-language classes and arranged certificate classes for Italian immigrants with skills but no 'Canadian experience.' The 1960s also saw the creation of the major construction unions, Locals 183 and 506. These were years of hard work and sacrifice. For most of the decade there was little time available for socializing except within the extended family or friendship structures. Gradually numerous clubs and associations based on Italian home towns of emigration were formed, and these clubs sponsored picnics, dances, sporting events, and little theatre.

By the 1970s efforts were under way to construct a home for the aged (see Chapter 4) and a community centre. An umbrella organization of all Italian-Canadian organizations with regional interests was established as well. Its mandate: to lobby governments on issues perceived to be relevant to the Italian community and to counteract negative stereotypes of Italian-Canadians in the press and within the broader public sector. It was first called the Federazione di Associazioni e Club Italiani (FACI) and later (1974) the National Congress of Italian Canadians. At the same time as these pan-Italian associations and institutions developed, local social clubs and sports groups were organized, and professional associations of lawyers, doctors, and journalists were founded. Labour unions with heavy Italian membership, such as residential home-construction Locals 183 and 506, created labour halls with a distinctive Italian-Canadian setting. Several women's groups were developed, including the Italian Canadian Women's Alliance and the more recent (1992) Voce Alternativa. Educational and cultural groups were formed as well, including Piccolo Teatro Italiano and Centro Canadese Scuola e Cultura Italiano.

Italian Canadians also gained access to power through the political process at municipal, provincial, and federal levels, although not in the civil service. At the local level, trustees were elected to the Metropolitan Separate School Board and Italian Canadians were elected as aldermen and alderwomen. In the early 1990s in Ontario, the largest caucus of Italian Canadians in provincial political history existed, with six members including one provincial cabinet member. At the federal level an equally large number of MPs of Italian heritage existed in the federal Liberal party. During the 1993 federal election people of Italian heritage ran for all three traditional major political parties in several ridings, in many cases against each other. In the municipal campaign in the fall of 1994 the Italian-language newspaper *Lo Specchio* announced that sixty people of Italian heritage were running for office in the greater Toronto region.

The Italian government has shown interest in the welfare, culture, and politics of the Italian-Canadian community since at least 1902, when a commissioner of emigration, Egisto Rossi (1903), conducted an inquiry into the conditions of Italian immigrants in North America for the Italian government agency Commissariato Generale dell'Emigrazione. Later, in the 1930s, active Fascist consular officers attempted to manage Italian communities overseas as colonies whose members were viewed as Italian citizens living abroad. In the post-1945 period, Italian politicians occasionally raised expectations that they would introduce legislation offering the vote in Italian parliamentary elections to Italian citizens overseas. In addition, the welfare-state agencies that developed in the 1940s and 1950s in Italy, such as FILEF, ACLI, or other *patronati* (benevolent funds) began to offer social services to citizens overseas.

The formal symbolic and diplomatic centre of the Italian government in Toronto is the Italian Consulate located in the former Casa D'Italia, the centre of the Italian-Canadian community during the 1920s and 1930s. At Dundas and Beverley Streets, it is now near the heart of one of Toronto's Chinese commercial areas. For many Italian immigrants, necessary trips to the consulate for government forms revive unpleasant memories of the tortuous Italian bureaucracy they had left behind when they emigrated. At the same time the Italian Consulate is the conduit through which over $300,000 is funnelled to teach Italian language and culture to Canadian school children. The Istituto Italiano di Cultura, a separate entity from the consulate, endeavours to bring Italian culture – artists, writers, cinema ... – abroad. Initially its mandate did not directly concern the Italian-Canadian population, but was intended to bring Italian culture to the broader Canadian public. However, recent changes in Rome have forced it to compete with other Italian-Canadian associations by catering to the Italian-Canadian community. Also at the national level, at least seven *patronati* of Italian national unions service the thousands of immigrants who still draw an Italian pension for the years of work before they emigrated. Finally, the Ministero Degli Affari Esteri has established an advisory panel of Italians abroad, whom it selects to represent Italian-Canadian interests to the Italian government concerning social, cultural, and political issues. Recently, each region (see Chapter 5) has established a similar advisory board.

The National Identity Debate

The dominant ideology in English-speaking Canada in the first half of this century was that immigrants and ethnocultural minorities should relinquish their languages and cultures and assimilate with the dominant English-speaking culture, one that was Anglo-Celtic in origin. It has become part of our national myth that previous to the mass migration of the postwar period, Canada's population was composed entirely of people of British and French descent. Of course, this perception masks the ethnocultural, class, religious, and regional distinctions within these two groups. The English, Scots, Welsh, Irish Protestants, and Irish Catholics displayed a heterogeneity with regard to associational life, residential segregation, language styles, culture, and religion. Further, Chinese railway labourers, Italian fruit vendors and navvies, Jewish garment workers, and Macedonian stockyard workers in Toronto, United Empire Loyalists of African descent in Nova Scotia and southwestern Ontario, and Finnish labourers clearing brush in northern Ontario, are just a few examples of the heterogeneity of Canada in the early years of this century. But 80 per cent of Toronto's people claimed British descent in the 1911 census. By 1941 this British-descent group within Toronto's 700,000 population still neared 80 per cent, with no non-British ethnic minority other than Jews comprising more than 5 per cent of the inhabitants.

The emergence in the 1960s of Quebec nationalist and secessionist feeling led the federal government to create the Royal Commission on Bilingualism and Biculturalism in 1963, 'to inquire into and report on the existing state of bilingualism and biculturalism in Canada and to recommend what steps should be taken to develop the Canadian Confederation on the basis of an equal partnership between the two founding races, taking into account the contribution of the other ethnic groups to the enrichment of Canada and the measures that should be taken to safeguard that contribution (1966: 151).' The 'other' ethnic groups, almost an afterthought in book four of the commission's report constituted nearly one-third of the population. What united them in the rhetoric of leaders and politicians was that they were not of French or British descent, but were composed of divergent groups who had arrived in great numbers in the post-1945 economic expansion: displaced persons from Eastern and Central Europe, immigrants from southern Europe, West Indians, Asians, and South Asians. As anyone familiar with some of the debate in the last two constitutional negotiations (Meech Lake and the Charlottetown Accord) is aware, some members of these minority groups at times felt slighted by a nation that, in the words of Prime Minister Trudeau, was 'multicultural in a bilingual framework.' To their minds the description indicated a hierarchy of rights within the Canadian Constitution that accorded privileges only to those of the two 'founding peoples': the British and the French.

I began my preliminary fieldwork among Italians in Toronto in the fall of 1992, just as the referendum campaign on the Charlottetown Accord was underway. At a rally by the Yes forces at Columbus Centre I spoke with Italian Canadians who expressed concern that people of Italian heritage felt left out of the Accord but would vote for it to save Canada. They felt that the idea of Canadian multiculturalism was not sufficiently recognized in the Accord, and that it seemed therefore that the postwar immigrants of non-British and non-French descent, and their children (known colloquially as the Third Force), were being neglected. Nevertheless, despite these concerns, during the referendum campaign the National Congress of Italian Canadians and the Federation of Canadian Italian Business Professionals Association urged Italian Canadians to vote in favour of the Accord.[7]

The formative years for Italian-Canadian institutions coincided, in the 1970s, with the height of the rhetoric and ethos about diversity of cultures by politicians, and ethnic and immigrant group leaders. This decade was also a tense period for working-age Italian Canadians, immigrants of the 1950s and 1960s who were now parents with children in schools that had little sensitivity to language and cultural diversity. Immigrant children began to face as well the language and cultural tensions with their parents that necessarily emerge in a new cultural and linguistic environment. It is since this change towards a more inclusive posture by governments concerning ethnic minorities that the associational life of Italian Canadians moved beyond social clubs, religious feasts, and picnics towards more complex social-service agencies and community-based cultural centres.

As shown in Table 5 (see Appendix), in the 1991 census people of Italian heritage in Canada topped the one million mark, with fully a third of this total claiming multiple ancestries. At the same time, Chinese surpassed Italian as the third most-common language spoken by Canadians (after English and French). More than just statistics, these two facts have symbolic significance concerning the changes facing both Italian Canadians and Canada. They also indicate potentially contradictory meanings for the Italian-Canadian leadership. On the one hand, wanting to claim unity of purpose for over one million Canadians creates the potential for greater political power; on the other hand, as Italian Canadians become further removed from the immigrant experience, the general commonalities within migrant life that might have encouraged communal solidarity are made more problematic by the differences between generations, classes, and regions.

Final Remarks

The following chapters address the efforts to construct communal solidarities and imaginings. But before we can discuss specific Italian-Canadian institutions, it is important first to explore the ties of obligation created by communal gift-giving. Gifts can secure the loyalties of friends and acquaintances. Gifts also create expectations of further exchanges. In part, these exchanges create the linkages that mark the social boundaries of imagining Italianness because they reveal who feels compelled or constrained to give, receive, and return a gift.

In the Italian-Canadian community, as in all communities, there are no free gifts. The anthropologist Mary Douglas captured the public, communal relevance of gifts when she wrote, 'Gifts are given in a context of public drama, with nothing secret about them. In being more cued to public esteem, the distribution of honour, and the sanctions of religion, the gift economy is more visible than the market. Just by being visible, the resultant distribution of goods and services is more readily subject to public scrutiny and judgements of fairness than are the results of market exchange' (1990:xiv).

The centrality of gift-giving to the construction of community is explored more fully in the next chapter.

3. Gifts and Ethnicity

To refuse to give, or the failure to invite is like refusing to accept –
the equivalent of a declaration of war; it is a refusal of friendship and
intercourse.

Marcel Mauss, *The Gift*

Early on in my fieldwork I had an ordinary experience for anyone
beginning encounters with new situations or even revisiting seemingly familiar territory with a new focus.

Fieldnote, 21 May 1993
I had been out with a friend, at a store that sold Italian ceramic dishes. I
was on friendly terms with the store owners, young people my age of
south Italian heritage, who had an exclusive import deal with a famous
ceramicist from the region of Puglia on the heel of Italy. I wanted to buy
several dishes as a gift for my mother and I had made this known to my
friend. At the store, my friend approached the proprietor about the
dishes, twelve in all, and arranged the sale below the marked price. The
exchange happened quickly, along with some conversation in Italian and
a few knowing nods. The conversation continued for another half hour,
while espresso and biscotti were served. As I paid for the dishes I noticed
the store owner hadn't charged us for the coffee, so I turned to my friend
to ask if I could pay for the espresso. Both he and the store owner
laughed and called me a *mangia-cake*, a term used to disparage non-

Italians' lack of appreciation for good food, but also, in a larger sense, their cultural practices and lack of social graces. Of course we did not need to pay for the coffee. As we walked out my friend noted my anguished look and knew immediately what was bothering me: just starting out in fieldwork, with people who appeared to appreciate generosity, I did not want to be seen as cheap. My friend said, with even more force than Mary Douglas (1990), 'Nick, remember, don't think Italians ever give you anything for free.'

I had read about the obligations and status issues surrounding gift-giving, and understood it in the abstract, but it was only when I heard my friend's words that I began to see gift exchange as central to understanding the mutually trusting relationships established within the Italian ethnic community. Later on in my fieldwork this experience let me look again at the obligations inherent in the giving, receiving, and returning at a larger communal level.

This chapter examines the role of the gift in the construction of community. It is not about the reciprocity between individuals or within families, but takes as its subject the central role gifts play in creating obligations to community and belonging among Toronto's Italians. Gift-giving is a material marker of social obligation to a community. The gift embodies social relations. A function of the exchange of gifts is to initiate an obligation for individuals or groups to interact and to sustain that social interaction. In other words, giving is both a material and a significant symbolic act. It is a way for elites to compete for claims of high status and leadership within the community. Material and monetary gifts are especially revealing of the ambiguities and tensions in a community. As Mauss (1967) contended, an aspect of gifts and gift-giving is the lack of clarity as to their meaning and interpretation for both giver and receiver. As Bailey (1971:24) points out, 'The overgenerous gift, so big that it cannot be returned, becomes a humiliation. In short, it is not that some exchanges are competitive and others are cooperative: all exchanges have the seeds of both these opposed things within them.' Interpreted either as competitive or cooperative, giving occurs in the context of mutually trusting individuals who together comprise a 'moral community.'

The Obligation to Give

In the life-cycle ceremonies of Toronto's Italian community (birth, baptism, confirmation, marriage) kin and extended kin make donations commensurate with the obligations implied by the social distance they are from the celebrant or the celebrant's family (N. Harney 1992; Sahlins 1965). Giving at these events is important for the maintenance of the good status and reputation of one's family within the community. As a host, one cannot try to save money, for example, by serving too little or poor-quality food. As a guest, one needs to offer a gift that is perceived as equal to your social distance from the host. But it is giving to a community of a larger magnitude that concerns us here. The act of giving to the community project implies a broadened notion of loyalty.

In the last twenty years Italian immigrants have expanded their social obligations beyond fellow immigrants from their Italian home towns of origin to others from the Italian peninsula. This broadening of loyalties has manifested itself in such diverse community fundraising campaigns as giving for earthquake relief in Friuli or Naples, or constructing community centres in Toronto. In the public policy initiatives of the postwar welfare state, ethnocommunities have been able to make use of patron-client networks and partnerships in government to secure state resources. Without such local community support, projects would not succeed. Ethnocultural associations assume obligations and duties on receipt of every gift. If they do not accord prestige and deference to the donor with the necessary ceremonies and/or with programs and activities, they run the risk of losing the support of their patrons and clients. Gifts of money, materials, and time help voluntary associations organize dinner-dances, cultural events, trips to Italy for children, or centre-building.

The social background of some Italian immigrants in Toronto may have much to do with the guarded way in which they contribute to Italian-Canadian communal projects. Largely from southern Italy – where both absentee landlords and corrupt bureaucratic governments encouraged primarily peasant people to construct defensive mechanisms to minimize exploitation and to protect their property, families, and well-being – Italian immigrants to Toronto have been reluctant to put their trust too securely in those who claim to have a leadership or communal purpose. Furthermore, among immigrants who arrived with little money and only the intention to build a nest-egg for themselves and their families, reluctance to give up hard-earned capital for unknown members of an imagined community persists.

In the case of gifts for communal projects such as Villa Colombo seniors' home or the more recent cultural centres planned by Italian-Canadian regional groups, donors are driven by the competition for status both within and outside the community, as well as by a moral sense of obligation to their ethnocommunity. The moral evaluation of a gift by insiders has less to do with its value in monetary terms than with how the act of giving is interpreted in relation to the donor's ability to give. A wealthy land developer or business person must contribute an appropriately large sum to match his or her economic wealth. Paradoxically, the more wealthy or powerful the giver, the greater the suspicion that self-interest is involved, interest that may not have the common good in mind.

The Obligation to Return

Mauss (1967) noted that the giving of a gift obliged the receiver to fulfil his or her part in the exchange by giving a gift in return. In this context a common practice among associations is to list the names of people and companies that have contributed, including the exact monetary worth of each gift. This of course is a crucial communal necessity, for several reasons. First, the receiver, the non-profit communal organization, must assuage the fears of contributors that funds may be unaccounted for. Second, the receiver may wish to exert moral suasion on others in the community to contribute similar amounts. Third, the giver will wish to have his or her reputation enhanced by the evidence of his name on a list accompanied by the amount he has given, signifying, much like a votive to the church, one's moral goodness. In the case of Villa Colombo and the Columbus Centre, a booklet was published with more than ten thousand names of donors. Some are listed with donations of as much as $50,000, others as little as $5. Of course donations were not limited to individuals. Businesses within the community contributed as well, in part because of a moral obligation to the community on which they relied but also because of their desire to be perceived as an integral part of that community. (A certain percentage was also tax deductible.) Those who contributed over $500 were recognized in larger print in a separate section of the booklet. This separate section demarcated the lines of status more clearly for those who wished to gauge the moral obligations of the community's wealthy.

For a business to contribute to capital costs of constructing a centre, renting a storefront for a social club, or sponsoring a festival in honour of a saint or the Madonna, the place of commerce in the exchange can have contradictory meanings. The relationship between religion and commerce is both ambiguous and sharply defined because businesses can advertise by sponsoring a community event but must not appear to be manipulating that event solely for commercial purposes. The contradictions are more precise when we speak of gifts for religious occasions, as the following example will show.

A number of immigrants, known as Ciociari because they emigrated from a mountainous area in the Ciociara region of Lazio in central Italy, have formed La Società Canneto to reconstruct a religious festival they celebrated in Lazio in honour of a representation of the Madonna. While there are several nights and mornings of prayer and Masses, the focus of the annual celebration is a one-day festival in August at the religious retreat of Marylake in Vaughan. The festival includes a procession with a statue of the Madonna, a Mass, and an immense gathering of families (almost 10,000 people) for a picnic. Each year the Madonna di Canneto committee produces a booklet that lists the six hundred or more community members who have contributed sums ranging from two dollars to one hundred dollars (the average contribution is twenty dollars) for the festival and for the upkeep of the Society's building, a small storefront in an industrial mall near Finch Avenue and Weston Road. These charitable contributions are, as Mauss wrote, gifts 'made to men in the sight of gods' (1967:12).

Photographs of the Madonna of Canneto during processions in

its town of origin, Settefrate, in the region of Lazio, are scattered throughout the booklet. Most of the pages are filled with advertisements from local businesses: metal manufacturers, real estate agents, construction and plumbing companies, butchers, physicians, and hairstylists. In one respect these are straightforward business exchanges: the sale of space in the booklet helps offset its production costs. Each contributor can also cut *una bella figura* (a good figure) in the eyes of their moral community and those of potential customers. However, failure to sponsor the event by an immigrant from that area in Italy could bring criticism and make the community disinclined to use the offending party's business.

Even as these commercial and social calculations are made by participants, the organizers of the event and La Società are explicit about their desire to limit the profane world of commercial transaction at such a sacred event. The president of the club confided that one member had been asked to leave the organization because he had been too forceful in his efforts to market his business within the circle of religious believers. Interestingly, the profane world of political activity is discouraged, too. Many political leaders attend local social-club events because of the obvious potential benefits they might accrue appearing at a community religious event. The organizers of the Madonna di Canneto festival have begun to discourage politicians from taking part unless they refrain from political activity and behave like other devotees of the Madonna.

For the organizers of ethnic projects the construction of a community of givers is paramount. In the case of Villa Colombo and Columbus Centre, apparent success has limited their ability to raise funds within the community; many look at the building complexes and activities and assume they are financially well off. Gifts must be seen to be repaid in services or in the construction of new buildings. One of the ways the ICBC/Villa Charities maintained community interest was with the staggered completion of projects over a fifteen-year period, since the mid-1970s. Each project could be interpreted as a focal point for giving by the community and then a concrete return on that gift by ICBC/Villa Charities. Yet just as taxpayers scrutinize governments, ethnocommunity members are concerned with how the money they have given is being used. Furthermore, the questions raised by community members can become personalized, and members may begin to suspect board members – often prominent elite from the real estate and construction trades – of profiting from their association with the organization. As noted earlier, because Villa Charities offers many services and has created building complexes, some have the impression that it is a source of unending capital from which to draw, and any attempt to seek more from the community is just greed.

The following brief fieldnote indicates the potential for misunderstanding and hostility inherent in a gift to communal projects:

Fieldnote, 17 October 1993
I was sitting at the Ristorante Boccaccio at the Columbus Centre with a husband and his wife, both middle-class professionals who had contributed to the fund-raising that built the Villa Colombo and the Columbus Centre. When the conversation turned to giving to community projects the man became livid. He said he did not trust community groups. He said he had given $10 in the early 1970s to buy a 'brick' to help build Villa Colombo, then in 1979 he had given $50 to buy a square foot of land for the Columbus Centre. Now he wondered if he had seen any results from his contributions. I mentioned that the Villa was built, that he was now sitting in a restaurant at the Columbus Centre, where numerous activities were being offered. But he still believed these accomplishments were not enough, that somehow money had been ill-spent.

Doubt as to the honesty of communal project organizers appears to occur in every sphere of their activity. Some Italian Canadians whose parents wanted to live at Villa Colombo accused the operators of wanting only to get control of the elderly residents' pension money. One man went so far as to threaten to leave his mother at Villa Colombo and use her monthly pension cheque for himself.

Status and Elite Gift Competition

The constitution of status gradations among immigrants is a complicated issue. Subtle differences in the size and type of landholding, specific artisan skills, or knowledge of Italy's bureaucratic system and the ability to get favours done by local and state officials may have contributed to one's prestige in the partially encapsulated world of the Italian agro-town, but these skills can become less relevant rather quickly in the new social and economic conditions of a foreign environment. While a small number of elite may be able to depend on old-country family status and education to garner prestige initially – and in fact some of these advantages may hold for a finely circumscribed subset of fellow villagers who have emigrated – such distinctions generally break down quickly. The new opportunities available to ambitious, hard-working immigrants in an urban, industrial, polyethnic city such as Toronto fracture the class and status structure of an agro-town. In other words, an immigrant's class of origin does not determine his or her class of destination. To accrue status within the new ethnocommunity, immigrant elites need to earn it. Because of the profusion of Italian Canadian voluntary associations in greater Toronto, the loci of competition are multiplied through the founding of new projects.

Donations to ethnocommunal projects occur in both egalitarian and hierarchical modes. A common egalitarian form of giving is the dinner-dance or picnic in which a set cost for the ticket ensures that all contributors give an equal amount to the cause. In the hierarchical mode, individuals can give to general fund-raising campaigns through pledges that they deem appropriate. Clever fundraisers of course arrange special dinners for those they suspect will be persuaded by 'moral' obligations and status consciousness. As events these dinners are symbolic acts, gifts in return. Invited guests are aware that they are part of a more exclusive and intimate group asked to make a contribution for some cause. Participation at such a dinner accords a person insider status for the project in need of funds. It is here that elites often compete to enhance their claims to status. The donations of these special guests can be regarded in some way as acts of *noblesse oblige*. As emblematic of their responsibility to community, the donations provide evidence of the donors' power and leadership in the community. As Blau states in Werbner (1985:373) these gifts found 'a claim to moral righteousness and superiority.'

One developer involved in fund-raising for several projects remarked that while the telethons and dinner-dances were important for the creation of wider community support for projects, a significant amount of the money was raised at these relatively small dinners, where there is a moral obligation on the part of those invited to give an amount commensurate with the status they have been accorded. Joe, a successful businessman and a member of several community boards, explained the fundraising process:

> I started off with a small nucleus of twelve people, to be exact, and I invited them to a dinner that I hosted at La Scala Restaurant [a posh Toronto restaurant since closed]. We had a nice evening there, and later I pointed out the need for an old people's home ... These were people of financial substance, people who I felt I could convince to make a contribution to this old people's home for the benefit of the Italian community ... We had a nice dinner, we talked things over very well, and I was able to convince most of them to pledge $50,000. And two of them pledged $25,000, for a total of $500,000 that night!

Once a project is completed there are new ways to acknowledge the gifts of donors that enhance their status and create further obligations upon them as community givers. One could name a wing of the building after them or place the names of larger contributors on a wall in a foyer. It is at this stage that one realizes that status seeking is not restricted to consumption within the community. For many of these elites there is a desire to be acknowledged by those outside the community as generous patrons and good citizens. As one man expressed it, 'I felt that by doing so [giving] it would be a good thing to be recognized by other people in the community, and I don't mean the Italians, and with elevating our stature and our status in the community.'

To talk about one's desire to do a lot, then not follow through with donations and gifts, can reduce one's status and prestige. Many of the older elite who were involved in the construction and development trades accrue some prestige for their ability to get things done. One informant called this the 'contractor mentality,' a single-mindedness towards achieving a goal. When one group was told to come up with hundreds of thousands of dollars in pledges in a short period, those who could give were quickly separated from those who talked about the need for giving. Distinctions were drawn between 'practical men' and others who just talked and in the end lost status. But while the talkers lost status, the givers were enmeshed in communal responsibilities.

In a polyethnic immigrant city, interaction with other immigrant and ethnic communities is critical to the development of knowledge about constructing ethnocommunity projects. Joseph Carrier, an entrepreneur and board member at the ICBC, spoke of the important assistance and advice given to them by members of the Jewish community, who had experience with their own communal projects. This is not an unusual connection, given that the leadership of both communities probably met through business contacts in real estate and construction. In addition, Italian and Jewish immigrants have settled in close proximity to one another on the west side of the city since the turn of the century. One wealthy businessman who had been involved in raising funds for Villa Columbo commented on how useful it was to observe how other communities organize:

> Well, I always have been a strong believer in following the experiences of people more clever and more experienced than I am in a particular field. Nobody does a better job, OK, in fund-raising in Toronto than the Jewish community. All through the years I have been a supporter of the United Jewish Appeal. I have business partners who are Jewish ... customers and so on. So I have a little background of raising money and following the patterns of the fundraisers in the Jewish community under the United Jewish Appeal or the Baycrest Centre for Geriatric Care ... I sat with some of those people and they gave me the directions to follow, and I followed them very closely.

Gifts and the Ambiguity of Status Enhancement

Another method of formal recognition is the naming of buildings or the engraving of names on monument walls. This recognition, however, encounters a cross-current interpretation by those in the community who believe these elites are overstepping the bounds of trust within the 'moral community.' Unkind gossip and rumours abound among tradesmen that elite contractors who have volunteered their time and expertise to help build several Italian community projects managed to make money through their involvement with the projects. For others, honesty, in the strict sense, was not the issue, but instead the motives of giving were questioned: big donors were just attempting to show off their wealth. We do not have to interpret this view of profit literally. It could be an encoded reference to status differentiation and the envy others feel that their project had not led to similar riches.

Part of the myth of origin for the ethnocommunity in its early years of migration and settlement in the 1950s and 1960s posits that all immigrants came here as equals, i.e., that they were all hardworking, honest labourers. As equals, therefore, one must not ennoble oneself, without considerable effort, above one's fellow immigrants. Of course in the intervening years some achieved greater economic or social affluence than others. A limited form of social control by those who have not attained the same economic success as the new elite seems to be the pleasure taken, say, in recounting a time when a wealthy developer was a poor and penniless labourer. All donors are aware of the dangers of overstepping their claims of status. However, there may be a disjuncture between a donor and the claims of obligation placed upon him or her by others. To counter this, a donor may choose to create a system of exchange with a new network of mutually trusting partners in a community; thus, the moral obligations associated with a previous or different subset of individuals may have a limited effect on his or her social status.

Defining the 'Moral Community' of Giving

Giving establishes a link of common cause to one's community. At the same time that it creates conditions for status enhancement or slippage, it is an expression of ethnic identity and community solidarity. Barth (1969) argued that ethnicity always involves social process, an aspect of a relationship rather than a reified cultural trait. Thus, gift giving becomes a useful marker of the process of ethnicity, which emerges from interaction with 'others.' Gift giving to communal causes or projects defines one as a member of a moral community, yet the scale of that community can change if one's ethnic identity is situationally constructed.

In Chapter 6 I discuss the ambiguity of Italian-Canadian identity and the emergence of subethnicities such as Calabrese, Abruzzese, Veneti, and others based on Italian regional areas of emigration. These other forms of self-identification are in turn supported by renewed expressions of belonging in the form of gifts. When funds need to be raised for a more circumscribed subset of people of Italian-Canadian heritage, new opportunities for status and prestige are available in the form of patronage with regard to regional centres. Recently the Italian-language press has featured photographs of members of locally based paesi clubs of emigrants from, in one example, Abruzzi, holding a cheque for $6,000 raised at a dinner-dance in support of a campaign to raise funds for the Casa D'Abruzzo. But the lines are not neatly demarcated along these administrative regional constructs. In several instances the clubs have solicited donations or pledges from the wider social field of Italian Canadians. In one instance I asked my Calabrese-Canadian host about a pledge he sought from a non-Calabrese, and he responded with a grin, '*Lui è cervello, anche se lui è Abruzzese*' (He is smart, even if he is Abruzzese). Others who have been involved actively in raising funds for pan-Italian causes have also contributed token amounts to new projects even if the needs of these clubs are limited in scope. The cost of not doing so would be detrimental to their own future fund-raising.

Good reputations are not a necessary requirement for community membership (Bailey 1971:7). In fact, community members with poor reputations help define the contours of acceptable behaviour and virtue for the community as a whole. Not all Italian Canadians contribute to communal events and projects. In fact some high-profile elite community members, some of them very wealthy, are considered poor communal citizens by community activists and fund-raisers. Because their livelihood rests on business interests that thrive on the niche market of the ethnocommunity, these non-contributors (or contributors of token sums) are also viewed by other elites as cheap, self-interested, and unappreciative. For example, one Italian-Canadian radio broadcaster is notorious for his unwillingness to do anything 'for free' to help ethnocommunity social agencies. At the same time his public persona is one of a gregarious grandfather and patron to the community who supplies his listeners with Italian-language news, sports, and entertainment. In fact his status could be called ambiguous. To those beyond the tightly circumscribed boundaries of elite giving, his reputation as a benefactor is secure, in the sense that he brings the comfort of the familiar language and culture to Italian immigrant families. Yet to others, particularly within the community's social agencies, he is considered lacking in generosity.

Final Remarks

The exchange of goods, money, and labour undergirds the construction of an ethnic group. To understand the dynamics of ethnicity we need to comprehend the multiple social fields in which ethnic identity and solidarity are inspired, shaped, and constructed. The symbolic exchange of goods and services initiates social obligations that scrutinize and expand the contours of community. Furthermore, the networks created by the exchange of gifts illuminate the multiplicity of fissures in what appears to be a corporate, homogeneous identity, and expose the differentiated social fields within an ethnic community. Public giving produces the structures that constitute and sustain the ethnic group. These structures are both social and material.

4. The Piazza of Corporate Unity

The reward for giving in support of communal imaginings is the actual construction of a project such as a community centre, which creates a field in which to view the obligations that are tied in to giving and receiving. Here, giving and status play are open to the scrutiny of the ethnic community and to the curiousity of the host society. Clifford Geertz has said that 'at base, thinking is a public activity – its natural habitat is the houseyard, the marketplace and the town square' (1973:360–1). A metaphor used by many to describe the Columbus Centre – the cultural-centre component of the Villa Charities' campus – is that it is the community's piazza: a forum in which ideas are exchanged and debated, where friends meet, business is conducted, families gather, and culture is expressed and produced. As Di Iulio expressed it, Columbus Centre is 'a bridge to ourselves and to the greater community. This piazza has helped to shed negative stereotypes and foster instead the vibrant values of commitment and multiculturalism' (1991). This metaphor of the piazza constructs the fictional unity of a community while acknowledging the limited diversity and lack of agreement associated with village life.

The Columbus Centre, part of the Villa Charities' constellation of four buildings (see Map 4.1) constructed by the Italian Canadian Benevolent Corporation (ICBC),[1] sits as a physical reminder of the presence of a corporate entity known as Italian Canadians. It is important to analyze the historical development of the ICBC, known since 1995 as Villa Charities, to examine the manner in

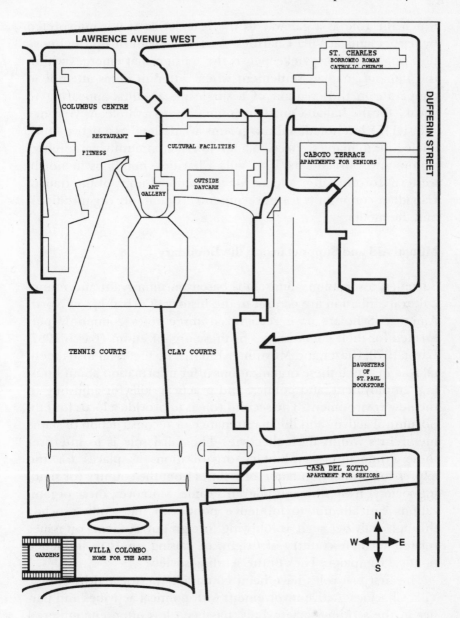

Map 4.1: Villa Charities Campus (Source: courtesy of the
Villa Charities; campus map not to scale)

which the role as a gateway to the broader society is interpreted by participants at Villa Charities. Associated with this pivotal position as gateway, or gatekeeper, is the tension that emerges within the Italian-Canadian settlement when different elites attempt to cooperate in the creation of a single piazza, thus appearing to speak for the Italian-Canadian community as a whole. As Werbner (1991:115) has noted, 'ethnic groups are defined as a fictive unity, analogous in many respects to a territorial community' by administrators and bureaucrats. The Villa Charities' buildings in northwestern Toronto offer a locus for the fictional unity of the Italian-Canadian community for governments, community organizations, and the media.

Mutual Aid and Support inside the Boundary

Societies, associations, and clubs based on immigrant and ethnocultural affiliation are central to the history of urban life in North America. Scholars have recognized three roles commonly performed for their communities by these organizations (Basch 1987; Bayor 1978; Glazer and Moynihan 1963). The first is an instrumental role in which these organizations offer information about housing, employment, and politics, and practical skills for adjusting to the new environment. The second role is to provide a locus for ethnocultural activity and the maintenance or reconstruction of status hierarchies within the collectivity. The third role is to interpret these ethnocultural voluntary organizations as places for the expression and continuation of politics from the country (or sending-society) from which immigrants came. Moreover, these organizations can attempt to influence politics in the sending-society through activities such as lobbying foreign governments on issues related to their country of origin, or raising funds to influence political campaigns back in the sending-society.

The first two roles have been commonly performed by ICBC/ Villa Charities. Active involvement with political activities and parties in the sending-society, Italy, has been less often encountered formally at the ICBC/Villa Charities other than for brief ceremonial receptions over the years during Canadian diplomatic tours by the presidents and prime ministers of Italy. These politicians invariably stop in this colony of 'their' diaspora to observe the success of *gli italiani all'estero* (Italians overseas). Officials at ICBC/Villa Charities are careful to point out when receiving Italian politicians that they are Canadians of Italian heritage and should not be seen as a colony of Italian citizens living abroad. An ongoing concern of those involved with ICBC/Villa Charities is their desire to be accepted as Canadians and to be seen as contributing to the welfare of Canadian society as a whole. In this context, the discourse and activities at ICBC/Villa Charities primarily revolves around Canada as a multicultural society and Italian Canadians as contributing members to that diversity.

This focus on Canadian citizenship has been influenced in part by two negative historical experiences that affected Italian Canadians as a collectivity. In response, a discourse that promotes Italian Canadians as equal, worthy, and willing Canadian citizens seeks to disarm those who would question the individual and collective rights of people of Italian heritage in Canada. The two experiences occurred with both pre-1939 and post-1948 Italian immigrants.

First, some of the older business and professional leadership, especially in the 1970s, remember the hurt and difficulty of the war years when Italian Canadians were classified as enemy aliens, made to report regularly to Canadian officials, and in a few cases were interned in a prison camp, Camp Petawawa (Ramirez 1988). Second, for post-1948 immigrants part of their identity was formed as a result of the discrimination they encountered when they moved into the Canadian labour market in the fifties, sixties, and seventies, and the difficulties their children experienced in the public and Catholic school systems that were reluctant and ill-equipped to respond to children whose home culture and language were different from their own. Nevertheless, the Canadian state's encouragement of a civic ethos of multiculturalism since the 1970s and the gradual economic success of Italian Canadians and their children encouraged Italian Canadians to affirm their links to Italy.

As the immense influx of new immigrants from Italy interacted with prewar Italian-Canadian immigrants and the host Canadian society and its institutions in the fifties and sixties, occasional efforts were made by businessmen, professionals, Italian-language clergy, and Italian-language newspaper editors to rally immigrants around a potential pan-Italian cause, to strive for *una piazza dell' immaginazione* (an imagined piazza). Many of these efforts reflected the desires of specific communities within the broader Italian-Canadian population. For example, the fight to retrieve the old Italian Consulate, Casa D'Italia, from the Canadian government (which had seized it during the Second World War) was spearheaded by prewar Italian-Canadian elites, professionals, and businessmen who wished to improve the image of Italians in the city and develop new associational life within the community.

Another site of social and cultural activities was the Italo-Canadian Recreational Club located near the intersection of Dufferin Street and Davenport Road on Brandon Avenue. The hall was popular with people from all regions of Italy but its central actors were from the region of Friuli in northeastern Italy (Grohovaz 1985). During these years there was also a bid to create an umbrella group to represent all Italian-Canadian clubs and associations in Toronto. One had collapsed in the 1950s as a result of misunderstandings between prewar Italians and the newcomers. It was revived, but not until 1969 when the postwar group became more firmly involved. During the difficult years of settlement in the 1950s and 1960s organizations such as the Italian Immigrant Aid Society and Centro Organizzativo Scuole Techniche Italiane (COSTI) worked to inform Italian immigrants about jobs, housing, training, benefits, and other forms of social assistance (Iacovetta 1992; R.F. Harney 1991). Also in the 1960s many began to make oral inquiries among Italians in Toronto about the eventual need to construct *'una casa di riposo per persone anziane'* (a rest home for elderly people) in Metro Toronto. The ideas and discussions around these efforts prepared the groundwork for such a project in the 1970s.

Origins of a Centre

The emergence of these coordinated efforts among some Italians in Toronto coincided with changes in the broader Canadian society. Twenty years of heavy migration had changed the ethnocultural character of Canada. In response to a changed demographic situation, politicians sought to address the new public and potential electorate of Canadians of non-British and non-French heritage (Tepper 1994; R.F. Harney 1988). In 1971 Prime Minister Trudeau said in the House of Commons:

> A policy of multiculturalism within a bilingual framework commends itself to the government as the most suitable means of assuring the cultural freedom of Canadians. Such a policy should help to break down discriminatory attitudes and cultural jealousies. National unity, if it is to mean anything in the deeply personal sense, must be founded on confidence in one's own individual identity; out of this can grow respect for that of others and a willingness to share ideas, attitudes, and assumptions.
>
> The policy I am announcing today accepts the contention of the other cultural communities that they too are essential elements in Canada, and deserve government assistance in order to contribute to regional and national life in ways that derive from their heritage yet are distinctively Canadian. (Trudeau 1971)

By the 1970s the Italian settlement patterns in Toronto continued to move northward from the initial receiving neighbourhoods around College and Grace Streets, St Clair Avenue and Dufferin Street, up towards Lawrence Avenue and Weston Road, and beyond. The expectations held by Italian immigrants that their families would care for them in old age were challenged as their children confronted the demands and desires of the North American industrial, suburban, and consumerist economy. As a result some aging parents were sent to nursing homes. Many Italian-Canadians recalled common experiences faced by older relatives when they needed care in Canada. The common narrative described a *zio* (uncle) or *zia* (aunt) who had suffered in an Anglo-Canadian rest home where the caregivers paid little attention to the quality of food or the *ambiente* (environment), and the patient's language could not be understood. As one story has it, perhaps apocryphally, the genesis of the Italian-Canadian home for the Aged, later known as Villa Colombo, was on a golf course in the late 1960s. A group of wealthy Italian-Canadian businessmen discussed the fate of '*uno zio*,' an old Italian immigrant they knew in an Anglo-Canadian home for the elderly who suffered from loneliness and cultural marginality. During a day of golf this group of businessmen (some from the Canadian Italian Business and Professional Association) and members of the la Federazione delle Associazioni e Club Italo-Canadesi (FACI) (some with experience in earlier cultural and social organizations within the Italian settlement) began the effort to raise funds for a home for people of Italian heritage and to create the Italian Canadian Benevolent Corporation. This kind of origin fed the criticisms, now muted, made by some Italian Canadians on the Left that Villa Colombo and the Columbus Centre were simply monuments that allowed the rich to enhance their prestige and create a place for their own aging relatives to live. In fact, however, for some members of the organizing committee – those who had lived through the difficult war years, then the arrival of masses of new Italian immigrants – the project was an opportunity to demonstrate to the host society that Italians were worthy citizens and that the Italian community was responsible and united. As one woman who had worked on volunteer committees for Villa Colombo and the Columbus Centre since the 1970s explained on the CBC series *Our Lives*: 'The significance of Villa Colombo and Columbus Centre has been the amalgamation of all the people from all the provinces of Italy to finally do something together. Something they are proud of. Something they agree on; and, something that they now see was right and feel good about it. Where one time it was all these little groups, all off by themselves, all pulling against [*sic*] each other, now we are pulling together' (Rosati 1994).

One of the initial organizers who was in charge of preparing a plan for the group (then unnamed) that wanted to build the home also sat on the board of a senior citizens home, the Pentecostal Benevolent Association of Canada (PBAC). He received help from the other board to prepare administrative and fund-raising plans and letters of incorporation for the new group. On 15 April 1971 the Italian Canadian Benevolent Corporation became a registered charitable institution under the Charitable Institutions Act, and was incorporated without share capital, with letters of patent issued by the Province of Ontario. At the same time a lottery was launched to begin the fund-raising for a seniors' home. Calls were also made to all clubs, associations, unions, churches, and other groups of Italian origin inviting members to participate in the first annual ICBC meeting, in August of that year, to elect an executive that would begin to steer the project to fruition.

In a 1974 feasibility study put together by the ICBC, more than forty-four Italian-Canadian organizations, clubs, unions, and churches provided support and personnel for the board of governors of the ICBC. The study noted that the Ontario Ministry of Community and Social Services' *Annual Report* of March 1971 stated the ministry's concern with addressing the needs of the province's ethnic groups, and to that end, ten homes for the aged were to be operated by ethnic groups with Ontario government assistance. The ICBC study stated that 'next to the British' Italians constituted the second largest ethnic group in Metropolitan Toronto, and that more than 12 per cent of that population was over the age of sixty. Finally, it argued that if smaller communities such as the Ukrainians, Germans, Chinese, and Japanese could have their own seniors' homes, then Italians certainly deserved government assistance to create a suitable home for the seniors in their community. A parcel of land was chosen on a three-acre lot near Dufferin and Lawrence on Playfair Avenue, where Villa Colombo was to be built. Other facilities providing services for the Italian-Canadian settlement were located near the proposed site for the Villa: two neighbourhood schools, the Dante Alighieri Academy, the Regina Mundi Elementary School, and the St Charles Borromeo Church.

The dreamers and builders of Villa Colombo not only wished to create a 167-bed home for their seniors – expanded in 1987 to 268 beds – they also intended to create an ambiente as well as a monument or symbol around which people of Italian descent could rally to show their pride. A self-made trucking magnate, the force behind the project, stated it clearly: '[We needed] a flag, a monument, a centre, something that when you say "our community" you associate yourself with this thing. And I found that it was something that we all could be proud of, and something that can attract the attention of the whole community ... we have a home that is probably the number one in the province of Ontario ... we have a home that is the pride of the province, and also, you know, our pride.'

Part of the effort to construct a proud Italian-Canadian identity and image in Canada by communal leaders and elites reflects the need to change the host society's stereotypes of the group: that Italian Canadians are involved in criminal activity (the Mafia), and that they are all from humble peasant origins. One man actively involved with the construction of Villa Colombo and Columbus Centre stated it bluntly: 'I felt we needed to prove we were good and hardworking Canadians, but of Italian extraction. What better way to do it than show some sort of civic responsibility, taking care of your own, by building an old age home. Sure, some of us came poor but we worked hard and did well. It was time to give back.'

A sensitivity about host-society attitudes does not lessen the ethnic group's accomplishments. It only underscores the relational dynamics of ethnic group competition and identity construction in a polyethnic society.

Villa Colombo's innovative design for senior care reflected the experiences and cultural expectations of Italians. Those involved in the planning believed that an integral role for the family was crucial, and that cross-generational activities would ensure that the cultural expectations of their seniors would be met. And, more than simply building a home, the ICBC sought to invent a replica of an Italian town within the home, complete with indoor piazza, chapel, barbershop, caffè, tuck shop, and fountain. To encourage the interaction of people of different ages a day-care centre was established and a banquet hall constructed that could be rented and used by all members of the Italian-Canadian community to generate activity and funds. As it was explained to me:

We tried very hard, and so did the others who were on the building committee, to try to carry out in Villa Colombo the atmosphere that will get the old people to mix and would have a place where they would not only stay in their rooms like they do in so many other places ... we tried to create an atmosphere of sociability, *la bella vita* (the beautiful life) ... with the piazza, the fountain, where people would come out of their room and come downstairs ... and play cards, have a coffee, or watch people coming in or out. And that is the atmosphere we tried to create so that the old people will not feel neglected ... that we have [these different parts] that were all part of the creation of a community. Villa Colombo starts on the second floor, the home is from the second floor to the fifth floor. The main floor is the community.

The ICBC organized fund-raising events to meet the needs of building a home for the aged with a day-care centre (Villa Colombo), which they estimated would cost $4,500,000. The most publicly visible form of both raising capital and broadening the support for the project within the Italian-Canadian collectivity and beyond was the annual Mother's Day telethon on Citytv. The ICBC's September 1975 *Report to Donors* described the extent of cooperation the ICBC found within the Italian-Canadian settlement and the wider society when it listed the donors and pledge amounts for the construction of Villa Colombo. Almost ten thousand donors, individual and collective, contributed through pledges, donations, and other forms of fund-raising in response to calls for their support through the telethon, the Italian-Canadian press, and the radio shows on the Italian-language radio station CHIN.

The ICBC also created its own construction company in order to build the home at cost, simply with the help of a voluntary committee of experienced people in the construction field (ICBC 1981). People involved with the construction project were able to encourage workers and subcontractors to charge minimal prices because of the communal nature of the home. Villa Colombo Home for the Aged was completed near the end of 1975, and in April 1976 Premier William Davis presided at its official opening. Though Villa Colombo was considered first and foremost a home for the elderly, it soon became a focal point for a number of other activities – dances, feste, and dinners – for people of all ages. It only took a year before the ICBC began active work to build another facility in which to channel other forms of social and cultural activities within the Italian settlement.

During the planning stages for the fourth annual Mother's Day telethon in March 1977 to raise funds for the ICBC projects, an opportunity arose for the ICBC to purchase one last piece of vacant land in the vicinity of Villa Colombo. A developer wished to demolish the old St Mary's Correctional School for Girls and construct a residential development on its twelve-acre site at Dufferin Street and Lawrence Avenue. Instead, in an agreement between the provincial government and the ICBC, the Ministry of Government Services purchased six acres of the twelve-acre site, including the old school, for $2.6 million and leased it to the ICBC for a nominal fee. At the same time the ICBC purchased the other six acres, land adjacent to the three school buildings, for $1.5 million. The ICBC agreed to pay the cost of both the renovation of the old buildings and the operation of the proposed cultural centre. Through further community fund-raising events such as dinners, bike-a-thons, a variety of community activities, and a Wintario grant, the ICBC hoped to complete renovations and pay back the lease to the government of Ontario within ten years.

An integral part of this effort to construct the Italian settlement into a community occurred during the raising of funds. The annual Mother's Day telethon on Citytv generated significant returns, not only in donations and pledges necessary to continue to plan and build the various ICBC projects such as the Villa and the community centre (Columbus Centre), but also as a public display of community existence and unity. Italian television and movie stars, such as Gina Lollobrigida in 1978, hosted, with the help of community volunteers, the various telethons.

A brief note about the scope of fund-raising is useful here. Pledges during the telethons and other events were receivable over a five-year period, which made mortgages and bank loans necessary to cover carrying costs and some construction. The ICBC's annual report to members in 1979 stated that since fund-raising had begun for the centre in May 1977 approximately $4.5 million had been pledged or donated, and an additional $4.2 million in Wintario grants were to be fully received by 1980. According to the 1979 report of the ICBC the projected cost for the Columbus Centre land and renovations was $13 million. In an article expressing gratitude to the Italian community in *Corriere Illustrato*, 20 May 1978, after the telethon, the ICBC again revealed the desire to articulate community worth and validity. The article praised the $725,380 in pledges and donations offered by Italians in Toronto. Here was evidence that the Italian collectivity was really a community: '*la comunità italiana è un'entità unica, solidale, unita, conscia dei propri valori e delle proprie responsibilità*' (the Italian community is one entity, solid, united, aware of its worth and its real responsibilities).

Almost $7 million of a projected $12.4 million cost was raised among Italian Canadians and supporters of the project, and an additional $4.2 million was received in the form of Wintario grants. However, the economy in the early 1980s faltered, and pledges and donations slowed. With the country in recession and interest rates hovering around 22 per cent, despite the pledges of support from government and from Italian Canadians, the Columbus Centre faced a difficult financial situation in 1981–2. Suffering from a shortfall of $500,000 in its operating budget the ICBC and Columbus Centre turned to Metro Council for a one-time grant for this amount, to enable the institution to adjust to the new economic conditions. According to the *Toronto Star* of 26 April 1982, after some debate the ICBC and Columbus Centre received the grant.

While the grant from Metro Council helped the Columbus Centre survive the poor economy of the early 1980s, equally important for the profile of the ICBC and Columbus Centre was the construction of Caboto Terrace, an apartment complex for seniors. According to articles appearing in *Corriere Canadese*, 5–6 December 1983, and in *Il Tevere*, 18 August 1983, the ICBC, taking advantage of the wealth of construction knowledge and labour power within the Italian settlement, managed to construct Caboto Terrace within the budget allotted to it by the Canadian Mortgage and Housing Corporation. This project generated publicity and interest, thereby encouraging participation by members of the Italian settlement in other aspects of the ICBC and Columbus Centre. It also reinforced the opinion of Ontario politicians and bureaucrats that the ICBC was a useful conduit for servicing a segment of the Ontario population.

What's in a Culture?

In a brief submitted to the Ministry of Culture and Recreation in 1978 for the purposes of gaining financial assistance from the province, the ICBC provided an extensive review of its plans to create a new community centre. The brief gave a short history of the ICBC and Villa Colombo and described the large population in the area of Dufferin Street and Lawrence Avenue that was underserviced by community recreational sites. It also outlined the consultation process with Italians that was underway in Toronto (part of which entailed the distribution of questionnaires to resident families), as well as planned cultural, social, and recreational services, building layouts, and financial information. The brief offered as well the philosophy behind the centre. The family, it stated, was the central unit for maintaining social and civic responsibility, and it was important therefore that a facility provide services for all members of a family, who in turn would help each individual 'to recognize and embrace the validity of the family unit.' The centre, with its Italian architectural traditions, would offer an immediate sense of pride for Italian Canadians which would 'generate a sense of belonging and a spirit of goodwill to grow together, cultivating traditional values in a healthy, modern Canadian environment.' Furthermore, the ICBC brief suggested other benefits that the centre might offer, such as leadership development, positive intra-community communication, and programs that would help promote integration and better citizenship.[2]

While it is true that a brief submitted to a government would reflect concerns for civic responsibility, its themes in this case also indicated something more about the attitudes of the applicants. The emphasis on the family not only as a traditional Italian cultural value but also as a potential benefit to Canadian society indicates a sifting of ideas by the applicants to find what they believed was a core ethnocultural characteristic that could be shared in a multicultural environment. The ICBC applicants posited the cross-generational family interaction as a core value, a 'lifestyle' for the transmission of cultural ideals, and the healthy construction of a new Italian-Canadian identity.

Of course this metaphor of the family had its limitations. To expect almost half a million Italian Canadians to express exactly the same family values despite a diversity of class, education, *paesi* (home towns), and lived experience in Canada was unrealistic. Even if all members of the Italian-Canadian community saw the family as a core value within their culture, and a metaphor for the unity of the community, this attitude towards the family has resonance in other cultures, too. But another point: for some in the Italian-Canadian community the creation of a home for the elderly contradicted their traditional sense of familial obligation and duty to live with and care for elderly parents. As one man stated, 'The difficulty that we had at that time, one we had to work hard to overcome, was what I call "the Italian sickness." *Si chiama vergogna!* (It is called shame!) The families were ashamed to send their parents to the Villa because ... this goddamn garbage ... "the Italians are looking after their own people" ... it is fine in Pratola Peligna or some little town that they come from, but here it doesn't work because of in-laws, the neighbours, busy lives.'

The early attempts to solicit funds from what one informant called people with a 'contractor' mentality – men of humble origins who found wealth in the building sector within the expanding economy of postwar Toronto – was not easy. Emigrants from a harsh peasant and postwar economy in disarray in Italy, these 'contractors' made their money through shrewdness, hard work, and frugality. In order to convince those reluctant to offer financial support because of their traditional sense of duty to care for their own parents, the fund-raisers sketched a different scenario. Joe, for example, explained that by drawing a scenario of the future for them, he could almost always get some funds:

We would go to ask for funds from successful contractors and they would say that a good family takes care of their own, so why do we need a home? So Mr Fusco, the successful transport businessman in charge of the ICBC, would say, 'Yes, you are right; but, don't think of now, think of twenty years down the road. Sure, you will take care of your parents but would you like this place for you?' ... and the man would look at his hockey-playing, Camaro-driving son and give out the cash.

With experiences and memories of communal life and multigenerational families in an agro-town in Calabria, Friuli, or Abruzzo, these immigrant parents initially expected to continue a cohesive familial and spatial intimacy. But the realities of their own nuclear families, raised in a North American industrial economy and conditioned by a North American capitalist concept of time and space, opened up new possibilities and constraints on their expectations. The exigencies of migration had already seen Italian immigrants enlarge their kinship networks, adopt *compari* (godparents) from disparate parts of the peninsula to cope with the practical, life-cycle, and emotional needs and difficulties of the migrant experience (Iacovetta 1992; Sturino 1978, 1990a; Yans-McLaughlin 1977).

The ethnocommunity was the next leap of loyalty in the concentric circles of allegiance that many Italian immigrants bridged to conceive a larger surrogate family, a fictional kinship. This new imagining of communal kinship that included all people of Italian heritage enabled immigrants to adapt their historically structured notions of filial obligation towards parents and to assuage the potential for shame in the face of new realities in North American urban and suburban life. Taking this view, young Italian-Canadian adults were not abandoning parents to an impersonal, foreign institution but instead to extended kin, thereby fulfilling their obligations as good children and honourable members of a community.

In the same brief from the ICBC to the Ontario Ministry of Culture, a section devoted to clubs and associations underscored a potential area of tension for the ICBC and the planners of the community centre. The brief suggested that since many clubs and associations were family based, an integration of these clubs into the centre with space allocated for their activities would strengthen the familial bonds of the centre and increase inter-regional activities: 'By having clubs and associations more centrally located, it will be easier to co-ordinate club and community activities, thus preventing competition and duplication of services and social functions.'

Competition inside the Boundary

Within the Italian-language Canadian press, such as *Corriere Canadese, Il Giornale di Toronto,* and *Forze Nuove,* during the 1970s there was protracted debate about the purpose, necessity, and desirability of a community centre. It could be said that this debate generally happened within the collectivity, since the linguistic barriers kept most dissension from the scrutiny of the host society. Some criticized it as a project for the wealthy elites, and the middle class, and their children, an impression that persists among some working and middle-class Italian-Canadians today. Here were the indications of a hegemonic struggle within the community.

On 17 April 1979 some of the tensions concerning the project within the Italian settlement, by those who were suspicious of the motives of the ICBC, spilled into the public sphere of the wider society in a meeting of the Social Development Committee on Estimates for the Ministry of Culture and Recreation. During this meeting several third-party NDP MPPs of Italian heritage questioned the minister of culture and recreation about the propriety of the land and lease arrangement mentioned earlier between the provincial government and the ICBC. The MPPs acknowledged a consensus among Toronto Italians to build the centre. However, among other concerns they wondered what assurances the province could give them that the site would be used for a community centre by the non-profit group. Furthermore, they wondered whether this assistance would be extended to other groups in a similar situation, or was it an exception made in this circumstance.

Responding three days later, a spokesman for the government stated that on 17 March 1977 the Management Board had decided to purchase the site and lease it to the ICBC until the group had sufficient funds to repurchase the land. The ICBC would be responsible for maintenance, upkeep, and taxes. Then on 28 November 1978 Cabinet directed the Ministry of Government Services to sell the land to the ICBC for the acquisition cost of

$2,607,125, with Council approving the sale on 11 April 1979. According to the minister, no formal policy had been adopted, nor had strict assurances concerning resale been written into the lease (Ontario Debates 1979).

One of the MPPs who asked these questions had been an ICBC board member in the early years, and as a result might well have been familiar with the corporation. The other MPPs also must have had some knowledge of the ICBC projects during the previous eight years. Their questions to the government about the project addressed four concerns: the potentially restricted and elite membership in the ICBC; the alleged prohibitively expensive membership fee to the Columbus Centre; the 'business' manner in which the ICBC was run; and, according to them, the lack of public scrutiny. The accusation that a non-profit group was run as a business we could assume was a coded reference to the class concerns the MPPs had about the project. One could speculate that the questions being raised reflected the concern that a community of working people and labourers might be priced out of its own piazza.

In a press conference on 25 April 1979 the ICBC refuted all these charges and expressed dismay at the allegations. The president of the ICBC pointed out that the ICBC annual report was made available to its membership and to interested members of the public, and that it was mailed to the Italo-Canadian media and was subject to scrutiny by the Charitable Institutions Act and Revenue Canada. Furthermore, he expressed his discomfort with the notion that the membership was restricted, given that 450 individuals belonged to the ICBC, of which 70 were delegates representing clubs or associations. The frustration of some individuals was expressed in the opening line of an article in *Corriere Illustrato*, 16 April 1979: '*Amici, qui si fa la comunità o si muore*' (Friends, the community is made now or it dies).

This public display of disunity, or more precisely, the differing opinions among people of Italian heritage, in full view of the provincial government and the broader media, ran counter to the image the ICBC wished to portray to the host society. It is difficult to determine the results of this episode, but it underscored the difficulty in conceiving of a monolithic Italian-Canadian community.

Perhaps one can judge the community response to these series of events by seeing the results of the annual telethon in 1979 after this affair became public. Hosted by Italian movie stars Rossana Podestà and Rossano Brazzi, the telethon raised $825,145 in pledges and donations. This response indicates that many members of the Italian-Canadian collectivity dismissed the issue as partisan bickering, or if they believed the charges, accepted them as the price to be paid for the Columbus Centre piazza.

A Territorial Centre and Community Guardian

Through the years a variety of Italian heritage-based organizations have used the Columbus Centre for meetings, office space, and cultural activities. As one informant told me, many regional clubs and associations use the Columbus Centre to meet and plan for the time when they will have their own. Nevertheless, a concern other Italian-Canadian cultural organizations have had since the late 1970s has been the potential hegemony and monopolization of resources and attention by the Columbus Centre and ICBC to the detriment of smaller, community-based groups. Internal differentiation exists within the perceived corporate unity as other scholars have noted (Saifullah Khan 1976; Werbner and Anwar 1991; Talai 1989). There was a fear that some in the ICBC wished the Centre to be the focal point of social and cultural activities. In the 1978 feasibility study the phrase 'preventing competition and duplication of services and social functions' was interpreted by some in that manner.

More recently another concern has emerged as the demographics of the Italian-heritage collectivity continue to challenge the state and the existing associations and institutions serving it. Italian-Canadians have moved in great numbers to the city of Vaughan, especially to the township of Woodbridge. In the last several years the ICBC has been approached by the federal, provincial, and municipal governments to bid on other lands designated by governments for the construction of affordable housing or seniors' apartments. Seeing the Italian-Canadian ethnic group as a corporate unity lessens the burden for politicians, but especially for bureaucrats who wish to maintain a certain amount of administrative efficiency. Politicians perhaps are more attuned to the finitude within the corporate unities (Bhabha 1990) than are bureaucrats, especially if they are themselves immigrants or children of immigrants. Community consultation requires time and labour. If a group exists that is already identified with a fictional community, it is more efficient to approach it for future projects than to negotiate with an unknown quantity. However, as the next chapter will note, contrary to Werbner's assumption (Werbner and Anwar 1991:115) in Ontario at least, administrative equity has not limited each ethnic group to one community centre or one seniors' apartment building.

In the last few years those involved with the ICBC have seen a need to address the changed demographic location of the Italian-Canadian community and initially they were interested in offering services to community members at several proposed sites further north and west from the present location. ICBC representatives told me it quickly became apparent, at municipal public meetings held to address these sites and others, that the ICBC was considered by some other community groups, principally ethnoregional Italian-Canadian groups, as a competitor. After this mood was assessed, the ICBC leadership told me it was more prudent to take on the role of benevolent older brother who would offer advice and technical aid to the Italian-Canadian groups interested in these specific sites.

Discounting the endurance of these alternative groups and the longevity of Italian regional loyalties on which many are based, several people involved with the ICBC assumed that in the future these groups would turn to the ICBC for assistance in the running of their seniors' apartments and centres. Maria, an active longtime member at Villa Charities, expressed some concern about regionalism: 'I do not agree with the regional outlook. I think to be Italian is to be Italian. I don't agree with regional differentiation. I don't know why people make it. I can say even with my cousins in Italy it is a big thing. I mean even if you're from the next town. It is such a big deal. I just don't agree with that, and that is probably, the main reason why I did not become involved with the Famee Furlane (Friulani Community Centre).'

Culture: Dante's or Dino's

One informant close to the ICBC and Columbus Centre explained
that the transition from 'the building of monuments to the running of a community centre' has not always been easy, especially
when developing cultural programs. The cultural arts section of
the Centre, understaffed and in deficit, offers a number of activities and programs, including voice, piano, ballet, and cooking
lessons, marriage preparation courses, Italian language classes,
folk festivals, children's drawing classes, *Coro Verdi* (choral music),
plays, art exhibits, and seminars in Italian-Canadian studies sponsored by the Mariano A. Elia Chair at York University. A notable
production was a play written by the Italian-Canadian actor/writer
Tony Nardi, called *A Modo Suo* (His Own Way), performed in the
Calabrese dialect.

In 1987, through a $1 million endowment from a benefactor,
the gallery became an accredited provincial art gallery. Since then
the gallery has exhibited First Nations artists and contemporary
Canadian and Italian-Canadian work, as well as shows devoted to
Italian artists and Italian cultural themes such as the Christmas
Presepio shows and the visual history of immigrants from Umbria.
Now officially incorporated into the arts bureaucratic mainstream,
the gallery stands at the threshold between the cultural needs of
the Italian-Canadian community and the expectations of a broader
public.

This brief list of cultural activities underscores the diversity or
inclusiveness conceived as suitable for an Italian-Canadian centre,
but its very diversity emphasizes a debate among those involved
with the Centre concerning what the ICBC should do in the area
of cultural programming. While many have lauded programs and
activities at the Centre, there is a sense that new effort is needed to
propagate, develop, and construct ideas and activities that will
bring forward forcefully the Italian language, culture, ideals, and
values to energize a new generation. It is more difficult for those
involved to agree always on which cultural 'content' or symbols to
encourage. With the emergence in the 1980s of Italy as an 'economic miracle' there has also been a sense that the Columbus Cen-

tre and the ICBC should be conduits through which the Canadian public might better understand Italy. One suggestion – to offer a travel service – had been floated but was rejected.

Culture is an ambiguous and contested concept. Anthropologists have stressed the processual dynamic of culture and ethnicity in part because of a concern that an emphasis on the 'cultural stuff' inside [group] boundaries would contribute to the excessive reification of culture and the reproduction of native stereotypes and ideologies (Eriksen 1993; Bentley 1987; Barth 1969). Yet even if culture is contested and provisional within the context of shifting internal group boundaries, schisms, identities, interpretations, and experiences, in the context of relations with groups and individuals outside the elusive Italian-Canadian boundary, people often act as if a bounded entity known as Italian or Italian-Canadian culture exists. Even more, some younger, second-generation entrepreneurs, restaurateurs, and professionals of Italian-Canadian heritage urge that Italianness be marketed as a commodity or product. It is argued that none are better suited to bringing Italian fashion, food, cinema, and refined technology to Canada than Italian Canadians themselves.

In a polyethnic and consumerist city what differentiates one ethnic group from another is its culture. Culture is an object to be marketed and sold. Handler's (1988:16) interpretation of Quebec nationalist culture is apt here, too: 'if culture is pressed into service to distinguish one bounded collectivity from another, it too must be bounded; that is, culture must be analyzable and identifiable, such and such a "trait" belonging to this nation or originating in that region.' Scholars of tourist art (MacCannell 1984; Graburn 1976; Barthes 1982) discuss ethnicity in this context. As Steiner (1994:93) notes in his study of Ivory Coast art markets, 'ethnic groups, like arts, can be colourfully mapped out on a poster from the Ministry of Tourism.' The complexity of ethnoculture is stripped of its subtlety, nuances, and ambiguities and marketed in its 'essential' form as a commodity for consumption as entertainment by others who wish to experience another culture, or ethnic 'dip.'

In some instances, Italian-Canadians have looked to other ethnocultural communities, especially the Jewish community, for examples of how they should proceed with cultural programming. One evening I was invited to participate at such a meeting. The Cultural Committee of Columbus Centre decided to convene its monthly meeting at the Jewish Home for the Aged at the Baycrest Centre for Geriatric Care (Baycrest), to see how it incorporated culture in its raising of funds. Baycrest has an extensive art collection that serves two roles for the non-profit organization: it provides both aesthetic pleasure and financial rewards. Much of the art at Baycrest is of historical significance to Jewish culture and was painted and/or donated by artists of Jewish ancestry. I recorded the following brief fieldnote at the meeting:

Fieldnote, November 1992
I noticed what appeared to be a sense of wonderment that overtook the small group from the Columbus Centre. They could not quite believe how well-organized and sophisticated the fund-raising was. After a brief tour of the building we were led to a boardroom to discuss the Centre's cultural programming. Along the way, we passed a room containing half a dozen volunteers preparing to solicit donations from a community list.

Later, as we left Baycrest, my Italian-Canadian friends expressed a complex mix of emotions: regret, a sense of failure, and envy. Over a dish of pasta at the Italian restaurant grano (the proprietor is a member of the Columbus Centre board), several vexing questions occupied the group: 'Why were Italians in Toronto so fragmented? Why didn't Italians understand the need for ongoing communal giving? Why was there an apparent disinterest in artistic efforts?' Nevertheless, the meeting ended with a sense of hope. Apparent in the creative Italianità design all around us in the restaurant was the possibility that Italian culture was sought after by the broader public, and that perhaps the Columbus Centre could indeed create within its walls a more complete cultural atmosphere.

What has emerged in discussions with informants and at cultural committee meetings is four different interpretations of the kind of culture most appropriate for the Centre to offer and pursue: (1) the Italian culture of Dante, Da Vinci, Caesar, Eco, and Pavarotti (the latter has performed twice to raise funds for the ICBC, in 1982 and

1985); (2) Regional and paesi culture of *presepii* (Nativity scenes), folk dances, cuisine, wine-making, sausage-pressing, and sheepskin bagpipe-playing; (3) Italian-Canadian-produced art, theatre, exhibits, and literature; and (4) basic lessons in the arts as part of general community-centre activities. Central to most of these deliberations is a conscious effort to anticipate and reflect back what the group perceives as relevant 'ethnic attributes' that the greater public wishes to experience. In other words, how can Italian-Canadians commodify Italianness; reduce it to a few manageable and marketable specific, observable traits; and attract others to it.

Being the Good 'Other'

It is important to recall that the political and cultural events out of which much of the present Italian-Canadian community leadership emerged were the societal debates in the 1970s about Canadian nationalism, Quebec separatism, aboriginal claims, and the advent of multiculturalism as ideology, ethos, and public policy. Two popular interpretations of that era held by many Canadian officials, Italian-Canadians, the media, and the ethnic/immigrant leadership are relevant here. One interpretation holds that ethnoculture and ethnocommunities have no longevity but simply have adaptive values, 'ethnocultural attributes' that, in this case, Italian immigrants can use to assimilate into Canadian ways. A second interpretation sees multiple and hybrid identities as having collective or communal values to pass on through the generations. A corollary of this second interpretation holds that a search for ethnic heroes in Canada's past must be undertaken, and once found, celebrated as great hybrid Canadians (R.F. Harney 1989).

It is the second interpretation that is superordinate in the discourse and public ritual of the ICBC complex. In this view ethnocommunities in Canada must share their cultures with each other, and intercultural events must become integral, ritualistic devices that the ICBC can use to reinforce the twin ideas of the adjustment and contribution of Italian Canadians to Canadian society and the legitimacy of hybrid, multiple identities in Canadian nationalism. The following examples explore this issue.

A series of social events sponsored by the ICBC and Columbus Centre speak to the symbolic role the Centre plays as an institution that interacts with the wider society on behalf of the Italian-Canadian settlement. Beginning a few years ago the ICBC and Columbus Centre began to arrange activities to commemorate the coming of Cristoforo Colombo (Christopher Columbus) and Giovanni Caboto (John Cabot) to the Americas 500 years ago. These events were explicit statements about the construction of ethnic sentiment within the debate about cultural conflicts in a multicultural society.

A search for ethnic heroes of the past to establish ethnic-group roots in the history of North American settlement should not surprise us. Robert Harney (1989) argued that North American ethnic-group status is linked to the length of time a group can claim a presence on this continent. He called this use of history 'Mayflowerism' in the American context, and related it to the Canadian concept of 'founding nations,' which confers special status for French and anglophone Canadians within a multicultural Canada. This version of history is used to legitimate their present-day cultural hegemony. The Italian-Canadian use of the names Caboto and Colombo is a reflection of the success of that hegemonic project.

As a cultural icon of North American society, Christopher Columbus, both the person and the symbol, has undergone a historical revision in the last five years, from that of a noble, bold discoverer to, at best, a person of his imperialist times and, at worst, a violent conqueror and destroyer of culture. This transformation has coincided also with a greater public recognition of the systematic mistreatment of Native peoples since that time and a greater public compassion for the cause of social justice for Native peoples. For Italians in North America, however, both Colombo and Caboto were and are potent symbols. To some they represent important historical forefathers whose accomplishment of 'discovery' has offered relief from some of the discrimination and hostility Italians have faced in their experience with the host Anglo-Celtic societies of the United States and Canada.

To reconcile the two current views of Columbus, an intriguing cultural event occurred in the context of discourse about multicultural understanding and sharing. The ICBC and Columbus Centre leadership was aware of the new interpretation of Columbus's place in history, but nevertheless desired some form of recognition of his 500-year place in history. As part of their series of events to commemorate the anniversary of Columbus's landfall and after consulting a noted writer of Ojibway heritage, the ICBC invited several Native artists from the Anishinabe First Nation of Wikwemikong on Manitoulin Island to exhibit their work in Columbus Centre's Carrier Art Gallery. Furthermore, on Canadian Thanksgiving Day (Columbus Day in the United States) guests gathered in the rotunda of Columbus Centre to attend an Anishinabe sweetgrass ceremony conducted by Bebaminojmat (the artist Leland Bell) to learn about the cultural meanings of this traditional purifying and cleansing ceremony. Certainly not all Italian Canadians attended or appreciated the programs arranged to address this changed status of Columbus in the pantheon of cultural heroes. Nevertheless, the events represented a conscious effort at renegotiating cultural ideas and symbols in a polyethnic society.

On another occasion at Villa Colombo the board of directors of the ICBC held a banquet to celebrate the relationship between Canadians of Italian and Portuguese heritage. Funds raised during the dinner were to be donated to help construct a Portuguese-Canadian youth camp. The relationship between Italians and Portuguese in Toronto offers an opportunity for insight into interethnic dynamics because of the close residential proximity of the two groups in the west end, and their common Catholicism and work experiences. An informal poll of priests and Italian Canadians I know would suggest that intermarriage between the groups is steady and relatively high.[3] Many Italian-owned construction firms that once employed only Italian labour have needed to augment their labour force with Portuguese workers as Italian immigrants retire and their Canadian-born children move to enter higher-status jobs. Some Italian Canadians I interviewed described interesting stereotypes of the Portuguese: that they are at times shifty and dishonest; that they are too Catholic; that their food, especially the seafood, is dull and of poor quality. During the 1994 World Cup, Italian Canadians resented the Portuguese Canadians' rooting for

Brazil on Italian-Canadian 'turf' (Dufferin Street and St Clair Avenue), while the Portuguese I spoke to resented what they saw as Italian-Canadian bravado. The banquet, then, was implicitly an opportunity for the successful, wealthy, and experienced Mediterranean cousins, the Italians, to help their newer fictive kin in the New World.

An event forty years ago served as the official genesis point of this encounter between the two communities. After a 1952 agreement between the Canadian and Portuguese governments, which enabled Portuguese workers to find employment in Canada's burgeoning postwar economy, transportation links needed to be established between the two countries. Since there were no direct passenger liners between Portugal and Canada, an Italian ship, the *SS Saturnia*, which brought Italian immigrants from the port of Naples, detoured via Lisbon to North America. It was this boat that, in addition to its Italian passengers, brought the first eighty-seven Portuguese men to Canada. In honouring these ties the rhetoric of multiculturalism was commonplace. Furthermore, Italian- and Portuguese-Canadian speakers suggested a sense of kinship through their common Latin heritage. More concretely, actual inter-ethnic marriages of couples who had met on the *Saturnia* and on subsequent journeys were honoured and celebrated as testimony to the quasi-familial ties between the two communities. As David Schneider has noted (1984:174), blood is 'an integral part of the ideology of European culture.' Blood is central to ideologies about nationhood, purity and the 'dangers' of miscegenation (M. Douglas 1966). 'Political alliances are portrayed in the language of kinship and affinity, and are often created through the "merging of blood" in dynastic alliances' (Herzfeld 1992:32). Intermarriage between Italian and Portuguese Canadians can be interpreted as 'morally' sanctioned by an ethnonationalist ideology that views the two groups as linked through blood and therefore extended family.

Through the evening a joking relationship developed between the speakers of the Italian community (as big brothers or godfathers) and the Portuguese speakers (as younger relatives). One Italian-Canadian speaker noted with a grin that, 'the Portuguese had pushed the Italians out of Dundas, then College, and now they had made it to Lawrence and Dufferin (the site of Villa Colombo); pretty soon it will be Woodbridge.' In one speech a Portuguese-Canadian politician linked the Roman Empire's failure to invade and subdue Portugal to the recent soccer match in qualifying rounds for the 1994 World Cup, which saw Portugal upset a heavily favoured Italian squad. In addition, he linked the common dislike of Rome by many Italian immigrants from southern and northern Italy, because of its bureaucratic domination of the country, to the historical experience of the Roman invasions of Portugal. Referring to an ancient bridge built by Roman invaders using Portuguese labour, he noted that both for Italian immigrants here with memories of Italy and for the Portuguese 2,000 years ago, the foreman was always Roman. The ideology of intercultural sharing and understanding is reinforced through the ritualized function of a banquet between leadership from two potentially competing ethnic groups in the city.

Final Remarks

Ethnocultural associations emerged within the Italian-Canadian community during the post-1945 years to respond to a complex set of demands and needs among Italian immigrants in Toronto, and to the increased intrusiveness of the welfare state in people's lives. One of these needs was the care of elderly, who, with little English, found life difficult in English-Canadian institutions. Converging with this social need was the desire of Italian Canadians, and especially the leadership, to find acceptance, status, and legitimation in the broader Canadian society, which they determined could be best achieved through the sponsorship of communal good deeds. Finally, in response to polyethnicity governments began to seek community-based organizations to deliver services to newer groups of Canadians. Throughout the last two decades the Italian Canadian Benevolent Corporation has constructed several buildings as cultural centres and seniors' homes, partly in the hopes of increasing community status and creating a focus for Italian-Canadian pride. The Columbus Centre has emerged as a focal point of interaction with other ethnocultural groups, the media, other Italian diaspora communities, and various levels of government. Moreover, because of its central role in the topography of polyethnic Toronto, its participants are constantly redefining Italian-Canadian ethnicity.

Those who have participated in the construction of the Italian Canadian Benevolent Corporation's multi-service buildings assume that future generations will continue to support the Centre. The perpetuation of the ethnocommunity is seen as inevitable. For believers the corporate unity of the Italian community must become more than just imagined. At the same time, the realities of economic survival for ethnocommunal projects and the cultural ambiguities of North American life encourage Italian associations to assess their role as resources on Italianness and storehouses of cultural knowledge for the broader public. As a result of the commodification of Italianness for consumption by the Canadian public, Italian-Canadian ethnicity is being altered by a constant shifting of ideas about ethnic attributes. But the diversity within the Italian settlement cannot be easily ignored by elites and leadership who wish to create a corporate unity. Community is an ambiguous and elusive concept, with constantly shifting frames of reference. An Italian-Canadian of Molisan regional heritage at the ICBC, when asked where Molise was, made an interesting analogy: 'Molise bridges the gap between the north and south in Italy. The Molisans do the same thing for the community here. In Canada we are trying to pull together the two regions on our backs.' As he spoke his knowing grin acknowledged the fiction of a corporate unity but also the symbolic and practical necessity of such a conceit in a polyethnic society.

5. Remembering the Apennines and Building the Centres: Italian Regionalism in Canada

Fieldnote, 4 December 1994
I attended the groundbreaking today of the Casa D'Abruzzo apartment
for seniors at the corner of Keele Street and Highway 401. It was a cool
dreary day, but that did not stop more than two hundred people from
coming to the muddy construction site to listen to speeches. Odoardo di
Santo, and Gino Ventresca, who spearheaded the project, hosted Premier
Rae; Anthony Perruzza, MPP; Tony Silipo, MPP and minister of community and social services (and the highest ranking cabinet member of Italian heritage); Joe Volpe, MP (I assume he took part because there is
federal CMHC mortgaging); Richard Allen, MPP and minister of housing; Metro Councillors Maria Augimeri and Judy Sgro. Silvana Pelusi,
assessora regional all' emigrazione, bilancio e cultura dell 'Abruzzo (minister of
emigration, budget and culture) attended as the representative of the
Abruzzese regional government. Conversations I heard in the crowd were
replete with community politics that I only partially understood. Personal
rivalries seemed to be at the heart of the matter: Who, for example, is the
most powerful Italian heritage politician in the province? I asked Joe, an
older man I had met at a few banquets and community events, for his
opinion. He was succinct and blunt, pleased with his turn of phrase:
'Nick, it's nothing; it's all about who is the "top wop" in Ontario. Look,
we're breaking ground today so Tony [Silipo] must have done something
for us.'

Over the last few months there has been a lot of pressure on Silipo, the
top provincial minister of Italian heritage, to attempt to help the different regional groups navigate the arduous process of applications to gov-

ernment ministries. One speech from the makeshift podium at this barren construction site suggested that Abruzzese Canadians, unlike other people, have never been linked to crime but are hard-working, honest people who have contributed a lot and are therefore deserving of this new building complex. It was not clear who the 'other people' were, but a few people around me, emigrants from other regions in Italy, shifted uncomfortably. There has been a sense of rivalry developing between the Abruzzese- and the Calabrese-Canadian leadership over who can (or should) get money to build a seniors' home/cultural centre. My friend John tells me that even his dad, an immigrant from Calabria who never shows interest in community events or projects, much less expresses a strong sense of Calabrian regional solidarity, remarked after seeing a brief news clip about the potential for a Calabrese home: '"We" deserve one.'

After a few speeches a priest blessed the rock of the new Casa D'Abruzzo, saying that, like the Gran Sasso mountain chain in the central Italian region of Abruzzo, it would be a house that includes everyone. I was told that neighbours in homes across the street, many of Italian heritage, are content that the Casa D'Abruzzo will be a seniors' apartment and not a *casa popolare* (public housing project) so their property values will not fall.

The crowd was well dressed for an event at a construction site, the women in heels, the men in loafers and shining new construction caps. As the brass band played triumphant tunes I looked at the improvised but sturdy podium and saw that it was bedecked in blue, white, and green ribbons, the (subnational? ethnoregional? transethnonational?) colours of the Abruzzese diaspora. Speeches praised Canada and the opportunities it had given the humble immigrants from Abruzzo. Premier Rae's speech honoured Gino Ventresca and Odoardo di Santo for the work they had done, and he intimated that his association with Italian Canadians had been a long one, first as a lawyer and then as a politician. He especially referred to the hard work Italians had done to help build the province. But even though Premier Rae had attended the groundbreaking, and the Ontario government was providing most of the funds for the project, it was the presence of the *assessore* (minister) from the region of Abruzzo that created the most excitement. For many with whom I spoke her presence had added an intangible emotional texture and weight to the occasion. Joe told me he had left Abruzzo with nothing, and when he went back to visit people there, he had felt for a while that they were ashamed of him, his need to leave Italy to find work, his archaic dialect, and his children's loss of Italian culture. Now, finally, somehow this Casa project indicated to him that the people from his place of origin recognized him and all he had accomplished.

I turned back to catch the end of the speech. It ended in an impassioned tone that concretized the presence of Abruzzese in Toronto and gave it wider meaning by placing it within the global migration projects of the Abruzzese. As the speaker said, 'the centre will create a dot on the map of Canada for Abruzzese around the world.'

In the 1960s Clyde Mitchell (1966) and others, during studies of urbanization and ethnicity (tribalism) in Africa, adopted the concept of 'situational selection' in order to interpret the multiple and potentially conflicting identities informants used in an urban setting as they interacted in different social fields. Downsview and Woodbridge, areas of considerable Italian-Canadian settlement, are a long distance from the urban centres Mitchell and others studied in the Copperbelt of Africa, but the authors' work on the selective use of identities, and processual change in identities, has resonance when we try to understand some of the changes occurring among emigrants from the Italian peninsula arriving in the greater Toronto region today. In the postwar period the Italian immigrant was well-prepared for the 'multiplicity of roles he or she need[ed] to play every day' (A.P. Cohen 1985:27) within the context of Canadian society because of his or her experience with a fragmented Italian nationalism. Moreover, the introduction of multiculturalism into public discourse in the early 1970s permitted immigrants from the Italian peninsula and their children to explore a wider social space within the concept of Canadian nationalism. Anthony Cohen (ibid:12) argues that 'community implies both similarity and difference. In other words it is a relational idea. The boundaries perceived by some may be imperceptible to many.' The case of Italian-Canadian regional identity is illustrative of the shifting boundaries and content of personal identity and community: 'The boundary represents the mask presented by the community to the outside world; it is the community's public face ... the boundary as the community's public face is symbolically simple; but, as the object of internal discourse it is symbolically complex' (ibid.: 74).

This chapter discusses and analyses one form of Italian-Canadian ethnicity or sub-identity that has become more current in both rhetoric and action in the past decade. The expression of Italian regional identities in Canada permits the public to glimpse ambiguous and complex realities concerning what it is to be Italian Canadian. The state, for its part, is responding to these shifts. First, I discuss the way in which those involved with associations and/or projects based on their Italian region of origin interpret their multiple loyalties in the context of Canadian nationalism. Second, I use two case studies, the Veneto Centre and the Casa D'Abruzzo, to illustrate how these imagined communities are made tangible with the help of state resources at various levels of jurisdiction.

If trying to determine the actual numbers of immigrants from various regions is fraught with difficulties, assessing the sentiment, sense of community, and identity of the immigrants in Canada who make up these numbers leads one quickly into uncomfortable analysis. As one friend said, 'about all we might agree on is that the Calabrese are by the far the largest, and then followed probably by the Abruzzese, Laziali, Friulani, and then the rest. What do you call my wife in these calculations? She has an Italian passport because she was born in Belgium of Italian immigrants there who had emigrated from Abruzzi when they were teenagers and then they came here. So what is she?'

Furthermore, in the case of the Region of Molise, the matter is more complicated. Until 1963 Molise was a part of the Region of Abruzzo. It was only after those emigrants who left the Region of Abruzzi-Molise between 1951 and 1963 had arrived in Canada that a regional government administrative structure known as Molise was created.

Political Changes in Italy

As emigration from the Italian peninsula slowed during the 1970s, new political jurisdictions in Italy created the circumstances for expanded contact and innovation in relations today between Italian immigrants and their children in Toronto and the social, cultural, and commercial interests in their ancestral Italian regions of emigration. The origins of these jurisdictional changes arose from decisions made in the immediate aftermath of the Second World War. In an effort to loosen the centralization of power in Mussolini's fascist state, the makers of the 1948 postwar Italian republican constitution had agreed to a devolution of power to twenty regional governments. But it was not until 1970 that there were elections for regional councils, and not until 1972 did the Italian national parliament proceed with this devolution of power by approving the constitutions of the regions and transferring power in two stages, in 1972 and 1977. This delay in power-sharing reflected Italian party politics. The Christian Democrats, who controlled the national government, wanted to prevent communists and socialists from gaining power in the regional juntas and acquiring the levers to many patronage positions the new level of government would offer.

Over the next decade the structures and responsibilities for regional governments established in theory in the 1970s were slowly and haltingly bargained over and negotiated by Italy's national government and regional politicians. Italy's political structures and classes have undergone swift transformations between 1989 and 1997. The political bribery *Tangentopoli* (corruption uncovered in Milan in the 1990s) and Mafia scandals coupled to discredit and topple the ruling Christian Democrats and their allies. These scandals led to several short-lived coalition governments and numerous other changes: a new hybrid electoral process that combined first-past-the-post and proportional representation, stronger regional parties in northern Italy, newly organized ex-communist and communist parties in the wake of the demise of the Soviet Union, a resurgent right-wing party with support in southern Italy, and the party of Italian media giant Silvio Berlusconi (Levy 1996). In this fluid context the powers appointed to Italian regions and their relation to the national government in Rome are likely to change as the country reorganizes its political life.

Nevertheless, by the 1990s the transfer of power to the regions included responsibilities for regional economic development and the delivery of social services. But the regions still depended on transfers from Rome for almost 90 per cent of their budget, of which fully two-thirds were non-discretionary payments, that is, payments for national health services or other fixed welfare-state activities. All laws passed by regional juntas must still be vetted to make certain they do not conflict with complicated and detailed national laws, with the result that many initiatives are slowed by party bickering and bureaucratic barriers (Hine 1996; Bartole 1984; Spotts and Wieser 1986). The regional juntas have also been criticized for not using all the funds apportioned to them because of the lack of programs, initiative, or political stability within some regional governments, especially in the south.

Included in the limited transfer of powers were activities relating to emigration, immigration, tourism, fishing, welfare and health services, pensions, professional and trade schools, agriculture, and forestry. During the early 1980s regional governments established *consigli* or *comitati* (councils) to advise *assessori* responsible for matters relating to emigrants. Representatives from regional communities overseas were appointed to these councils. In December 1993 I attended a meeting of the Consiglio Regionale per l'Emigrazione e l'Immigrazione for the Region of Abruzzo, in a resort town on the Adriatic coast north of Pescara, as the guest of Renzo, the *consultore* (councillor) for Abruzzo, who lived in Toronto at the time and was a longtime and active participant in projects and organizations within Toronto's Italian settlement. Individuals from major communities of *Abruzzesi all'estero* (people from the region of Abruzzo abroad) advised the minister in charge of matters for the Region of Abruzzo on ways to serve Abruzzesi overseas more successfully. Suggestions ranged from the sponsoring of tours for retired immigrants back to their land of birth and the organization of summer language and tour programs for immigrants' children who had never seen their 'homeland,' to lobbying the Italian central government on behalf of immigrants for the right to cast votes overseas in Italian elections.

These new efforts have received considerable attention by

regional governments seeking to tap the potential financial resources of former residents now in Canada, South America, other European countries and Australia, both as tourists or as investors. In the 6 April 1993 issue of the Italian-language newspaper *Lo Specchio*, distributed in the northwest suburbs of Toronto and the surrounding Italian-Canadian enclaves in Vaughan, Italians of Abruzzese origin were assured of greater access to their region of origin by a major tour carrier to Italy. The carrier had signed an accord with the *assessore* of Abruzzo that would allow direct flights from Toronto to Abruzzo, bypassing Rome. While the economic impact migrants have had on their land of emigration through remittances has been well studied (Philpott 1973; Watson 1977; Lopreato 1967), that of tourism has not. As one acute observer noted concerning the changing financial link between migrants and the land of emigration: 'Regional authorities find in the tourist and trade possibilities of increased ties with emigrants, a financial resource which should more than compensate for the decline of remittances which comes naturally with the maturing of a migration cohort overseas' (R.F. Harney 1993:114).

As noted earlier, the consultore is appointed to the regional advisory council by the region. There are no elections, and as one consultore in Toronto told me, the advice they give is considered that of an individual not a community; nevertheless, since access to both information and functionaries in Italy is part of this broker's position between the community and regional governments, we can assume he is often asked to speak for the larger community. However, though one's selection to the post of consultore gives the appearance of being based on an individual's political and personal networks within regional governments, the inevitable factions and competing interests within an ethnocommunity often translate into intense distrust of leaders who are allied with one state resource or another. In some instances the resulting conflicts arise from ideological differences, but they may also arise when there is unequal access to material resources. For example, even if a consultore has good personal relations with other Italian-Canadian spokespeople, the potential for conflict is inherent in the position. The perception that one is speaking for all the Abruzzese or Calabrese or Laziali in

Ontario creates friction and suspicion, and calls for more democratic access to the region in question. Others complain that the regions are just attempting to exploit the emigrants as a colony. Still others see those involved with a region at this level as those who are after political patronage and somehow too tied to their land of origin. While the financial largesse of these comitati may not be that significant, the status and prestige accorded to members and the need to find an identity more connected to the places they know from their everyday lives, makes this position a valuable award.

It should be noted, too, that the Italian national government has appointed committees in various forms going back to the fascist years under Mussolini. The most recent advisory groups are called the COMITES (Comitato italiano all'estero; Committee for Italians Abroad). The council in this case advises the Italian government on policies towards emigrants. A heated debate between the National Congress of Italian Canadians, an umbrella organization of associations of Italian Canadians, and the Italian government over the legitimacy of the Italian state concerning activities in Canada is recorded almost every week in the principal ItalianCanadian newspaper *Corriere Canadese*.

Constructing Italian Regionalisms in Toronto

In the last decade Italians in Toronto have begun to organize their paesi clubs into federations and associations based on the aforementioned regional identities, which are more significant than the home towns. Some of the most prominent and active are the following: Confederazione Calabro-Canadese, Federazione delle Associazioni del Lazio in Canada, Federazione delle Associazioni e Club Abruzzesi Greater Toronto, Federazione Clubs e Associazioni Venete-Ontario, and The Federation of Sicilian Clubs (Carella and Chianello 1990; Buranello and Lettieri 1993). The relative economic success of Italian-Canadians, an increase in leisure time for the immigrant generation as it approaches retirement, the social space created by the discourse of multiculturalism, and the activities of Italian regional governments, have all encouraged this flourishing of organizations.

The supra-local federations based on administrative realities in Italy, as well as memories and loyalties in the individual and collective minds of diaspora Italians in greater Toronto, are still, however, constituted by local paese club realities. These federations are both more and less than the amalgamation of the many paesi or home-town clubs that have organized themselves in these larger orders of institution. As I demonstrate later, federations are more in the sense that they constitute a significant political force that is able to accrue state resources; yet they are less to some extent in that they survive only through the activities and sentiments of home-town clubs. In almost all situations the presidents of the paesi groups are the officers of the federations. Exceptions to this locally based infrastructure of regional federations are emerging, and these indicate what Mitchell and others have called *processual* rather than *situational* changes in identity (Mitchell 1966). Within the Veneto federation some groups have emerged that are solely based on this wider territorial fictive kinship base, the region.

One could speculate that there are many reasons for this development: (1) the necessity of meeting the needs of immigrants and their families from a town that sent too few families to sustain the activities of an association; (2) the existence of children who prefer the *Veneti* (people from the Region of Veneto) community with its larger pool of people the same age within which to meet friends; (3) the limited historical memory and emotional bonds based on the personal experience of children of immigrants, for whom a knowledge of the paesi of emigration consists of a few visits in the summers to cousins or to *nonni* (grandparents), and the stories of parents and relatives; (4) the hegemonic influence of the Veneti as a form of self-identity reinforced by the successful, that is, impressive, physical structure of their centre and grounds, and through the larger economic, demographic, and political resources available to the Veneti as a group. This is not to discount the power and influence of some of the subgroupings based on the province or town of origin, but to suggest that in the competition between different boundaries in the symbolic construction of community, under existing conditions, the regional one has the potential for wider affiliation. I will return to the Veneti and their associations later.

With the recent upsurge in regionalism in Toronto, one friend who works in a pan-Italian institution told me that it is hard to find friends any more who want to be simply Italian Canadian. Many are developing their regional ties: 'There are just too many of us, so I guess each person is trying find something in their past that's more intimate.' The literary critic Homi Bhabha has written about the space created within a nation's discourse for expression and experimentation by minority groups: 'Once the liminality of the nation-space is established, and its "difference" is turned from the boundary "outside" to its finitude "'within,'" the threat of cultural difference is no longer a problem of other people. It becomes a question of the otherness of the people-as-one' (1990:301).

In my fieldwork experience, the liminality of the nation-space is better understood in the context of global flows of migration, technology, and transportation. Italian regional television networks create and market flashy videocassettes of historical sites, cultural events, commercial products, or illustrious citizens of the 'homeland.' Newspapers and magazines such as *Friuli nel Mondo*, *La Regione Calabria – Emigrazione*, and *Abruzzesi nel Mondo*, published in Italy and exported along the networks of the diaspora, contain articles about the region and the other colonies of the diaspora in Australia, Belgium, France, or the many countries of Latin America. Associations send information about the local activities, for example, of Abruzzesi in Toronto, so that cousins or fictive kin in other parts of the diaspora can read about or see faces in the larger 'imagined community,' which are sent through the papers, letters, and magazines of 'print capitalism' (Anderson 1983) and the videos and cinema of 'electronic capitalism' (Warner 1992; Lee 1993).

But the affiliation with one's land of emigration does not preclude a 'rootedness' in the new land (A.P. Cohen 1985; Appadurai 1993). In the speech of those involved with these associations, Canada is seen as a fortunate migration choice by a part of that broader migrating community, especially when the situation here is compared to the economic and political instability of South American countries such as Argentina and Brazil. In several instances during my research I was informed of or read community material about organized trips to Friulan or Abruzzesi associations in Argentina and Brazil. The tone of the stories always seemed the same: while there was joy at discovering cousins and fictive kin in other lands who had created a piece of their home town some-where else, ultimately it was impled that the cousins were less fortu-nate in their choice of a new home. For example, one newsletter of the Famee Furlane organization in Toronto reported on a trip some of its members had taken to South America to meet Friulans there: '*Friulanità* (Friulan ambience) survived and is prospering in both Americas, but the people present could see that destiny was kinder to us in Canada.'

The 'Finitude Within' the Nation-Space

I want to turn here to the way some Italian-Canadians talk about these multiple identities and 'communities of belonging.' For some there appears to be a finitude for self-expression within the Canadian nation-space, even if the aggregate Italian-Canadian boundary masks that diversity to outsiders. The following quota-tions are lengthy, but their thread is indispensable for seeing this complexity as lived experience:

1. If you are Welsh it is okay if you talk [in public] about different regional aspects, and some categories apply; but here in Canada it is more difficult to speak of yourself as Molise because they think of you as Italian. But being Molisani, it is the same thing as Welsh ... Here they [Anglo-Canadians] cannot control the process. One cannot have a future if you do not have a past. Jews epitomize the strength of good Canadians ... inner strength comes from a certain sense of history ... there is fragmentation of the concept of Italy. To our children we are saying that you are Italian, but also from Molise and the town of so and so. There is a 'genetic link' to where your ancestors were in Molise ... you try to instil the history in your child of Petrarch and the Sannites, but there is still a 'genetic culture' of where you are from.

I brought my kids there to Molise ... What is it? A mountain? It is nothing. I brought my seven-year-old for the first time and we looked over the castle built by the Longobards, and the history of that place and castle will always be with him ... I bring my children here for a week like I would to the Plains of Abraham. There has been history in Molise ... it is not just a mass of rocks or brown agricultural and natural hills. From these rocks have emigrated thousands of people all around the world. When my son comes here, he is not a Molisani, but it gives him something, a better sense of history, a better sense of the world, and it makes him a better Canadian to have this cultural link. We have organized many happenings here in Canada to continue the cultural links ... in 1984 a soccer club from Campobasso played at Varsity Stadium, paid for by us.

Research into the Sannite history of the region was done by a Canadian at McMaster University ... historically Sannites predate the Romans and fought them in Campania and Molise. These early Sannites formed confederations of tribes, and thus what we see there is sociohistorical precedence for the confederations here in Canada. In knowledge of our history we are ensuring continuity of the memory and landscape, and we are insisting our children be aware of this continuity even if they go to Osgoode or Harvard.

2. I started working here at the Veneto Centre and realized that Veneti are not dark-haired and dark-skinned [like me] ... but I was speaking the same dialect, same language. There were so many of them, a critical mass existed. I had found a community. I started learning the story of these people, the history of the Veneto, and I started to take pride in it. In law school everyone has their own little cause, no one is calling themselves Canadian. Meech Lake was just for the French and English and the next agreement was just for the French, English, and Indians. Those events focused and spurred my identity because it was talked about so much.

So you ask, who am I? This place [Club Veneto] offered an answer. At school I am Italian and I make no bones about it. I think of myself as Italian and less as an Italian Canadian. You need to separate the notion of nation from state. In terms of state and elected officials, law, and so on, I am Canadian. In terms that connect people together – it doesn't matter where the border is – I'm Italian, I'm Veneto. I'm a particular breed who happens to be born in Canada, Sao Paolo, Paris, New York, or Argentina for that matter. Somehow I feel I belong to that nation. Indians don't look at borders, so why should I?

Now I don't feel an allegiance to the state of Italy if Italy goes to war, but I'm Italian. I am from the Veneto and that is why at certain times I think the way I think. Why not do a series of half-hour video productions on the Veneto and Veneti? But not the one back in Italy ... I also believe there is a Veneto here – let's export [my Veneto-Canadian experience] to Veneti in Brazil, Australia, and so on – and I have this corner here to start to nurture and market myself. This place [Veneto Centre] I would like to make a premier cultural centre, and not just with polenta and sausage ... the high culture stuff is okay as long it can be diffused into the masses.

3. So what are the concerns we have? Parents would like to see the children not lose their heritage, their ties with the country of origin. It is part of their history. I tend to agree, in effect, that if you do not know your region you cannot be a complete individual. You can reaffirm yourself better if you know where you come from. We feel ourselves Canadians in all respects. It is a matter really of being better citizens. If people do not know where they come from they are not complete individuals; they cannot reaffirm themselves within the society as they could if they had this base where they could feel strong and protect themselves.

You have to know the history of Calabria. Calabria has been occupied by many different races – Greeks, Romans, Byzantines, Ottomans, Albanians – from all over. We're talking about maybe ten different races. It would be very difficult really to have Calabria analysed. You go from one town in Calabria to the next and the dialect is different. In Calabria we still have communities of Greeks who speak Greek and they are Orthodox. They still have conservative views about religious issues and language. In this institute we would build there would be some suites for researchers from overseas. And this institute would have the task of studying Calabria and Calabrese overseas, and bringing scholars, and linking with other institutions that have a similar interest around the world. It could really become a focal point for Calabrese around the world.

These statement contain several recurrent themes concerning Italian regional identity: (1) that the knowledge of one's regional history, ancient and recent, makes one a more complete person;

(2) a corollary of the latter point, that a more complete person is a better Canadian citizen; (3) that membership in a diaspora or transnation (Appadurai 1993) offers the security of a sense of belonging; (4) that the transnation is a potentially exploitable resource, not only concerning personal identity but also for its possible exportable, commercial value, such as ready-made markets and networks of like-minded real and fictive kin who are members of a symbolic community.

Sentiment and Cement: Building Regional Centres

The sentiment of regional identity has been announcing itself visually, in concrete realities, in the suburbs of greater Toronto. As noted earlier, federations of clubs and associations have been created in the last ten years by emigrants from specific regions in Italy, most of whom, in turn, have been sponsoring, planning, and seeking government and community funding for construction projects such as cultural centres, seniors' apartments, and sports complexes. In one small area in the northwest part of greater Toronto, on the northern edge of Downsview and the southern part of Woodbridge, at least four regional associations have either constructed multi-use centres or have requests pending with the provincial or municipal governments. The area bounded by Weston Road in the east, Steeles Avenue to the south, Highway 7 and its adjacent lands to the north, and Martingrove Avenue to the West, is the geographic space of most interest, since it caters to the Italian-Canadian enclaves within Metro Toronto and the suburbs just beyond, such as Woodbridge and Maple. Some groups, such as the Famee Furlane and the Federazione Clubs e Associazioni Venete-Ontario, have complexes that are built and operational. Efforts have been under way by two other groups: one that is claiming to represent the Laziali, and another – one that wants to represent CALM, a combination of the four regions of Calabria, Abruzzo, Lucania, and Molise – that has made a submission to Vaughan council for sixty-four acres of green-belt land. An article in *Lo Specchio* included architectural plans for the latter multi-regional complex, which includes two soccer fields (one for seniors), a stadium, social-club buildings, tennis courts, and bocce courts, and baseball and softball diamonds. This combined group has since broken down into its component Italian ethnoregional parts, each part pursuing its own project. The Abruzzese group is constructing seniors' apartments and a community centre in Downsview.

Werbner and Anwar's (1991:23) perceptive analysis of Black and South-Asian ethnic associations and leadership can help us interpret Italian-Canadian associational life and leadership. As they have noted, state and local governments attempt to address economic structural problems and/or welfare state imperatives through the funding of ethnocultural communities: '"Ethnic" claims to collective consumption or representative status are, it must be remembered, made by associations and their leaders in the name of deeply felt symbolic requirements and experiences ... The primary aim of these associations is, after all, to ensure the autonomy of the immigrant community and establish the basis for its future cultural continuity and reproduction' (ibid:28).

Two ways to ensure this autonomy are (1) to convince different levels of government that one's group constitutes an ethnic group and therefore a political entity and constituency, (2) to build a physical plant, not only as a material testament to one's existence but also as a symbolic and material resource. In two recent examples, segments of the Italian-Canadian collectivity emerged as ethnocultural entities in the competition for state resources: the Veneti and the Abruzzesi. A brief description here of their federations and projects will give us a sense of the dialectic between regional identity and government sponsorship at work in the construction of new symbolic communities in a multicultural society.

The Veneto Centre

The Federazione dei Clubs e Associazioni Venete dell'Ontario was created in the fall of 1984. The five original clubs of the Federazione, and later its Veneto Centre, were the San Marco Club (70 families), the Associazione Trevisani Nel Mondo (350 families), Club

Piave (40 families), Club Vicentino (80 families), and Famiglia Belunese (70 families). Later, four other clubs joined the group: Toronto Boccefila (50 to 60 families (some are also Friulani), the Montegrappa Society (70 to 80 families), Gruppo Regionale (100 families), and Gioventù Veneta (65 to 100 youth). Today it is estimated that about 800 families belong to the Veneto Centre. It should be noted also that the present consultore was the president of one of the original five clubs, and now, as a representative of the region, he sits on the cultural committee of the Veneto Centre.

In 1984 the original five clubs got together, as informants, say, for convenience only, to pursue the purchase of a piece of Crown land available in the Kipling and Highway 7 area. It was better, they felt, to approach the government as a group. The Famee Furlane, a multiuse complex organized by members of the Friulani community and just a short distance away, was seen by other Italian regional groups as an example of how to build a community project. With an opportunity to acquire Crown land, raconteurs say that the thinking in the mid-1980s was that this land would be used for picnics and outdoor sports, and rented to other Italian-Canadian groups and to non- Italian civic groups in Vaughan, such as the Woodbridge Soccer League and the baseball leagues. The land could also be used for the picnics of other Federazioni (Abruzzesi, Molisani, Laziali), feste, public events sponsored by CIAO (an Italian-language radio station), and Channel 47's wine festival, Mosti Mondiali. Through these events other Italian-Canadian regional groups glimpsed the possibilities for their own sites.

According to members, the concept of a centre emerged after organizers saw the site plan. Because many people of Veneti origin are involved in the construction industry, a site plan was a familiar tool for many involved. One member mentioned with a smile that his group's membership had expertise in every part of construction except drainpipes. In 1989 the Veneto Centre received a $400,000 lottery grant from the province to begin the building project, and a fund-raising campaign among the members raised an additional $1.2 million.

Organizational unity has not always been easy, as rivalries and personality conflicts between the leadership of constituent clubs has lead to conflict for hegemony of the whole (segmentary conflict). Some have also seen the energies devoted to the Veneto Centre as draining the resources of locally based club sites and activities. In addition, several of these organizations (as Italian-provincial or locally based clubs) have infrastructures and networks of their own that extend throughout the world. For example, there are international organizations of these local clubs, based in the Region of Veneto, which distribute newsletters. However, the region has recently reduced funding to the Veneto provincial groups, such as those from Treviso, in favour of Veneto-wide programs of exchange and promotion.

Inevitably the Federazione, through its physical presence and legitimization by state funds, has emerged as more than an extension of the original five clubs. One young man active in the Centre seemed to understand the importance of print (Anderson 1983) to the process of constructing an ethnic group: 'To those of us who are involved with the place it has begun to look as if it has a life of its own. A newsletter is published here, letterhead is created, contracts are signed. I feel like one of a real entity.'

The material changes in the status of the Centre from campground to clubhouse, banquet hall, and multi-use facility create a physical structure that gives presence to the identity for people from Veneto. A *processual* change in identity is also being constructed by the Centre through the creation of two new clubs that are constituent members of the umbrella federation and therefore voting members. Gruppo Regionale (100 families) is an arm of the Federation created for anyone who did not belong to a paesi club. It has complete rights, i.e., representation on the Veneto Centre Board, as does the Gioventù Veneta (65 to 100 youth). As another young woman said, rather innocently, 'Day by day the other clubs are losing power to the Federation.'

Casa D'Abruzzo

As the age pyramid of the Italian-Canadian settlement edges towards retirement, new projects by community groups to gain access to funding from state and local state governments to construct seniors' apartments emerge as more central in the debates about what communities should do. Governments appear to be seeking ethnocultural communities as well, to assist with these welfare-state programs. In the early 1990s some Italian-Canadian regionally based groups have obtained monies from the joint federal-provincial (Canadian Mortgage and Housing Corporation and Province of Ontario Ministry of Housing) program for community-based seniors' housing. One of the issues surrounding the public financing of facilities for ethnocultural communities is that the Human Rights Code of Ontario prohibits discrimination on the basis of ethnic identity. The stipulations of the code, one Italian-Canadian leader expressed to me, were not always easy to relay to someone who wanted to donate to a seniors' home or cultural centre built for people from his place of emigration. Often, such a donor thought all his money would go to his paesani. Werbner and Anwar (1991:32) have noted the importance of this government intervention in the modern polyethnic state: '... community groups are *entitled* to state funding as citizens and taxpayers; they often need this funding in order to build ethnic institutions which are not dependent on the largesse of wealthy community members ... State giving ... implies symbolic incorporation of ethnic groups into the wider moral community. It objectifies equality and citizenship rights. Such giving therefore has a symbolic dimension, whatever its instrumental utility.'

A group of Canadians of Friulani heritage in Windsor and another in Greater Toronto, respectively, constructed several hundred units of affordable apartments for seniors through this program. Federazione, Associazioni e Club Abruzzesi Greater Toronto also obtained state funding for its project Casa D'Abruzzo (on provincial land at Keele Street and Highway 401), which includes the construction of apartments for seniors and a community centre.

The first approaches to create the Federazione Abruzzesi were made in 1982 by Club Abruzzi (founded in 1957), with the advice and encouragement of two consultori, who had been involved in a number of Italian-Canadian community activities in other capacities. In the club's 25th jubilee magazine, a sense of the larger regional community already existed. Its editor responded to a

Toronto journalist who had used as rhetorical resources a mix of national, regional, and local identities:

> Some hard-headed, red-neck, pseudo-writers who fill editorial pages of the Toronto junk press seem to think our love for the Queen is not as pure as it should be because we don't repudiate Pietro da Celano and what goes with it. The point seems to be that we can't be good Canadians and remain (with our children and the children of our children) good Italians at the same time ...
>
> Well, we as Abruzzese people have an answer for these ignorant bigots. 'Not only do we keep the hyphen, but we add another one.' Therefore you call us Abruzzese-Italian-Canadian because that's what we are. We take the opportunity to suggest that our beloved friends, the other 'hyphenated Canadians,' follow our examples so that you will have Macedonian-Greek-Canadian, Andalusian-Spanish-Canadian, Azorean-Portuguese-Canadian, and so on. (Guardiani 1982:3)

In 1988 and 1989 the Federation was realigned to include Greater Toronto: Mississauga, York, Vaughan, and Markham. Each club delegates someone to represent it at the federation level, and every two years there is a new board of directors. Informants say the Federation is needed to collect the community, maintain ties to Abruzzo and Italy in general, expose children to cultural and linguistic traditions through events, sponsor exchanges for students and *anziani* (the elderly), and generally carry out a variety of projects for the Abruzzese community in Toronto. The regional government of Abruzzo has told the Toronto community that they have the greatest number of Abruzzese outside of Abruzzo.

The Casa D'Abruzzo is not officially an association. For legal reasons it would be better to think of it as a non-profit charitable organization. The Casa D'Abruzzo Benevolent Corporation will get funding (approximately $16 million) for the shelter part of its construction (175 seniors' apartments). The extra $3 million or so it needs for the non-shelter component (library, offices, meeting rooms, a banquet hall ...) is not included in the funding program of the Ontario Ministry of Housing and the CMHC; it therefore has to be raised by the Abruzzesi community, although a portion of that total will be received as part of a grant from the provincial government's JobsOntario Community Action program. The contribution of the Region is multi-pronged. In addition to $250,000 as a contribution, the region also develops networks for cultural exchange, tourist travel, and educational materials. It has also promised to supply the materials for the library.

At a meeting of a group of Canadians of Abruzzesi origin gathered to discuss the Casa D'Abruzzo project I asked one member, in the gathering of fifteen or so, Why a Casa D'Abruzzo? Why not an Italian Centre or the United Way? He replied that those other causes were good but first 'we must take care of our own.' Within the same room there were people who had emigrated from towns in the mountain areas of L'Aquila and Avezzano, and still others who were from the coastal towns north and south of Pescara. As the conversation wore on, gentle and lighthearted ribbing persisted between these groups. It culminated in the reaction to the architect's drawing of the Casa D'Abruzzo, which had several architectural features reminiscent of the geography of the region, including a series of stone supports that had mnemonic resonance with the medieval aqueduct of Sulmona. The terms of the fundraising and the project were clear and accepted. All those in the room were soundly behind the project. It seemed, however, that the aspect that caused the most controversy, even though unquestionably friendly, was whether the architect had drawn an image of the Apennines from the appropriate side of the great mountain range that dominates the region. Should it be a view of the Gran Sasso, one of the majestic, snow-capped mountains seen from Teramo? Or should it be from L'Aquila or from the Maiella of the Marone chain as seen from Chieti and Sulmona? All of them provided appropriate nostalgic references for the prosperous immigrants who were now creating a physical locus of sentiment for the imagined community of the roughly 70,000 Abruzzesi Canadians.

Final Remarks

A submerged identity of a more supra-locally based loyalty among immigrants from the Italian peninsula has achieved a certain degree of reality within the context of Canadian society. With the aid of plural state policies and resources, these solidarities are given added currency. Within the social space of the Canadian nation, members of the larger Italian-Canadian community have defined a smaller moral community within which to express, adapt, and defend themselves.

Social space is not shifting, either more locally or globally, but there is a rearrangement or reordering in the relationship between them. In a sense, the growth of regional activities and other transnational practices among Italians in Toronto, as discussed in this book, offers signs of changes in the social organization of time and space that social theorists have detected in the postmodern world of late capitalism (Harvey 1989; Giddens 1984; 1990). The time-space compression that Harvey observes has occurred for Italian-Canadians. The instantaneous time of advertising and television allows for products from each region in Italy to be consumed by Toronto's Italians. The region the emigrant has left has now literally come to set up shop next door, to encourage tourism and investment. Regionally sponsored cultural centres with libraries and exhibits provide information not only about famous poets, folklore groups, or tourist attractions in one's 'homeland,' but also about the newest technological breakthroughs in mechanical engineering or design and olive oil and other food products of companies in regions of origin. The centres also create seemingly familiar places to meet officials from the regional governments, who, for example, can help negotiate Italy's public pension maze or investment rules. At the same time, Giddens's notion of 'time-space distanciation' also occurs. No matter how much effort is exerted to inculcate one's children with experiences, ideas, and nostalgia for their ancestral homeland, social activity to enhance these identity-forming experiences must depend on those who are further away in both time and space. This distance reinforces the physical and temporal reality that the separation has occurred through the migration experience.

Tentative plans are under way for the construction of a centre/ institute for the largest subcommunity among Italian-Canadian immigrants, the Calabrese. According to speeches at community banquets the Calabrese community can number as many as 200,000 or as few as 120,000. It is perhaps too large a group – from four different provinces in Calabria (Reggio, Cosenza, Vibo, and Catanzaro) – to sustain the unity its members need to satisfy nervous bureaucrats and suspicious community donors concerning their plans to construct one centre for all. In the welfare-state reality of the 1990s, in which governments seek to become more community based in offering services, the life course of some of these solidarities implies multiple citizenships and sentiments within at least three nations: Canada, Italy, and the transnation or diaspora of each Italian regional heritage.

6. Culture, Calcio, and Centro Scuola: Italian-Canadian Collective Pedagogy

This chapter interprets a site of ethnocultural leadership and social thinking, Centro Canadese Scuola e Cultura Italiana (the Canadian Centre for Italian Culture and Education). Centro Scuola is a cultural storehouse for the Italian-Canadian community. It leads the effort to sustain its polity through cultural activities, language, and sports education for youth. It is also the central institution that mediates the flows of Italian culture and manufactures linkages with educational and cultural sources from the Italian peninsula. This chapter examines the layers of meaning and interests of this cultural institution's leadership in the sociocultural field. Consider it an archaeology of the cultural practices and cultural production of Italian-Canadian ethnoculture as it is constituted by Centro Scuola.

While the offices of Centro Scuola sit on the second floor of Columbus Centre, a new threshold of understanding needs to be crossed to interpret its cultural practices (Carstens 1994). Framed collages of newspaper articles recording the successes of soccer, basketball, volleyball, and track teams the centre has sponsored in tournaments in Italy cover the walls approaching the offices, interspersed with well-designed mounted posters of Italian theatrical productions of *La passione* performed by the Teatro Stabile Dell'Aquila, or Pirandello's works by Toronto's own Il Piccolo Teatro, arranged under the auspices of the centre. Passing through this montage of visual chronicles is akin to a rite of transition (Van Gennep 1910 [1910]; Carstens 1994; Turner 1969) or a liminal state during which the fieldworker is aware of a transformation into a social space with new realities and layers of meaning to be comprehended.

The business of culture here is not passive. The chatter of the Italian language heard emanating from the offices is emblematic of the focal point of the institution; whereas the Italian language may be used informally in many aspects of the quotidian activities of the Columbus Centre, the language of official dialogue is more generally English. At Centro Scuola the Italian language is used at least equally in official work and is perhaps superordinate in the offices. In fact, since the mid-1980s Centro Scuola's annual report has been written in Italian. The chatter also is in Italian, as are the playful word-games that are spoken in a mix Calabrese, Abruzzese, Italian, English, and Italiese, the ethnic dialect comprising all of them, created by the lived experience of Italian immigrants from different parts of the peninsula (Clivio 1985: Danesi 1985). These kinds of conversations among the workers give the place an energetic bustle. Meanwhile, the bookshelves are packed with the Italian-language instruction books produced by the centre, books that incorporate Canadian experiences in their instructional stories for Canadian youth, and in the numerous artistic, literary, and scholarly monographs of Dante, Da Vinci, Vico, Gramsci, Di Cicco, Mazza, and Edwards.[1] Mixed with these literary and artistic forms are a plethora of silver- and gold-coloured sports trophies, some draped in the tricolore (red, white, and green) of Italy or the *azzurri* (blue) of Italy's national sports teams that acknowledge partnerships with local Italian clubs or sporting associations. The display of these trophies and plaques from the many tournaments in Italy, South America, and Canada in which Centro Scuola has participated, testify to the active and passionate promotion of sport as an instrument of pedagogy.

Centro Scuola is one of the ethnocultural core institutions and perhaps the only pan-Italian institution that, because of its outreach into the schools and the arts and sports communities, affects most intimately the relationship between parents and children and their continual negotiation of Italianness in the greater Toronto area (GTA). On a typical day in the offices of Centro Scuola one might encounter the education officer from the Italian Consulate in Toronto dropping by to ensure that plans for a language program are on track; young Italian-Canadian men and women from volleyball or soccer teams sponsored by Centro Scuola preparing for a sports/education trip to Atri, Rome, Bologna, Florence, Brescia, or Messina, or to a summer language program in Abruzzo; heritage language teachers from the Metro Separate School Board arranging a workshop; or a visiting modern-dance troupe from Italy. It is out of this convergence of activity and material culture that one begins to interpret new cultural meanings, practices, and politics.

Ethnocultural Entrepreneurs

At the nexus of these different currents of cultural resources are brokers, intermediaries, and social agents who interpret, mould, and distribute cultural capital to an ethnic polity. Much as other brokers of the middle classes such as travel agents, notaries, lawyers, and doctors mediate between the local, national, and international economic and political systems for the community, the ethnocultural entrepreneur provides an integral service as an agent of identity negotiation and community building for members of the ethnic community in the social and cultural blur of messages and codes in the global cultural economy. Young (1976:45–7) coined the term *cultural entrepreneur* in his study of new nationalisms in Africa, to distinguish the social position of those middle-class community leaders who mobilize ethnic solidarity through the enhancement of cultural expression and capital. Since language is one of the most crucial cultural devices because of its link to identity, the cultural entrepreneur attempts to create a modern universal language in order to overcome regional dialects and to create a medium for literary and cultural production that can be the basis for an emerging cultural solidarity. Another archetype Young describes is the political broker who may mobilize ethnicity for collective social and political advantage (Eidheim 1963). I find it more useful to combine these two elements into a single intermediary, a cultural broker whom I refer to as an *ethnocultural entrepreneur* because of the score of roles the leadership at Centro Scuola plays and the nature in which politics is embedded in its cultural activities.

An ethnocultural entrepreneur's political persuasiveness arises out of the cultural capital he is able to accumulate through the production and distribution of culture. These leaders are the community-based agents of the reallocation of symbolic resources that Breton (1986;1984) delineates in his discussion of Canadian nation-building and multiculturalism. If the twin notions of bilingualism and biculturalism are elements of the hegemonic discourse about Canadian nationhood, then those central foundations have been confronted with the counter-ideology of multiculturalism, not exclusively as proposed as government policy but as enacted upon by ethnocultural minorities. As an ethos endorsed by many ethnocultural communities after Prime Minister Trudeau's announcement in 1971, multiculturalism has created for many a broader nation-space that incorporates their ideas about citizenship in Canada.

Reams of literature on the issue have been written in the years since its announcement. Many critics have interpreted the policy as a cynical attempt by politicians to attain votes, control minorities, reduce the legitimacy of Quebec ethnonationalism, and limit the construction of horizontal class movements (Porter 1972; Brotz 1980; Peter 1981; R.F. Harney 1988; Fleras and Elliott 1991). Yet as Breton (1984) has noted, even as the policy implies co-optation and control it also reflects deeper shifts in the political and cultural symbolic order of society which are beyond the mechanical manipulation of politicians. The myth of the Canadian nation as composed of two founding peoples, English and French, has been ruptured by this new discourse. In this context ethnocultural entrepreneurs have attempted to capitalize on the opportunity to change the traditional symbolic order and invest it with new meaning, responsibility, and power.

The Origins of Centro Scuola

Before we can elaborate on the social field in which Centro Scuola performs its cultural entrepreneurship it is necessary to sketch the origins of this community-based institution. Italian immigrants who had arrived in the 1950s and 1960s at or near the age of pro-creation or with small children began to see their children enter the Canadian school system in the 1960s and 1970s. At this time a number of issues arose that motivated parents, community leaders, and the Catholic Church to respond. The genesis of Centro Canadese Scuola e Cultura Italiana in 1976 arose from a con-fluence of circumstances in the 1970s that affected the Italian-Canadian settlement in Toronto:

1. The children of immigrants of Italian heritage were streamed by an unresponsive school system into vocational schools and discouraged from pursuing higher education.
2. The internal cohesiveness of the Italian-Canadian family was perceived to be threatened in part because of the lack of a com-mon language between generations; parents were fluent in regional dialect or standard Italian and the children in English.
3. Some Italian-Canadian leadership wanted to reduce barriers between immigrants from different regions of the Italian pen-insula and to construct and maintain an Italian-Canadian com-munity.
4. Members of the Italian-Canadian collectivity took seriously the federal policy of multiculturalism and its rhetoric that encour-aged the retention, nurturing, and sharing of immigrant and ethnic cultures.

In the late 1960s and early 1970s the Italian settlement and the Cath-olic Church began to address some of these concerns through the teaching of the Italian language in parish halls on Saturday morn-ings. By 1971 a partnership between the Dante Society of Toronto and the Italian Pastoral Commission created the Comitato Scolas-tico Italiano di Toronto. With funding from the Italian Consulate and the Italian Ministry of Foreign Affairs the Comitato attempted to standardize the pedagogical, curricular, and administrative teaching of the language for the Italian-Canadian community. It drew over 6,000 children in its first year (Danesi and Di Giovanni

1989). In 1974 the Italian Pastoral Commission of the Metro Toronto Archdiocese, under the leadership of a priest who was also a separate school trustee, began a pilot project with the Comitato Scolastico Italiano which permitted the Italian language to be taught during regular school hours in some Catholic schools that had high percentages of Italian-Canadian school children.

In 1976 the Comitato was reorganized into a non-profit organization under the auspices of the umbrella group of Italian-Canadian associations, the National Congress of Italian Canadians, and changed its name to Centro Canadese Scuola e Cultura Italiana (Kuitunen 1993), with a board of directors composed of parents, teachers, community activists, university professors, and other citizens. Centro Scuola's objectives have centred around the teaching of Italian language and culture in the school system, the study of social and cultural problems facing the Italian-Canadian community, and the sponsorship of linkages with Italian literary, film, performance art, musical, and sports groups.

Heritage Languages

One young student studying the Italian language in greater Toronto in 1997 was asked who the father of the Italian language was. Instead of reciting the standard response – the literary genius Dante – the child answered, 'Alberto Di Giovanni,' the Italian-Canadian who is director of the principal community-based sponsor of the Italian Heritage Language Program (HLP) in Ontario, Centro Canadese Scuola e Cultura Italiana. Ethnocultural institutions and associations are constituted by the collective expectations of ethnocommunities. It is argued by many scholars that ethnocommunities are imagined and constructed both by the state, through official largesse, and by ethnocultural leaderships who create associations 'with global cultural, political, or religious aims' (Werbner and Anwar 1991:21). But leaders and governments achieve degrees of community solidarity by earning the assent of the collectivity's members and by tapping unarticulated concerns. In the case of language retention, teaching, and encouragement, that assent seems to be more easily forthcoming because of its centrality to familial communication. One parent and community activist articulated a refrain I heard over and over again:

> Our children are being given the impression that the language of their parents is not as important as English and French. By deduction they could take this to mean that the culture of their parents is inferior to that of the English and French, and again by deduction, that they themselves as Italian-Canadians are inferior to the English and French ... If we really believe in multiculturalism then we should put all languages on the same level.

The teaching of ancestral or familial language by immigrants in makeshift schoolrooms in the basements of religious institutions or in the back rooms of boarding houses has a long tradition within migration history. A corollary of this learning has been the programmatic efforts by host-country educational authorities to eradicate any traces of 'foreign' languages or culture and to inculcate in immigrants (or Native peoples) Canadian standards of behaviour, comportment, and speech (Harney and Troper 1975). Since the turn of the century Canadianization has been a central ideological ambition of school teachers, social activists, civil servants, public health officials, and religious leaders. Within the contemporary nation-building debate in Canada the hostility by charter group spokespeople and some in the press to state encouragement, through funding, of non-charter-group languages in schools has been vocal and at times nativist and xenophobic (Cummins and Danesi 1990). Ethnocultural communities have countered with assertions concerning the pedagogical advantages of multilingual education as well as its social and other benefits: familial cohesion during the difficult migration process, the rights asserted by the UN and other international bodies that people maintain their culture, and finally, the potential economic advantages to the Canadian economy of a multilingual workforce. Most important, since its inception heritage-language proponents have urged the integration of courses within the regular school day that will raise the status of all 'non-official' languages within the curricula hierarchy in Canada, and the reduction of the kind of stigmatization engendered when young children must stay after school or go to school on Saturdays to learn their native languages.

In a more recent initiative, in 1994, in order to receive higher status and legitimacy, ethnocultural communities convinced a sympathetic Ontario provincial government, several of whose members started their political careers as public and Catholic Separate School trustees in Metropolitan Toronto, to change the name of the program to International Languages Program, to set the stage for more proactive initiatives and to indicate its usefulness as a resource for global trade and economic and cultural exchange. However, for the purposes of consistency I use the term *heritage languages* throughout this book to specify the general program, because it is used currently by community groups and because the change in terminology is so recent.

As an aside, it is instructive of the resistance to third-language teaching within the educational bureaucracy to this day to note that at present the Ministry of Education in Ontario does not place international languages (HLP) under the jurisdiction of the prestigious and powerful central curriculum division. Instead, it places this program and anti-racism and ethnocultural equity programs outside the main bureaucratic structures with their own, and less influential, assistant deputy minister. Moreover, to the consternation of many ethnocultural HLP activists who see HLP as an indispensable educational program for youth in the global economy, this assistant deputy minister emerged out of the quite different tradition of teaching English as a second language, and has no history of involvement in the teaching of heritage languages.

After the Canadian federal government introduced the concept of a multicultural society within a bilingual framework in the early 1970s, ethnocultural minorities began to pressure politicians to respond to their needs about culture. Echoing some Quebec nationalist sentiment and academic discourse, ethnocultural minorities argued that without language culture was dead. Furthermore, some ethnocultural educators and parents argued that multicultural policies needed to include initiatives to encourage the acquisition and use of 'non-official languages.' In 1976 the Federal government's non-official languages study (O'Bryan et al.

1976) concluded that ethnocultural minorities strongly supported the inclusion of non-official languages in educational curricula, especially at the elementary level. For example, in a York Board of Education survey of its citizens, many people of Italian-Canadian heritage were asked if they wanted Italian introduced at the elementary level and administered by the board. The idea received 89 per cent support, with 69 per cent preferring that the language be taught within regular school hours. Nevertheless 89 per cent still believed English should be the first language of instruction and Italian the second (Kuitunen 1993:117).

In the years 1975–6 the Italian government contributed $187,000 to the Metro Separate School Board to help pay for Italian-language teaching. As Berryman (1986) suggests, the embarrassing threat to the Province of Ontario's jurisdictional integrity clearly influenced the Ontario government to begin limited funding for a heritage language program. In 1977 the federal government established a cultural enrichment program through the Multiculturalism Directorate to help teach heritage languages.

Over the years Centro Scuola has created a number of activities to respond to the needs of community workers, parents, and school boards involved in heritage language teaching. The organization also helps interview candidates and assists in hiring qualified instructors. It organizes professional development workshops and seminars for hundreds of instructors and develops curriculum guidelines, text books, and teaching aids. It supplies books and curriculum material to students and classroom teachers and provides community resources and community assistance to the heritage language instructors. Finally, it helps organize multicultural events in schools and provides speakers and/or artists for the schools. For almost two decades an annual average of 34,000 school children have studied Italian at the elementary school level and another 6,000 students and adults have participated in the Centre's programs.

Centro Scuola's success has also enabled it to share its ideas and programs with other community language groups in implementing heritage programs in many languages, including Chinese, Greek, Polish, Ukrainian, Spanish, Portuguese, Korean, German,

Croatian, and Bengali. An annual heritage language symposium is held to encourage teachers of different languages to discuss their programs and develop different pedagogical efforts; it is also meant to signify implicitly to politicians, especially those elected in polyethnic neighbourhoods in the GTA, that the organized, multi-lingual, education community is a constituency that they cross at their own political peril. In this context, around the issue of heritage language, extensive networks of individuals and community-based organizations have been created from different ethno-communities concerned with their respective ethnolinguistic and ethnocultural heritages. These organizations coalesce at times to lobby school boards or the Ministry of Education when funding cutbacks are considered. One participant noted an unintended result of these cross-ethnic encounters:

> Through the heritage language activities, we maintain links with other communities and develop further links with other community groups which created the base for other kinds of linkages in the cultural, social, and economic arena ... I think the sympathy that existed ... in the fight to retain languages developed a sense of cooperation in other areas, and a form of dialogue ... I think, for example, that when you elect a trustee for a board of education, whether he is of one background or another is relevant up to a certain point ... What is relevant is whether they also experience the same struggle in language retention that you have ... That way you can easily see an Italian-Canadian voting for a Ukrainian and vice versa.

A coalition of ethnocultural communities attacked the federal Progressive Conservative party for its withdrawal of $4.1 million in heritage language funding in its wide budget-cutting efforts in 1990, and accused the party of linguistic genocide. The group mobilized Liberal party opposition support to attack the budget cuts, and in the 1993 federal election, PC candidates in the heavily polyethnic and immigrant GTA were all defeated. It might well be speculated that their losses were partially due to their neglect of these constituents.

One of the common laments of Italian ethnocultural leadership (and many others) is the inability of the ethnic community's own

leadership to mobilize the polity. The one exception to this griev-
ance is the transmission of language. The fight with the educational establishment (boards of education, teachers' federations,
and ministries of education) to offer heritage languages, and in
regular school hours, has been and is a central issue on which ethnocultural mobilization occurs. It is a direct result of what Breton
(1984) calls the symbolic allocation of resources, echoed here by
Alberto Di Giovanni, director of Centro Scuola:

> The idea of multiculturalism gives the strength, as I said before, to
> stand in front of Canadian institutions and say that if this has to be a
> multicultural country, as the policy officially states, then what that
> means – which was not initiated by the government – is that the gov-
> ernment has to pay attention to the newer communities. The policy
> must encourage more than just banquets in the basement of a
> church. This is not just folklore. What it means is that our language
> education has to find a rightful place, that our presence has to be
> reflected in the different institutions, that those institutions have to
> take into account our approaches and our views concerning how
> they should operate.

In the effort to reorient Canada's institutions and make them
more responsive to the new diversity, the educational system has
been at times slow to change. In the case of heritage language
teaching continual political pressure through parents' organizations and ethnocultural entrepreneurs has been essential to prevent the retrenchment of budgets for HLP.

As an ethnocultural entrepreneur the director of Centro Scuola
has helped mobilize unarticulated community strength and resources on several occasions during the recession of the early nineties in the GTA, to fight budget cutbacks in school boards for the
HLP. Aside from presenting academic studies that support his con-
tention that the program has pedagogical advantages, one of the
more effective ways Mr Di Giovanni has tried to raise the status of
the HLP is by pointing to statistics that show that the courses are
not simply transitional devices to help immigrant children adapt to
Canadian life, nor does he wish to retain them for ambiguous heri-

tage reasons. Statistics show that nearly 33 per cent of those studying Italian in HLP, for example, are not of Italian descent, and it is estimated that 95 per cent of those of Italian-Canadian heritage taking HLP were born in Canada.

Several examples of Centro Scuola's involvement in the program will serve to illustrate its critical role as ethnocultural entrepreneur. In 1992, with the York Region Separate School Board facing severe budget limitations, there were proposals to slash its financing of HLP, much to the dismay of many of the Italian-Canadian parents who had moved to this new 1980s bedroom community. These families, who had lived in the older neighbourhoods of St Clair and Dufferin or in Downsview in the Metropolitan area, had been expecting the HLP to continue in the new suburbs. At several public meetings, Separate School trustees were confronted with three to four hundred parents (who threatened to mobilize over four thousand people) protesting the proposed cutbacks to funding and demanding retention of the programs. Alberto Di Giovanni helped mobilize these parents to develop a solution to the York Separate School Board's budgetary problems. In order to offset a shortfall of approximately $250,000 Centro Scuola offered to provide more than $150,000 in services and materials to help maintain both the teachers and the program (*Corriere Canadese, Lo Specchio, The Liberal*, April/May 1992).

Facing further budgets cuts in the spring of 1993 a document that chronicled some opinions of principals and workers within the Metro Separate School Board indicated how fragile was the support within the educational bureaucracy for third-language teaching (HLP). The report suggested that HLP 'diminishes Canadianization' (*Corriere Canadese*, 29–30 January 1993). Upon receiving a copy of this informal collection of opinions, Mr Di Giovanni made the issue public. In his view parents needed to attend the upcoming budget meetings at the board to make it clear to the school trustees that this blatant and misleading attack on heritage languages should not create grounds for excessive cuts in the budget. At the following public budget meeting the board members disassociated themselves from the idea that HLP 'diminishes Canadianization,' and said there was an error in the transcription.

As these examples demonstrate, the ethnocultural entrepreneur seeks to articulate a collective and mobilize communal activity around an ethnocultural core value. Italian heritage language becomes one of those communal core values for two reasons: (1) many parents want the respect, obedience, and understanding of their children and see this best achieved through the retention of a common language: Italian; (2) the continuance of HLP in the Canadian institutional setting of schools legitimizes the status of Italian Canadians as equal citizens in Canadian society.

But the ingenuity of ethnocultural entrepreneurship in a global cultural economy is not simply related to the mobilization of communal sentiment around symbolic and emblematic projects within one's own state. The intricate work of the ethnocultural entrepreneur surfaces in his or her ability to skilfully occupy an interstitial point between several ideological and national streams and power blocks, and to manoeuvre them for the advantage of different communal projects.

Since the gradual lessening of Canadian federal government spending on cultural enrichment programs in the last decade through the office of the Canadian Secretary of State, Centro Scuola has augmented its funding base through grants from the Italian Ministry of Foreign Affairs. In the budget year 1982–3 Centro Scuola received just over $10,000 from the Italian Consulate and over $90,000 from the Canadian federal government. Ten years later Centro Scuola received more than $270,000 from the Italian Consulate and only $27,000 from the Canadian Secretary of State. Moreover, an additional sum of close to $60,000 was received from the Italian government through the Comitato Olimpico Nazionale Italiano (CONI) program to develop youth athletes of Italian heritage in Canada. (Incidentally, since 1989 Centro Scuola's director has been CONI's representative in Canada.) Centro Scuola has received continual but lesser funding from Ontario provincial governments under the leadership of all political parties over its more than twenty-year existence. Centro Scuola has dispensed much of these funds to help the Ontario school system, directly or indirectly, to maintain its heritage language programs.

An illustration of the deftness of Centro Scuola's director, who must operate in situations not completely in his control, occurred during an event held to honour the visit of the new undersecretary of foreign affairs for the Italian government. The luncheon banquet was sponsored by Centro Scuola at a restaurant within Columbus Centre. Following the meal she was given a tour of both Columbus Centre and Centro Scuola and given copies of several academic publications about Italians in Canada, and pedagogical works produced and published through Centro Scuola.

Of the approximately twenty guests who attended the luncheon, there were two provincial government ministers, several other MPPs of Italian-Canadian heritage, municipal politicians, several university professors from Italian departments, the chair of Centro Scuola (who was also chair of University of Toronto's Governing Council), a couple of representatives of the National Congress of Italian Canadians, the executive director of Columbus Centre, the director of the Istituto Italiano di Cultura,[2] and me. If one reads a brief Geertzian narrative into the list of invited guests one can see the different layers of meaning that the ethnocultural entrepreneur wished to relay at the event. The two ministers from the provincial government served two different purposes. Minister of Culture Anne Swarbrick oversaw a ministry that occasionally gives small grants for one-time projects run by Centro Scuola. Minister of Community and Social Services Tony Silipo was an Italian immigrant from Calabria via Australia, who had earned political respect as a school trustee in the early 1980s fighting for heritage language. Fluent in English, Italian, and French and cosmopolitan in demeanour, his presence helped our ethnocultural entrepreneur say several things to the group: (1) that Italian-Canadians had achieved significant political and economic 'success' in Canada, and not at the expense of cultural learning; (2) that trilingualism was beneficial in the global cultural economy because it facilitated warm, personal relations with representatives from other countries; (3) a corollary of the second point, that symbolically the banquet instructed the participants in the notion that the support of these cultural and linguistic activities among ethnocommunities is legitimate and accepted within the concept of Canadian citizenship.

The assortment of other guests, such as university professors, ethnocommunity leaders, and municipal politicians, enhanced the status and reputation of the ethnocultural entrepreneur in two distinct ways: (1) to the invited guests from Toronto he had demonstrated his capacity to reach, and influence, powerful individuals within Italy's political culture; (2) to his Italian guests he had demonstrated his ability to command the appearance of two provincial ministers, a score of local politicians, a university governing-council chair, and several university professors, which underscored the support he appeared to have within the community and among other power brokers in the city and province. The event enabled him to cultivate what Galt calls a 'real system' that uses human, personal contact to facilitate goals, as opposed to the cold 'official system' of an unresponsive bureaucracy (1974;1992). He created a personal rapport with someone his institution depends upon in Italy and he renewed personal relationships with other persons of power within Ontario.

Something also needs to be said about the gender politics of the event. Our ethnocultural entrepreneur implicitly underscored his progressive views concerning gender equity, which did not go unnoticed by either the guests from Italy or the minister of culture. The presence of the chair of his board, Annamarie Castrilli, implicitly indicated to the Ontario minister of culture, whose government had expressed concern over the need for more gender equity, that stereotypes about chauvinist Italian males were not appropriate for understanding Centro Scuola. It also indicated to the undersecretary from Italy that the widely projected image of the Italian immigrant Toronto community as dominated by cultureless male contractors and labourers was not an accurate interpretation of the reality.

The event did not come off without a hitch; at one point, just as the main course was served, the Istituto director, simply an invited guest, ushered the undersecretary away for an interview on Italian-language television leaving the organizer, the director of Centro Scuola, to utter angry aphorisms about the proper role of guests. If one sees the Italian government's resources as limited, Centro's reliance on investment from government to ensure the teaching of the Italian language to Canadian children and to encourage Italian cultural activities in Canada puts it into conflict with the ministry's own service agency in Toronto, the Istituto Italiano di Cultura. This appears so even if the Istituto's unstated preference but clear intention is to serve Toronto's non-Italian cultural elite and its relatively small community of more recently arrived Italian professional and better-educated immigrants.

Diaspora through Sport: Giochi della Gioventù

For anyone entering the offices of Centro Scuola a remarkable feature is the density and number of sports paraphernalia, the trophies, the kaleidoscopic colours of tournament banners, the team photos. It is a scene that by the intensity of its sensory stimulants almost defies 'thick description' (Geertz 1973). Sports can be an interpretive device for understanding the emblematics of ethnicity and negotiable identity. By watching and supporting Turin's first division soccer team, Juventus, and by participating in North York's Azzurri youth soccer team or Centro Scuola's summer soccer camp instead of spending time at hockey schools or watching the Toronto Maple Leafs, Italian-Canadian youth indicate to the world some of the daily lived emblematics of ethnicity.

In Naples I joined a teenage soccer team sponsored by Centro Scuola which had been playing tournaments and touring the northern Italian region of Trentino. Centro Scuola had organized a special side-trip to Naples, halfway across Italy, to see the Italian national soccer team in a friendly match against France. Such a trip emphasized the link between amateur soccer in Canada and the premier league in the world in Italy. It also aimed to orient the youthful team towards sports heroes and sports information networks other than North American ones upon their return to Canada.

Sport can also be seen as a sign of group solidarity. The continuance of appreciation for a sport of the *madrepatria* (motherland) such as soccer, or fluctuation between one world of sports or the other, demonstrates the shifting and complex quality of ethnicity. Centro Scuola has attempted to engage Italian-Canadian youth with the culture of their parents. It has responded to two core communal beliefs of many Italian-Canadian parents: (1) that language is a critical instrument of communication between generations and the transmission of ancestral culture and must be learned, (2) that sport, and specifically soccer, as a nostalgic reference for immigrants, is an important cultural experience parents wish to share with their children. Furthermore, Centro Scuola's director believes sport is a useful pedagogical instrument because students enjoy it. Sports educators also see sport as a way to combat the difficult and alienating demands of a North American consumer economy that often sees both parents working and youth with too much free time and too little supervision. They argue that sport can create a sense of community and responsibility, foster teamwork, and provide an opportunity to make friendships while at the same time being a vehicle for learning about Italian culture.

Since the 1982 victory of Italy in the World Cup of soccer and the post-victory parade in which an estimated 300,000 people took part on St Clair Ave. West in Toronto in the heart of the Italian-Canadian settlement, Centro Scuola decided to integrate sports within its cultural and language education. The Heritage Language Soccer Tournament created and organized by Centro Scuola for all students attending heritage language classes in grades five through eight, has awarded the winners a summer trip to Italy to meet soccer stars and play in friendly tournaments with Italian regional soccer federations. In 1983, with the assistance of Italy's Federazione Italiana Giuoco Calcio (FIGC), the winner of the Toronto Heritage soccer cup, none other than Centro Scuola's Azzurri squad itself, went to Italy to participate in the Italian *Giochi della Gioventù* (Youth Games). By 1986 the Italian-Canadian team sponsored by Centro Scuola was able to win the cup in the tournament against Italian-based youth clubs and Italian heritage teams from Belgium, Argentina, Switzerland, and Germany. Centro Scuola had the best team for the year 1986 among the community of Italians and 'Italians overseas' that the Italian government strives to encourage as a potential source of and base for cultural and economic trade. Under the auspices of Centro Scuola CONI Canada itself has, with the help of the Italian Consulate, participated in a Canadian version of the youth games for school children in Italian heritage language programs. Prizes for Centro Scuola's annual essay writing contest for school children in Italian-language programs are awarded after the annual Giochi della Gioventù, which is sponsored every year by various school boards and York University.

In 1993 Centro Scuola operated twelve soccer teams. Another 120 students/athletes participated in its soccer school, two female teams and one male team of volleyball, two female teams and one male team of basketball and four other teams in swimming and track and field. In the same year, aside from language programs arranged for students in Italy, Centro Scuola brought, on four separate occasions, Italian-Canadian-based teams (not all members of the teams were of Italian heritage) to compete in tournaments or friendly matches in Lazio, Veneto, and Abruzzo. It should be noted that although Centro Scuola is a pan-Italian organization, its networks with regional groups and the centre, both in Italy and Canada, have enabled it to maximize its access to opportunities of exchange in both southern and northern Italy. Parents whose children have gone on these soccer, basketball, volleyball, and language exchange trips become fiercely loyal to the director and to Centro Scuola for what they see as the important work they do in providing familiar culture and sports activities for children who have been raised in an environment and culture alien to that of their parents.

In theory, the ethnocultural entrepreneur located at the nexus of several global cultural fields orchestrates the possibilities of these different fields to construct new opportunities for cultural synthesis. In the case of Centro Scuola's director, a measure of this orchestration is the program he has devised to take full advantage of resources in two different countries. Aside from the many language exchanges and sports trips Centro Scuola sponsors to Italy throughout the year, since 1991 it has also created a more extensive program to expose Italian-Canadian youth to the culture of Italy. Centro Scuola has established a program called Project Atri to allow a small group of students to immerse themselves in daily Italian life for an academic year. The program is named after the small town of Atri, located north of the coastal city of Pescara in the Italian region of Abruzzo, in which the students billet. Each year with the cooperation of the Ministry of Public Education in Italy and the Metropolitan Separate School Board's Continuing Education Department in Toronto, nineteen Canadian students have studied from September to April in an Italian high school, earning credits for their Toronto high school degree. At the same time they have participated in a special soccer school that has teams that compete in regional soccer tournaments. The director's long activism in HLP in Ontario, combined with his knowledge of the system in Italy and his contacts with networks of educational institutions in Abruzzo (such as the teachers' federation, IRRSAE, and the language exchange program he established with the Abruzzese cities of L'Aquila and Sulmona) have contributed to his ability to establish the Atri program.

One of the more ambitious activities that reflect the effort by Centro Scuola as a locus of ethnocultural entrepreneurship for the remaking of the symbolic order of Canadian cultural practices – in an image that suits the global and multicultural ethos it articulates is the Canadian version of Italy's Giochi Della Gioventù. For eleven years, with the help of the Italian Ministry of Foreign Affairs, through its consulate in Toronto and CONI, Centro Scuola has organized youth games on a June weekend in Toronto, most recently using the facilities of York University for teams representing Italian-Canadian communities in Quebec, British Columbia, Alberta, and northern and southern Ontario. More than 4,000 students participated in the 1994 tournament.

Teams coming from out of province are composed of players of Italian-Canadian descent. Because they are of Italian heritage their transportation and lodging are paid for by the Italian government. The GTA teams are polyethnic and multiracial in composition since most are based on teams coming from specific schools within, predominantly, the Catholic separate school system. This polyethnicity is encouraged by Centro Scuola. The encouragement of diversity and sharing coincides with the efforts of our ethnocultural entrepreneur to legitimate Italian culture as an object of study as important as English and French culture in the contest over educating Canadian youth. It is also a message to his Italian sponsors about his expertise in coping with diversity in Canada. Centro Scuola and its practices should be seen by Italian officials as a potential resource to draw upon, as Italian governments at all levels confront the new immigrant diversity that has transformed Italy in the last fifteen years from a sending country of migrants to a receiving one.

At the opening ceremonies on the York campus, a commemorative booklet was given to parents and participants at the weekend games describing the ten previous years of success, the booklet contained letters of congratulations from Canadian federal and provincial politicians and from the president of the Italian National Olympic Committee, the Consul General of Italy, and the Chair of the governing council of the University of Toronto. Also included were photographs of past sporting events at the Giochi della Gioventù in Italy and Canada and the names of athletes of the year. During the proceedings the director of Centro Scuola was given a plaque from federal Minister of Citizenship and Immigration Sergio Marchi on behalf of the prime minister, in honour of Centro Scuola's work in education, youth activities, and multiculturalism. A faxed statement praising the event from Prime Minister Silvio Berlusconi of Italy was read aloud. Although many were uncertain about Berlusconi as a politician, the ambivalent qualities of ethnonationalism surfaced in the pleased looks and nods of approval this message received among some participants at the event, who seemed more satisfied with this electronic message than with the crowds of Canadian politicians. It is not just a matter of preference for one loyalty over another; rather, the response is indicative of the elusive, fractured, and creative force of cultural production among ethnocultural minorities in polyethnic societies, one that defies simple dichotomization.

The evening was also filled with classical music performed by children who played violin and piano. There were school choirs, a guest modern-dance troupe from Treviso, Italy, and the Coro di San Marco singing a medley of Italian regional songs. Near the end of the ceremony, after greetings were delivered by representatives of the two levels of Canadian government, both Italian immigrants themselves, and the Italian consul general, awards were made for the best essays at the annual literary essay competition. The three different subjects for 1997: 'Sport is Togetherness, not racism; Sport is Friendship, not violence; Sport is Life, not drugs.' Out of all of this ceremony, pageantry, and platitudes, two important impressions emerged from the event. First, through the act of sponsoring the event the Italian government was laying claim to a community overseas. Second, with the presence of officials from several Canadian levels of government Centro Scuola continued to legitimize its project of bringing Italian culture within the sphere of Canadian citizenship. In the commemorative booklet given to all guests, one article spoke to the place of Italians in the development of multiculturalism as an ethos. In fact it argued that Italy was the first true multicultural society able to integrate yet celebrate the diversity of its heritage. In order to support this view the author cited the history of the Etruscans and Greeks in creating Rome, the Arabs and Normans in Sicily, the Spanish and French in Naples, and the literary work of the city-states in Florence and Venice. In the task to create a counter-ideology all fields of culture and history seem open to interpretation.

Final Remarks

In the 1970s Italian-Canadian parents and community leaders sought to address the growing concern that their children were losing the ability to communicate with them and with their grandparents. The language and culture of the schoolyard made it more difficult for parents to communicate with their children in their original language and culture. In order to offset this concern, parents rallied around the idea of teaching heritage languages to their children in the schools. The quality of this language education has not been an issue in this chapter, but it should not be overlooked that these cultural and educational practices depended upon volunteer community workers and underemployed teachers without Ontario teaching certificates. The HLP program created employment for individuals, mostly young immigrant women, who were caught in changing and demanding economic circumstances and new unresolved expectations about gender roles. Out of the social movement of parents and educators and in the concomitant climate of federal and provincial-government multicultural policies, community-based organizations found support for projects that responded to the needs of parents.

Centro Scuola has occupied an interstitial point between two societies: Italy and Canada. The situational use of subethnic loyalties based on regional Italian cultures runs counter to the Centre's institutional and intellectual need to construct a pan-Italian-Canadian cultural relevance for children of Italian immigrants and for a broader cosmopolitan Canadian community. As a purveyor of culture Centro Scuola's director needs to find access to cultural and educational resources in Italy in order to maintain his position at the transnational creative points of cultural production.[3] Through an innovative program of pedagogy based on sport and language Centro Scuola has tried to ease some of the inevitable and overwhelming cultural differences that arise between immigrant parents and their children. Furthermore, it has steadfastly promoted the historical tradition of Italian humanist values to encourage cross-ethnic and racial communication.

One of the ways an ethnic polity attempts to construct a collective identity is through a set of core values and cultural practices chosen to articulate ethnoculture within the community and to the host society. Ethnocultural leadership is indispensable in defining, interpreting, and constructing this ethnocultural core, and in reifying cultural practices. As ethnocultural entrepreneurs these social imaginers originating out of the middle classes act as agents of articulation, and they participate in the active development and promotion of ideas, values, and beliefs as the immigrant community confronts its emergent condition as an ethnocultural minority in a new setting.

7. Locals in a Global Village

Fieldnote, 21 March 1994

I was having a cup of espresso with my informant, Fortunato, in the house of the president of a paese social club whose members are primarily composed of immigrants from a small town in Reggio Calabria, the southernmost part of the Italian peninsula across the Straits of Messina from Sicily. An impressive painting of Fortunato's home town, a shining city on the hills looking out over the Mediterranean, soon caught my eye amid the honorary plaques and family photographs. On the dining room table were labour union notices, newspaper clippings of Italian-Canadian social functions, and a tray of biscotti. We had been chatting about politics, union work, Calabria, and his experiences every so often for a few months. We continued our conversation:

NICK: Were there people that you met from San Giorgio who had emigrated before the war?
FORTUNATO: Yes, Giorgio I believe his name was. He was living south of College on Clinton Street. One day we went to see him. He was retired at that point. I asked him how long he had been here and he said for twenty-five years. I looked at my cousin and said, 'Jesus, he has roots here, eh!' I have been here forty-two years, so the time flies.

You see, Nick, people from San Giorgio are in every city of Italy. We have people in Germany. We have people in France. We have people in Switzerland. We have people in every country of Europe, including Russia. We have people in you-name-it. We have a large number of peo-

ple from San Giorgio in any country in South America, all over the
United States, Canada, and Australia. Everywhere you find San
Giorgesi. They went to all these places for only one thing, to work.

San Giorgio Morgeto, which is in the province of Reggio Calabria, is
a beautiful place. We don't have 200,000 people, only a few thousand.
The people of San Giorgio have emigrated all the time, since the world
was created. I recall before the war and during the war, people from the
north coming to my place, people with cameras taking pictures and I
was laughing. I said, what did they see that was so special about this
place that they want to take a picture? I did not appreciate the beauty of
the place of my birth during my life in Italy. I do now. Everything
around San Giorgio is flat territory covered with olive trees, and then
there is the sea. On special nights when the fishermen are out it is
beautiful with the lights on their boats. San Giorgio looks right out
at the Mediterranean. It is something, really. The location is really
fantastic.

NICK: Did you ever think you would go back?

FORTUNATO: I went back many times, not only to Italy and my place of
birth but even to Europe and South America, the United States, California. But you cannot find a place better than Toronto. I have roots
here.

NICK: How did you decide to come here?

FORTUNATO: My cousin Luigi, who sponsored me, worked first as a
bricklayer. He emigrated in 1949, and I came for the first time in 1952.
First I was going to go to South America because near San Giorgio
there was an office that was taking applications to settle people in
Peru. One day I said I wished to apply to go, and I was ready to go but
they told me that office was no longer there. These were fly-by-night
operators, funny like a three-dollar bill.

So then I had a good friend who went to Australia, and he said, 'As
soon as I get there I will do everything I can do to get you over there.'
My cousin came from Canada and said, 'If you wish to come I will sponsor you,' and I said, 'Do it fast.' In no time, in 1951, he sent me the call.
I went to Rome and they gave me the visa for landed-immigrant status,
and then on the 7th of February of 1952 I left San Giorgio and headed
for Naples. From Naples I took the boat to Salerno. The boat was killing me. I felt sick, and said I would return home when we hit Palermo.

Then the boat stopped and I felt better and I said, 'Well, let's forget about getting off. I can make it to Canada.' I was not thinking that stopping was different from travelling. So when we reached Halifax I was not able to stand on my feet because I had been so seasick from Palermo. I could not eat anything. I was the only one from San Giorgio on that particular trip.

I was surprised when we got the train from Halifax to Toronto. In Italy I was travelling by train all the time. The train was in really bad shape here in Canada. The first thing we had was sliced bread, which is soft, and I said, 'My god this bread is good for people who have no teeth, but not for me.' We were used to this home-made bread, and I thought this bread was awful. So it took two days from Halifax to Toronto and I believe I got here on the 22nd or 21st of February. When we got to Toronto Luigi was there at the Union Station.

It was a different world altogether. It was cold. I stayed first on Brunswick Avenue and then on Clinton Street. My cousin was like a father for me. This other cousin, Joe, spotted the construction boots in my suitcase. I opened a suitcase because I brought a bottle of liquor for him from San Giorgio ... I never forgot his wife, Esperanza, who made a beautiful supper, everything was there on the table. There was steak, pasta, you name it.

I was really hungry but I had to wait until after Joe gave me a speech for twenty minutes. I was listening to him: 'Don't forget that you left your mother in Italy who is depending on you. You left a younger brother and a sister. They depend on you. Don't think that you are here and they are forgotten. Try to hang out with people better than you or at least at par with your level, not with others, because you can end up in trouble or in jail. You are here to try to build yourself up. Don't burn what you earn. Be a good administrator of your cheque. Don't forget that money is round. If you are a lousy administrator this money will roll away from your hands.

A common lament by Italian Canadians who worry about their Italian identity within polyethnic Ontario is that so many immigrant Italians who arrived in the 1950s and 1960s still retain social networks circumscribed by *campanilismo*, a parochial pride in their town of origin. Most Italian immigrants to Canada did identify themselves, in fact, more readily as people from their paese or their *comune* (municipality), rather than as members of the Italian nation (Zucchi 1988).

I will focus now on those home-centred identities as they are revealed today in the cultural artifacts of the Italian home town or provincial club. Forty years ago the Toronto newspaper *Corriere Canadese* reported that for the 50,000 Italians in Toronto there were 38 organizations (Sidlofsky 1969); but by 1984 that number had reached 240 (Ministero degli Affari Esteri, 1984) and by the 1990s more than 400 (Buranello and Lettieri 1993). Some of these social clubs dot the urban and suburban landscape of greater Toronto in storefronts along major arteries such as Eglinton Avenue, Dufferin Street, Keele Street, and Steeles Avenue, or are tucked away in the back of strip malls and industrial zones near Weston Road and Finch Avenue and the new commercial parks in Woodbridge. Still others use the basements of members' homes to store banners, plaques, saints' statues, club paraphernalia, and minutes in between the clubs' communal meetings, picnics, and dances. These institutions are nodal points in the cognitive maps constructed by immigrant and ethnic actors as they interpret their lives and construct their new identities in Toronto's industrial megalopolis. These local, communal identities grounded in the linkages, both real and imagined, with geographic areas of emigration in Italy are another expression of Italianness that flourishes in Toronto.

The word *campanilismo* (parochialism) is a derivative of *il campanile* (the bell tower) of an Italian town. In southern-Italian agrotowns the church is situated on the central piazza, the heart of community life and social interaction. The ringing of the town's bell has multiple meanings for townspeople. The range of its chimes marks the boundary between *la famiglia* (family) and *compaesani* (fellow townspeople), who are known and at times can be trusted; and *stranieri* (foreigners), whose intentions are suspect. The different rhythmic patterns of church-bell chimes also signal the significant ritual events that reaffirm family life and solidarity, such as birth, baptism, marriage, and death. Douglass (1984:1) notes that the community loyalty imagined by those who operate within the cultural framework of campanilismo is based on an assumption that the community's boundary encompasses a 'distinctive moral and social universe.' This universe exhibited itself in style of dress, food consumed, oral history, and even dialect. The author Ignazio Silone noted the significance of language as a signpost of communal membership in his classic book *Fontamara*, about a town in Abruzzi: 'Let no one get into his head that Fontamarens speak Italian. The Italian language is for us a foreign language, a dead language, a language whose vocabulary and grammar have grown complex without remaining in touch with us, our way of living, our way of acting, our way of thinking, or way of expressing ourselves (Silone 1934:xviii).

Even within this context of strong locally based identities and loyalties, Italian immigrants were pragmatic in their efforts to improve the economic conditions of their families. Southern-Italian peasants and, in turn, Italian immigrants may use campanilismo as an ideological construct to interpret their lives, but in daily activities a more pragmatic, subtle, and inclusive way of thinking operates. The tensions, ruptures, and incongruities in campanilismo temper its coherence as an ideological system. People employ their identities selectively. In social situations in which sociocultural knowledge of distinctions in Lazio, Calabria, Abruzzi, or Sicily have relevance for the participants, local identities, meanings, and assertions frequently shade the conversations. Today, among the immigrant generations in Toronto, these distinctions take the form of good-humoured joking about dialects spoken in nearby towns, or the cheapness or dim-wittedness of the people across the valley or down the coast. The beauty, power, or culinary habits of the women in another village are also common distinctions. The following jokes are typical:

1. On dim-wittedness: Two guys from the same home town went hunting for crickets. They chose a huge wheat field to hunt their prey. Each man took an opposite side of the field. Eventually a cricket landed on the chest of one hunter. The other hunter, upon seeing the cricket, fired, killing both the cricket and his fellow townsman. When he returned to the village alone he was asked how his hunting went. He replied, 'It was even. We lost one of ours and they lost one of theirs.'

2. On stinginess: A man passing through a neighbouring town in the afternoon was asked if he had eaten. He replied no. The townsman responded, 'If you had said yes I would have invited you in for some wine.' The next day he walked by the same townsman, around lunchtime, and the townsman asked if he was thirsty. The man responded no. The townsman said, 'If you had said yes I would have offered you something to eat.'

As Sturino (1990:8,207) notes, the commune of Rende did not suffice as an analytical unit to understand socio-economic interaction in his study of emigrants from that Calabrian town. He needed to expand his work to include surrounding small towns. The anthropological literature about southern Italians had tended to stress the 'village-mindedness' of peasant interaction and loyalty (Banfield 1958; Moss and Cappannari 1962). In Sturino's study, although rivalry still existed between people of different neighbouring towns, the people of the Calabrian Crati valley were connected through extensive economic and friendship links, both manifest and latent. Furthermore, the attitudes that manifested themselves in campanilismo were able to change in the face of challenges in the migration process, such as the need to find employment, housing, and social life. Through flexible concepts of kinship and chain migration networks, immigrants extended their notions of community in order to migrate, and, once abroad, to ease life in new settings where it was necessary to rely on people who had not emigrated from the same home town (Sturino 1990; Gabaccia 1984; Yans-McLaughlin 1977; Cronin 1970; Boissevain 1970; MacDonald 1964).

Italians have been able to extend family membership and offset potential conflicts between family and other personal relationships through the institution of *comparaggio* (ritual kinship), which incorporates into the family friends encountered at work, in the neighbourhood, or through the church, by giving them familial status as ritual compari (godparents). A compare does not need to be of Italian origin, but could be a friend met through work or neighbourhood life and then formally incorporated into the kinship structure. The nearness of kin and *parentela* (relatives) created the necessary social conditions to limit the need, at least at first, for formal ethnocommunity associations. Nagata (1969) noted a similar pattern among Greek immigrants in Toronto. Immigrants, both men and women, worked long hours in factories or on construction sites to accumulate some material security in Canada. Little time was left to establish clubs. Italian-language theatres on Sundays, church events or dances at Brandon Hall, the site of the Italian Canadian Recreational Club, sufficed for social encounters. The Italian immigrant settlement was also initially in a tight geographic area. Concentrated near College Street or St Clair Avenue in the west end, people could see each other during evening walks, in cafés, or shopping in neighbourhood stores. However, once they had attained some economic security and bought homes further north and west in the suburbs of Lawrence and Downsview and then beyond, in Woodbridge, daily contact was less frequent. The dispersion of suburban life and centrality of kin networks were critical factors that significantly spurred the elaboration and number of sociocultural voluntary associations in the seventies, eighties, and nineties. This change in living style, which reduced daily contact between kindred, encouraged people to form organizations that would create occasions and places (such as storefront clubs) to develop and maintain a social life with relatives or people who had common experiences. A critical mass existed, of people with the same nostalgic references and shared memory culture who found sustenance in the reunion with people with common experiences, language, and cultural expectations, as well as prestige and status in creating their own clubs.

Local Toronto Clubs

Literally hundreds of social clubs can be found in Downsview, Etobicoke, Mississauga, and the city of Vaughan. In part these clubs are contemporary versions of the mutual-aid and benefit societies created by European immigrants in the late nineteenth and early twentieth centuries before the elaboration of the welfare state (Briggs 1978; Nelli 1970). These associations provided some financial relief for members who were injured or sick, as well as death benefits to help survivors offset the cost of burial, or sometimes to cover the transportation of a body back to Italy. But in addition to sickness and death benefits many associations organized language classes, cultural activities, and employment and business networks.

In the context of welfare assistance elaborated by the state in the postwar period, the nature of a club's or society's utility has changed from direct welfare to a communicative *piazzetta* (little town square). Italians who arrived in the 1950s and 1960s have reached the age of retirement in the 1990s. The communication or *la chiacchera* (gossip or chatter) that fills the afternoon and evenings at club espresso bars and card tables gives the members and their network of friends and acquaintances opportunities to become informed on a number of issues that confront them in their daily lives. These include Canadian and Italian pension requirements, workers' compensation procedures, Canadian citizenship applications, and job opportunities for themselves or their children. These clubs also provide new opportunities to catch up on family gossip, old town and diaspora community news, Canadian news and gossip, and so on.

The family is the basic unit of membership in most of these clubs; thus, the formal organization is traditionally patriarchal. The participants are predominantly male between the ages of forty-five and seventy. The club is a public space for males to gather after work hours, after dinners for an espresso, on Friday evenings to play *tressette, scopa*, or other Italian card games. As a result, most Italian social clubs in Toronto follow conservative gender roles. During my research, in a few rare instances I found women involved as club officers in associations based on small towns in Abruzzi, Veneto, Sicily, and Calabria. Unfortunately, the lack of formal titular recognition of women masks their enormous contribution in the organization and running of association events.

This gender bias is not only at the local level. One woman involved in both a local club and a pan-Italian organization talked about her frustration as a member of the board of the pan-Italian organization:

There has been a lot of talk among some of the female members of the boards. A lot of them are not happy. We are not involved in the committees. A lot of the decisions are made before we ever get there. We are now much more active than when I first got there. When I joined two years ago we said nothing; the meetings were completely different. Now everyone is very interactive and loud. But now sometimes I feel like they [the men] just don't pay attention. Lately I have found I lose my temper a little bit, hopefully not in front of them. When I was there the first year and a half they always forgot to call me. I was the treasurer, but I didn't go to one finance committee meeting and they didn't even notify me until eight months into my term. I would call and say, 'What's going on? What is this?' And it was obvious I was just a figurehead. I don't know if they didn't want me involved, or I don't know if they thought I couldn't handle it, you know.

A lot of the other women feel they go to a lot of meetings, they make recommendations, and nothing ever gets done from their recommendations. I don't know if it is a sexist thing or if the decision-making powers are with a small group of people that I don't even know if I can identify yet.

Social Clubs and Social Life

In clubs that enjoy either rented or owned space there is typically a small kitchen, an espresso and wet bar, card tables, a television for viewing soccer and hockey games, photographs of club events, and tourist posters from the members' town or region of origin in Italy. Some have had indoor bocce courts. Some associations have bought additional sites as a future investment. When a clubhouse is not in use, it is sometimes rented to other organizations, thus earning it extra income to support community events.

Each social club usually organizes two or three dinner-dances per year, in autumn and spring, at one of the many Italian-owned banquet halls that have flourished in the northwest suburbs of the city. Summer picnics usually include a celebration of the Catholic patron saint revered in the town of origin, complete with a Mass, a procession with a statue of the saint, and games for the children. The generational mix of these dinner-dances usually includes

younger children, but the Canadian-born and/or educated children between the ages of seventeen through to the early thirties
tend to miss these events.

Different generations approach community events with different perspectives. As fifty-five-year-old Anthony said concerning the
usefulness of the banquets: 'It is nice to have people from my Italian home town in Toronto, sometimes coming from Ottawa, Buffalo, Welland, Guelph, and Kitchener ... What happens sometimes
is that people have been away and they haven't seen each other. In
some cases the kids meet and get married. If not for these meetings to meet these parents and kids I guess they would marry some-
body else.' And as one twenty-seven-year-old man complained, 'I
am so sick of being asked by every relative, every cousin, every
uncle at these picnics, 'When are you going to get married?'

Parents view these gatherings as one of the few social situations
under their control in polyethnic and consumerist North American society, and therefore they are the perfect opportunity to
scheme about marriage partners for their children, even if the
plans meet with limited success. These semi-annual events also
serve as meeting places for compaesani who may have emigrated
to more distant cities in southern Ontario, or for cousins who have
settled in the United States. At the dinner-dances generous
amounts of food are served, often with specially prepared local
foods common in the town or province of origin.

Music too can do more than mark social boundaries. Music can
stimulate memories and nostalgia for place, thereby encouraging
collective memories, shared experiences, and the moral cohesion
of the group. It can also transform social space for immigrants,
allowing them to transcend the limitations of their immediate
social and spatial conditions to recall and reconstruct other identities in other places (Stokes 1992). I have seen for myself the trans-
formative effect of music on groups of middle-aged Calabrese,
Abruzzese, or Laziali, whose emotions and excitement grow when
they listen to a mix of Italian regional folk music performed by
local bands, with songs such as 'Arrivederci Roma' or 'Cala-
brisella,' a version of the beautiful country girl genre. These songs
feed the nostalgia for place and a longing for the pastoral hills that

have been left but can be reconstituted in memory through song. With this music, which also includes American rock 'n' roll of the 1950s and the songs of Frank Sinatra, the memory of youthful years in Italy can be intensely recalled at these events (Del Giudice 1992).

Honoured guests usually include a politician from the municipal or provincial level in Ontario, an editor of an Italian-language newspaper, and often a wealthy community benefactor who is accorded special status for his ability to navigate the economies and/or the bureaucracies of both Canada and Italy. Inevitably the mayor or vice-mayor of the Italian home town is there with greetings from relatives who have remained back home or have emigrated to other targets in Australia, South America, or Europe. A subtext of the presence of Italian home-town representatives is the imagining of this greater community of people around the world who share a common birthplace and ancestry. Even more, however, especially in parts of southern Italy, the life and economy of the agro-town is aided by the diaspora community. Town councillors and priests from many Italian towns that sent emigrants abroad try to keep wealthy *canadesi* or *americani* interested in the vitality of the town. These town leaders often will make trips to different migration targets around the world where people from their home towns have settled. Donations are encouraged as well, to fix the town's church, or build a retirement home, or otherwise infuse capital into the weak economies of southern Italy.

Dramatic changes in telecommunications and transportation have helped to revitalize these local identities further, in four obvious ways. First, the ease of both local and international telephone calls enables frequent communication between relatives and fellow townspeople in greater Toronto, southern Ontario, and around the world, to announce births, weddings, and deaths, and to gossip (Sturino 1990b). Second, in addition to the Italian-language radio stations CHIN and CIAO, which serve the GTA, the satellite television and cable stations Telelatino, CFMT's Telesera (now Studio Aperto), and Incontri bring Italian news reports and programs direct to Canada, thus offering a common basis for popular culture. At the same time, videocassette technology helps distribute family events and messages from grandchildren to nonni or from cousin to cousin in other parts of the world. Third, many paesi social clubs in Toronto have begun to produce their own glossy news magazines, such as *Il Laghetto dei serresi nel mondo* (Serra San Bruno, Calabria) and *La Lumera* (Vallelonga–Monserrato, Calabria), originating from Italy; and *La Cisilute* (the periodical of the Fogolârs Federation of Canada) and *Terra Veneta* (a bulletin produced by Italian Canadians from the Veneto region), all of which include stories from the town's diaspora communities, rites of passage announcements, and photographs. Fourth, less expensive and more direct air travel through newer international airports in Pescara, Abruzzi, or Lamezia in central Calabria make linkages between the diaspora and the towns of origin more accessible for those who wish to visit their birthplace or introduce their foreign-born children to their ancestral agro-town.

More recently (as discussed in Chapter 5) paesi clubs from specific Italian regions have formed themselves into federations. These new aggregate groups respond to three conditions: (1) the elasticity of kinship and quasi-kinship, and the reduction of campanilismo that resulted from the necessities of migration and the experience of meeting people from other parts of the Italian peninsula; (2) the political realities within a larger Italian-Canadian community as people try to distinguish themselves from one another; and (3) new political structures in Italy itself, based on the regions that encourage subnational identities.

San Giorgio Morgeto and the Steelworkers

At least twice a year immigrants from the small town of San Giorgio Morgeto, in the southernmost peninsular province of Reggio Calabria, gather for a banquet in a hall in Downsview or Woodbridge to reaffirm their sense of community. As previously noted, a small contingent of immigrants came to Toronto before the war, and many have lived in Canada for more than thirty or forty years. A mountain town located near the Aspromonte mountains, with a view of the Straits of Messina, San Giorgio Morgeto today has a population of no more than 6,000 people. In southern Ontario

today there are roughly 10,000 San Giorgesi of different generations and birthplaces.

In the early 1960s the San Giorgesi began to celebrate their
patron saints, San Giorgio and San Giacomo, in the last week of
July. During this religious feast San Giorgesi families who had
immigrated to other parts of Ontario, such as Guelph, Kitchener,
Oshawa, Ottawa, Welland, and Woodstock – even as far as Albany,
New York – would gather to renew friendships and introduce their
children. Both newspaper reports and oral testimony say that
between 13,500 and 16,000 people would converge on the monastery at Marylake, just north of King City, to honour the patron
saints of their town of origin and to reconstitute the overseas San
Giorgesi as a community. By 1974 some of these San Giorgesi had
created their own social club, Circolo Morgezio, unrelated to the
saints' day celebrations and under the leadership of a charismatic
and energetic steelworker/union organizer. It is this specific meld-
ing of the paese group with the universalist notions of the union
that is of particular interest. In their 1974 constitution a global
rather than a parochial understanding of their place in the world
is asserted. Its purpose: 'to gather people originally from San Giorgio Morgeto, and others coming from any regions of Italy, and now
residing in Canada, and to organize and promote activities for the
purpose of communication, promoting Canadian citizenship, Education, information re: Unemployment Insurance, Workmen's
Compensation, Canada Pension Plan, and social activities.'

At these banquets, which continue to this day, aside from the
greetings from various politicians and notables the San Giorgesi
recognize several of their own. Tradition holds that at each
banquet a couple that emigrated from San Giorgio is accorded
honoured status in commemoration of the journey they have travelled through a long life of migration. A brief biography of the
couple is recounted, and roses are presented to the wife. In addition, a bouquet of roses is presented to the oldest San Giorgesi at
the gathering. Each banquet is videotaped, then edited to a half-
hour program to be featured on a local community cable station's
show on labour issues, hosted by the president of the social club
and sponsored by the United Steelworkers. Several photographers

are present to ensure that numerous prints are submitted to all four Italian-language newspapers so that the event will be recorded for posterity and dissemination. Each paper is supplied with story material and copies are sent to relatives and town officials in San Giorgio and to other San Giorgesi living around the world. Some of the money raised at each dinner-dance is donated to the Humanity Fund of the United Steelworkers, some given to Villa Colombo, some used to help restore the church in San Giorgio, or donated to other charitable causes around the world.

During an annual banquet sponsored by the Circolo Morgezio at the Mona Lisa banquet hall (since closed) near Caledonia Road and Lawrence Avenue, Fortunato described with pride some aspects of the club and its activities:

> The best part is that I have a group of people in the executive who are very fine. We made one of the best constitutions, and no other social club I think has done one like ours. We have a reference to assist people who need help. We also have a reference where we encourage people to become Canadians and to be active in the community. We help a lot of people become Canadians who have been in the country for twenty years. Some have been afraid to go to court to face the judge. We have explained that the judge from the citizenship Court is not a criminal judge. But a lot of people have said, 'We have never been in court, we have never had to deal with the law.' And we say, 'This is a different thing altogether. If you have been living in this country for several years you should know something about Canada.'
>
> Each time we do a dinner and dance the tickets go quickly because we include a great meal. There is always plenty of food. We negotiate with the catering person in order to serve the right antipasto, pasta, meat, and fish. We usually go to a banquet hall run by a friend from Reggio Calabria.
>
> We also give a donation to the Villa [Colombo] because it is doing a fantastic job. We gave money to Caritas for a community [effort] against drugs. Our money is given even to the food bank in Toronto.

Rhetoric about home, whether the new one in Canada, or the old one in Italy, is always a significant part of speeches at these banquets. Canada is always seen as a country that offered work, food, and economic stability for these immigrants and their children. The migration journey, the establishment of a home, the pleasure of seeing children and grandchildren raised in a safe and prosperous country are also recurrent themes. Finally, the contributions made by these men and women as workers, labourers, and parents are singled out and repeated as though they were cathartic incantations. Italy is seen as home, but foreign. It is recognized that for the vast majority of immigrants, political instability, bureaucratic complications, and economic imbroglio in southern Italy have mitigated against returning, at this stage, other than for vacation.

Since the leadership is tied to the labour movement, banquet guests in the past have included former Premier Bob Rae of the Ontario NDP government, New Democratic MPPs Tony Silipo, Rosario Marchese, Tony Rizzo, Anthony Perruzza, and George Mammoliti, Liberal MPP Gregory Sorbara (whose father was a San Giorgesi), and labour leaders such as Bob White and Buzz Hargrove. Pan-Italian-Canadian community representatives such as Palmacchio Di Iulio from Villa Charities, community leaders such as Ben Bellantone, the Canadian envoy of the Calabrian regional government, Dan Iannuzzi of the Italian-language newspaper *Corriere Canadese* (sometimes jokingly referred to as *Corriere Calabrese*, because of Mr Iannuzzi's heritage), and leaders of the Confederation of Calabrian Clubs in Ontario have also attended.

The mix of political leaders and speeches filled with platitudes concerning Canada have a performative effect. Politicians of Italian heritage symbolically strengthen the legitimacy of migration projects. If one or more guests also speaks Italian or a dialect and has achieved a prestigious status in Canada, all the better. The presence of non-Italian-Canadian politicians indicates that the community is relevant to the broader Canadian society. The stock phrases reinforce and reassure the participants that the struggle of their migration project and the price of cultural change for their children were worthwhile.

These participants need a communal ritual to assert that the

migrant journey was necessary and fruitful despite the disloca-
tions, ruptures, and hardships that forced them to leave their family, friends, language, and terra firma for a foreign and sometimes
hostile Canada. They also need reminders that to return to Italy to
live would result in some social cost, especially for those who did
not return in the intervening years (King and Strachan 1980:177).

Two different forms of social abuse can also occur at the hands
of those who remained behind in Italy. A derisive term used to
describe migrants who have returned to Italy from the poorer
economies of Latin America, *vu torna* (you who have returned),
chastises the migrant for his loss of language, culture, and children
to foreignness and his failure to achieve economic stability or success. Another problem returning migrants face is that their Italian
cousins or fellow townspeople expect some financial gift, because
they perceive all migrants as rich. A corollary of this view is that
wealth has brought with it hubris and laziness. Migrants can also be
accused by those who have stayed behind as being neglectful of
their home town.

The Sense of Place

A recent meeting of an Italian-Canadian university-student federation – one that sparked a discussion about which community organizations might support a conference for students on the subjects
of potential careers and Italian-Canadian culture – led to an
intriguing exchange about sense of place and its relationship to
ethnicity and ethnic identity. One speaker, a child of immigrant
parents, suggested the group contact some paesi clubs, and she
mentioned 'Sora' as an example. The Sora Club derives its membership primarily from the town of the same name in the region of
Lazio, about an hour southwest of Rome. It is an area from which
thousands of Italians have migrated to Toronto. The facilitator of
the meeting, an immigrant in his forties who came to Canada from
Calabria as a child and was now an established Ontario politician,
asked, 'Where is Sora?' Several students responded, 'It is on
Steeles' (Steeles Avenue, the east-west arterial road that also serves
as the northern boundary of Metropolitan Toronto). The facilita-

tor, understanding, grinned and asked again, 'Where is Sora in Italy?' This time he received the appropriate response.

The toponymy of the Italian settlement in greater Toronto speaks to the complexity of social space and the semi-deterritorialization of ethnicity in a polyethnic and immigrant city. To understand the 'human ecology' of Toronto's Italian settlement one could look first at the spatial ordering of the original immigrant settlement, and then at the successive movement of immigrants and their children that has corresponded to the expansion boom in the residential housing industry in which Italian Canadians figured prominently as builders and labourers. As we know, the first waves of immigrants in the postwar period settled near College and Grace Streets in the southwest of the city. Then, through the years, the community gradually grew outward to the north and west. Not surprisingly, this move in residential concentration, while it may be seen as part of the larger movement of urban people from smaller dwellings in the city's core to larger suburban homes, also coincided with the gradual movement of jobs in industry, mainly manufacturing and construction, in the same northwest direction. This shift in economic activity also corresponded to the increased importance of the airport (in the city's northwest) as an economic engine, as compared to the railway (centred in the downtown core). At the same time a small Italian settlement in the east of the city, on Danforth Avenue, has also dwindled as its people have moved farther north and east into Scarborough.

Nowhere in Metropolitan Toronto's twenty-eight wards do Italian Canadians constitute a numerical majority. At their highest concentration, in North York Humber, they constitute the plurality at 34 per cent (1991 Census). In these new neighbourhoods the simple sign announcing a home-town club's meeting site is often situated next to other business units.

Even if Italian residential concentration reaches a plurality in several municipal wards, to think of Italian-Canadian ethnicity as constructed within a bounded communal territory does not fully explain the complexity of the issue and the intercultural encounters in workplaces and markets. Instead, it would be better to perceive it also as 'a communicative community – more often than not dispersed – whose bounds are limited by a social, not a territorial field' (Kenny and Kertzer, 1983:6; A.P. Cohen 1985). As the anecdote regarding the town of Sora portrays, the cognitive maps of immigrants and their children create some intriguing disjunctures in the relation between space and community. In the transnational social field of Italians, the mapping of Sora includes a social club in a strip mall in northern Toronto. This site is not only a signifier for those who emigrated from Sora but also for many other Italian Canadians who are in the process of negotiating the spatial dimensions and thresholds of Italianness in the world (Carstens 1994). Italian anthropologists have called this phenomenon *apaesemento* (mondialization) (Pitto 1990; Douglass 1984). Employing a sending-town-centred approach to understanding migration these studies approach migrants as part of diasporas (Clifford 1994) creating multi-locale social fields through networks of communication such as newsletters, videotapes, and glossy magazines, all of which link chains of immigrants and their descendants in migration targets in the Americas, Australia, Africa, and Europe.

At the same time that place takes on more subtle and complicated meanings in a diaspora or immigrant community, territory and place within the city's ecology are crucial for what de Certeau (1984:36) calls 'the mastery of time through the foundation of an autonomous place.' Immigrants become deterritorialized by their migration to new cities and countries. The social clubs and picnic sites in Downsview, Rexdale, Woodbridge, and Maple provide an opportunity for them to remake history by recapturing the piazza of their place of emigration, a familiar cultural space. This is not simply a re-creation of the old but a fostering of a new sense of belonging in a new community and a new place, with extended kin and friends, while simultaneously asserting a continuity with the land of emigration. It is also about the guarding and enhancing of familiar cultural spaces in the face of the encroaching foreignness of the larger city.

Final Remarks

A noticeable feature of Italian sociocultural life in Toronto is the ubiquity of social clubs based on sending-town loyalties. These associations indicate the persistence of the strong local attachments people feel towards their historical homelands and the importance of these affections to kin and friendship networks in the new land. Nevertheless, the relevance of campanilismo should not be overdrawn. Italian immigrants to Canada have been quick to establish new relationships within the broader Italian migration stream in order to adjust to a new industrial setting. Social life has necessitated and created new opportunities for fellow feeling. As one young woman whose parents emigrated from Sora told me, 'I was chosen Miss Ciociara even though I am not from the town of the club sponsoring the event. They didn't have anyone the right age or willing to do it, so they asked me.' These clubs, however, do constitute a sociocultural space that creates a place to construct a member's past, present, and future. They are critical points on a map of Italianness for Italian Canadians in Toronto, but they are also significant locations in the webs of kin and compaesani networks that comprise the global village of small towns.

8. The Journey of the Saints and Madonnas

Fieldnote, 22 August 1994

Immigrants from a mountainous area in the region of Lazio in central Italy have formed La Società Canneto to reconstruct a religious festival they used to celebrate in Lazio in honour of a representation of the Madonna. There are several nights and mornings of prayer and Masses, but the annual all-day festa in August at the religious retreat of Marylake, in King City north of Vaughan, is the most anticipated event.

I arrived at the Marylake Monastery at around eight in the morning. Already, groups of devotees (men, women, and children) were gathering around the stone-arched entrance to the retreat in anticipation of the arrival of the Madonna. Many were dressed in the traditional red, black, and white embroidered vests, skirts, and pants of their home town. Toronto Italia band members milled around, warming up their brass instruments, looking over their sheet music. Cars began to arrive and park in neighbouring farmers' fields. Out of each car came what seemed an improbable number of prepared foods, tables, and chairs. The Madonna was on the back of a blue pick-up truck. She had made the trip from the clubhouse through north Toronto's streets to the gates of the monastery in King City. The blue pick-up truck was usually used for construction, but today its bumpers were wrapped in powder-blue cloth like the skirts of buffet tables at an elegant wedding. The Madonna herself was bedecked in garlands, crêpe paper, and blue carnations. Soon she was hoisted from the pick-up's flatbed to the shoulders of six men dressed in white and red robes. The Toronto Italia band played now religious, now march music as it lead the procession up the winding, half-mile, tree-covered driveway to the church.

Several women in the peasant dress of Lazio followed the band, holding in their hands cloth-covered wooden boards of gold-embroidered design laden with pinned banknotes of various denominations; photographs of children, husbands or wives; gold trinkets, necklaces; and prayer cards of the Madonna and other saints – each a plea for the Madonna's intervention. Following the statue were a group of women singing 'Evviva Maria.' The procession continued to trail the main body of devotees, composed for the most part of separate groups, each bearing its own or another's representation of the Madonna. When I asked about the significance of the various Madonnas I was told they were meant to show respect for the miracles of the Madonna di Canneto. In front of the church an outdoor Mass began for the 10,000 or more people who had gathered.

I walked towards the vast green fields of the monastery campus that had gradually been filling with cars and trucks, barbecues, and children's playpens. Although the Mass was in progress, many people were milling about in the fields chatting with friends, kicking soccer balls. Young men and women were furtively exchanging glances and beginning to exit from the area in which their parents were congregating to more remote and serene surroundings on the grounds. Although there was a core of a thousand or more devotees following the Mass intently, for more people it seemed a preparation for a long day's cookout.

This festa is one of scores of religious observances that begin with the Good Friday procession on College Street and continue throughout the summer months in Italian parishes throughout the city. The feste are central ritual events in the construction of Italianness in Toronto. In 1991 94 per cent of Italians in Canada professed to be Catholic.

This chapter explores the 'popular religion' of Italian-Canadian Catholics and the way it is expressed through the rituals for saints or the Madonna at feste in the GTA. Religious symbols and rituals provide a sense of order in times of dislocation, and promise in the face of an unpredictable future. Religious institutions provide an organizational framework in which the form of groups can be constructed. Religious rituals also nourish and encourage a sense of communal solidarity.

The term *popular religion* carries a panoply of meanings and interpretations that should be differentiated before I continue. Some interpret popular religion as comprising the bizarre or peculiar practices of people outside any formal institutional religious structure. Still others romanticize a peasant spirituality they interpret in the folk wisdom and magic of popular religion (Orsi 1985:xiv). In the case of Italy, and especially southern Italy, popular religion can include the use of incantations to ward off the evil eye; herbal healing practices; amulets in the shape of hunchbacks, red *corni* (horns) to hang in doorways or on rearview mirrors, or as protection from the envy of others; or the observance of communal feste that honour patron saints or specific representations of the Madonna.

The categorization of these as popular culture also implies the existence of an elite religion. These are the 'two tiers' of one religious system. Using this distinction popular religion is considered somehow less refined, less structured, even a misconception or corruption of elite religion (Brown 1981:13–22). As a result popular religion is not considered a legitimate meaning system by many religious leaders. Despite some of the problems associated with the category of popular religion, I think it can be usefully applied in a limited and prudent manner. For example, Badone (1990:5–6) offers a practical definition of popular religion as 'those informal practices, beliefs, and styles of religious expression that lack the formal sanction of established church structures.'

Italian peasant popular religion combines pre-Christian sources such as polytheism, sorcery, and animism with Christian sacraments (Rami 1972; Chapman 1971; Bo 1984; Orsi 1985). It is intensely bound up with the world of campanilismo (see Chapter 7), wherein each paese reveres a specific saint or the Madonna, whose assistance and intervention with God is called for in times of need. Some scholars link an individual's personal devotion to a patron saint to the everyday reciprocity practices between people of differing status and wealth in the Mediterranean. Social structure in this area encourages patron-client relationships, and the saint and follower are an extension of that relationship (Boissevain 1977). Di Tota (1981:238) suggests that the patron-client relationship between saint and devotee is a metaphor rather than a direct reflection of the patron-client relationship in the social system. Each is based on expectations of reciprocity, but she cites several examples to illustrate the different qualities exhibited by the two relationships.

The annual celebration in honour of a patron saint or a representation of the Madonna forms the apex of a villager's year. Marco, a twenty-two-year-old who grew up in Toronto but whose parents emigrated from a small town in Reggio Calabria, told me the annual feast was the most important event of his year. It was even more important than Christmas or Easter because it marked his survival for one more year, and his patron saint needed to be thanked properly for protecting him. This festa commonly includes an elaborate procession with a statue of the saint or the Madonna adorned with jewellery and flowers, followed by religious society members, clergy, throngs of faithful, and brass bands. Games, fireworks, pork roasts, and other sumptuous foods complete the celebration.

The 'informal, unofficial practices, beliefs and styles of religious expression' (Badone 1990:4–6) outside church structures for Italian immigrants extend beyond negotiations with the divine over tragedy, misfortune, and calamity in this world and the next. The meaning system encompasses numerous spirits, both good and evil, which are believed to influence illness, unemployment, and marriage breakdowns. Spells or incantations uttered by sorcerers to ward off *mal'occhio* (the evil eye) (Migliore 1997) or to discourage the envy or ill-wishes of others, and palm readers who predict the future, are still important for many Italian immigrants in the city. A sure sign of the adaptation of these religious practices and beliefs to an urban industrial setting is that these services are now offered over the phone (Iacovetta 1992:139).

Maria, whom I met along the procession route for the celebration of St Anthony's feast, said she considered herself a devout Catholic, but that she had been told by her priest not to believe in the evil eye or wear protective amulets. She did stop wearing the amulet to church, but still believes in the power of the evil eye, as do her sons, who were born and raised in Canada. Many of my

Canadian-born informants, children of immigrants, have also incorporated this meaning system into their daily lives but not all are completely convinced of the value of these incantations, spells, plastic amulets, and gold trinkets. They have argued, however, that it is better to be safe and follow the rules than face unfortunate consequences. One priest commented on the Italian popular religious tradition of hanging gold bracelets on a statue of the Madonna or a patron saint to thank them for assisting with a particular problem. He said he thinks about this periodically and sometimes doubts whether these people are really Christians.

Italians and the Catholic Church in Toronto

With the advent of the migration from the Italian peninsula at the turn of century, the Catholic Church became concerned about the spiritual state of these migrants. Several male Italian and American orders – Redemptorists, Franciscans, Oblates, Salesians, and Dominicans – and the female Carmelite nuns began to 'missionize' Italian communities overseas. A new order founded by Bishop Giovanni Scalabrini, named the Scalabrinian Order, focused specifically on Italian immigrants. The term *missionize* might strike the reader as odd given that the overwhelming majority of Italian migrants were Catholic. But as several scholars have shown (Zucchi 1988; Cumbo 1993; Pennacchio 1993) the hierarchy interpreted southern Catholicism with some suspicion and condescension because of its mix of formal structured church practices and unsanctioned popular practices and beliefs. Its 'otherness' suggested that Italian peasants needed to be taught formal Catholicism as a means of integrating them into Canadian ways.

Zucchi (1988:118–40) argues that the church and clergy helped Italian migrants construct a pan-Italian identity in the prewar period in part because they treated all migrants as if they held Italian nationalist sentiments. The clergy neglected the village origins and local identities that were central to immigrant identities, a practice that caused some conflict between the church and its parishioners. Cumbo (1993) studied Methodist social gospellers and other Protestant missionaries who actively proselytised to Italian migrants.

Their inability to understand the practices and meanings of the popular religion for immigrants also limited their success.

Even if only a few Italian migrants converted to Protestantism, the Catholic Church hierarchy was sufficiently disturbed to react. In 1908 the Archdiocese of Toronto decided that there were sufficient numbers of Italians in the city to require the establishment of a national parish. St Patrick's Church, originally an Irish parish, was duly reconsecrated as Our Lady of Carmel. Because a national parish bases its membership on ethnicity instead of place of residence, creating national parishes became a common method for the Catholic Church in North America to minister to non-English-speaking immigrant communities. One could choose to belong to either a national parish or a territorial one, but membership in both was not acceptable. Further, if there was more than one national parish, each had its own territory. Through the prewar years, two new parishes, St Agnes in the area of College and Grace Streets and St Mary of the Angels at Dufferin and Davenport, both run by the Franciscan order, began services in Italian.

The postwar arrival of Italian immigrants in immense numbers generated areas of friction and adjustment between Italian Catholics and the English-speaking church and its parishioners in Canada (Iacovetta 1992:130–42; Marchetto 1985:106–9). Over the next thirty years the archdiocese adjusted to this new inflow of Catholic faithful by the massive construction of parishes to ameliorate church overcrowding. In turn the hierarchy tried to increase the number of Italian-speaking priests in the city by visiting the secular priests in Rome's Ufficio Centrale per l'Emigrazione and encouraging members of the aforementioned religious orders to come to Canada. Some clergy also followed kin who had migrated to Canada. By 1971 there were thirty-three parishes and sixty-five Italian-speaking priests throughout Metropolitan Toronto. At this time Italians accounted for one third of the 841,740 Catholics in the city.

Since it was not until the 1970s that the archdiocese building projects reached fruition, other changes were required to serve the increasing numbers of Italian parishioners. The national parish system adopted in the prewar years needed adjustment. In areas of considerable Italian settlement, older, generally Irish territorial parishes became bilingual and began to offer Italian services. As well, some large suburban parishes were divided and bilingual parishes established, offering Mass in Italian (Iacovetta 1988). As a result the intervening years created tensions between English-speaking and Italian-speaking Catholics. Often, Italian parishioners who had moved into areas previously settled by Irish and Scottish Catholics but were now becoming Italian neighbourhoods, were forced to attend Italian-language religious services in the basements or auditoriums of the parishes, while English Mass was held in the sanctuary. Italian-speaking parishioners and their Italian-speaking clergy regarded this as unfair, and on many occasions they made their feelings known to the hierarchy. Also, inevitably, some conflict arose when older English-speaking parishioners encountered southern Catholicism's elaborate public rituals, professions of faith, and feste. But as Iacovetta shows (ibid:131–6), church leaders agreed with their Italian parishioners in many of these conflicts and encouraged English-speaking Catholics to be more charitable. This concern may have reflected a desire to welcome immigrants into the Canadian Catholic church. Certainly, the possibility of changing the numerical balance between Catholics and Protestants in the city appealed to the hierarchy's sectarian impulses.

In 1970 the archdiocese created an Italian Pastoral Commission to coordinate Italian-language priests and parishes and to give them a greater say within the church's administration. Just as the Italian-speaking clergy at times felt slighted by the hierarchy, the relationship between Italian-speaking clergy and their congregations was not always free of friction. In part, different geographic, class, and cultural origins separating parish priests from parishioners reinforced the long-held mistrust for the clergy (Vecoli 1969). Although congregations were largely composed of southern Italians, nearly a third of the Italian-speaking clergy came from northern and central Italy. Only 14 per cent originated from southern Italy and another 12 per cent from the United States (Tomasi 1975). By 1993 there were more than eighty Italian-speaking priests providing pastoral care to Toronto's Italian Catholics. In comparison, the next-largest group of priests (fifteen) spoke Portuguese, and the next group (five) spoke Polish.

The present-day clergy, especially members of the Italian Pastoral Commission (IPC), have two distinct strategies for coping with the popular religious festivals. One strategy calls for bureaucratic incorporation of the festivals into the church's sphere of influence. However, since each feast is sponsored by a lay religious or social club with roots in a town of emigration, resistance against the authority of the church is a recurrent theme. The second strategy, similar to the first, attempts to control the formal Catholic spiritual elements within the feste.

To implement the first strategy the hierarchy has instituted a number of regulations to control the use of statues and the performance of feste rituals (Archdiocese 1981). I will highlight several important features of these rules. First, each January the presidents of social clubs or religious societies that sponsor feste meet with the head of the Italian Pastoral Commission to formalize plans for the coming summer's celebrations. Second, some societies ask a parish to sponsor a saint to avoid internal community rivalries over the celebration. The church now refuses to permit different groups from the same home town to hold more than one saint's festa. Parish sponsorship also legitimates a saint and a festa, and as a result increases the prestige of the sponsoring religious society and its Italian home-town origins within the social field of religious celebrations. Once a statue is accepted by a parish and its priest it becomes part of the church. But not all societies will relinquish control of their feasts and sign an agreement to hold a religious service in accordance with the IPC's restrictions. Third, priests are no longer permitted to celebrate Mass for religious societies or social clubs in banquet halls. In the view of the Italian Pastoral Commission (IPC), since the Mass celebrates the eucharist it is an inappropriate juxtaposition of the sacred and profane to charge fifty or sixty dollars for banquet tickets which include both a Mass and a secular party. Fourth, in the past devotees pinned money to the statues during the processions as offerings to the saint. The IPC saw this as a clash between

secular and religious worlds, and demanded an end to the practice if societies wished clerical participation. Fifth, all club members pay a nominal fee to insure the church and the club (for up
to $2 million) against litigation from the city in the event that
civil agencies (fire, police, ambulance) are required in an emer-
gency. Each one of these initiatives increases the bureaucratic
authority of the church over what was originally a communal
popular religious event that used the services of a priest but was
for the most part operated outside the formal structure of the
church.

The second strategy articulates the spiritual ambitions of the
Catholic Church in creating the former bureaucratic rules to gov-
ern the feste. As was noted, the president of a club must ask for
permission to hold a festa, to use the church building, or have a
priest say Mass. However, to secure these services from the
Church the clubs must give up possession, hence practical ownership, of their statues to the Church. Clubs are reluctant to give up
the ownership of a statue because they fear the priest will exclude
them from choices about the celebration. But in the clergy's view,
placement of these statues in a church creates a larger and more
accessible space for devotees to honour a saint. Instead, the saint
would often be housed in the home of a club officer or in a separate room in a clubhouse. Placement in the church also maintains the possibility of clerical control over the form of devotion
expressed in honour of the saint. One Italian-speaking priest
mentioned that the idolatry of saint worship made him feel
uneasy, but he felt that if the devotees at least came to church
they might deepen their sensibility concerning Catholicism. With
a resignation brought on by years of ministering to the Italian-
Canadian community, he continued to indicate his acceptance of
saints' feasts: 'All things considered, any time to pray is good. Italian immigrants are still very faithful to the Madonna, and you fac-
tor that in and think something must be rubbing off ... If it also
shows the young respect for their grandparents, that's good. You
hope the faith comes through in the celebrations to all these
saints. As long as there is a catechism something might stick.'
This view contrasts with the hostility to feste and saints' proces-

sions that Brettell (1990:57) found when doing fieldwork with Portuguese priests in Toronto.

Madonna di Canneto in Toronto

A reading of Italian-Canadian Catholicism needs to move beyond the formal church structures that support the faithful to the numerous communally based organizations and practices that give meaning to popular celebrations. In 1992 fifty-five processions were sanctioned by the archdiocese; in 1993 there were sixty-two. Several priests lamented that instead of disappearing, they appeared to be increasing in frequency.

This section briefly highlights the origins of a club that celebrates a representation of the Madonna. The ethnohistory that follows is a reconstruction of the stories recounted by several informants who are members of La Società di Canneto, a religious social club with its own storefront clubhouse in an industrial zone around Finch Avenue and Weston Road. Throughout the year members gather one night a month to hold prayer sessions of devotion to the Madonna, whose statue is kept in the club and not at a church.

Canneto is in the mountains of Lazio, near the town of Settefrate, from which the core group of the La Società di Canneto comes. Legend has it that in Roman times there was a temple there dedicated to the Roman goddess Mephites. The area was well-known for its mountain breezes, forests, and spring waters with reputedly curative qualities. It is believed that Hannibal met the Romans at Canneto, and during a battle there the temple was destroyed. People are not absolutely certain where it was, but nevertheless the temple was never rebuilt, and eventually it was covered by dirt, stones, and the debris of centuries.

A legend tells us how this spot was converted from a temple in honour of Mephites to an area associated with the Madonna: A young girl was tending the family's sheep in the valley. One day as she was watching over her flock she was met by the Virgin Mary, who asked her to deliver a letter to the priest in town. The girl said she could not go because if she did not bring water to the sheep they would die. Thereupon the Madonna pressed her hands to the rock and a flowing river of mountain water appeared for the sheep, so that the girl could deliver the letter to the priest. In the letter the Madonna told the priest to build a church for her in Settefrate.

A more recent story of the location's religious importance tells the story of monks on a pilgrimage. On the northeast side of the Apennine mountains sits the monastery of the brothers of St Vincent. The monks on their pilgrimages used to stop in Settefrate to rest, and in their rest area they built a little wooden chapel dedicated to the Madonna. Over the years several hundred miracles have been documented in Settefrate by the church of Canneto. Gradually the little chapel, built by the monks, became a church, and their pilgrimages expanded from one day to five days a year. Pilgrims would walk barefoot for three hours from Canneto singing praise to the Madonna di Canneto and as they rested by the road local peasants would give them water. Today there are major pilgrimages from 16 August to 22 August.

In the mid-1960s in Canneto, the Madonna di Canneto festa, which had been controlled traditionally by a public, nonecclesiastical committee, was taken over by the clergy. The parish had made a decision to take power away from the people and to change various parts of the celebration in order to reduce the scale of the festivities. Local people protested that the festival had been theirs for centuries and should continue to be theirs. A number of them corresponded with immigrants in Toronto who every year had organized an unofficial committee to collect money for Canneto to help maintain the little church and to insure that the celebrations for the Madonna continued. When the Toronto people heard of the changes in Settefrate, this unofficial group of a dozen or so people decided to form a pro-Settefrate committee against the Church. They wrote letters of protest to the Pope and to the Catholic leadership, but did not receive a satisfactory response. They then wrote to the archbishop of the area stating that since the Church failed to comply with the wishes of the people of Settefrate, the people of Toronto would have their own celebration in Canada. Still they received no reply. As one informant said, 'They probably thought we were joking.' The people began again to collect money and to inform others, and in four

months the committee grew from twelve to fifty people, all originating from Settefrate.

After all these people got together they decided to raise money
for a new statue of the Madonna, to be carved in Italy. Members of
the committee began visiting people from Lazio, Abruzzi, and
Campania in the evenings and on the weekends. Many were enthusiastic about bringing the celebrations to Toronto. No one refused
to give money, including people from New York State. The committee then incorporated itself, to make its status legal and to
silence any criticism that funds were not being properly controlled.
In anticipation of the arrival of the statue from Italy for the celebration, announcements were placed on CHIN radio. At the
opening ceremony, in August 1968, politicians from all levels of
government, including the premier of Ontario, came to Marylake
to celebrate. Initially the organizers assumed that at most a couple
of hundred people would participate. As it turned out, Keele
Street was crowded with people and had to be blockaded as devotees arrived from all over Ontario and New York State.

Local church authorities in Italy were angry when they heard
about a new statue and another feast, which further cemented the
resolve of the Toronto committee to continue the celebration in
Canada as long as the clergy in Settefrate controlled the event.
After three years the church in Italy gave the festa back to the lay
committee. In turn, the Toronto committee duly changed its name
to the Canneto Society, registered itself as a charitable institution,
and resolved to build a church in a place resembling Canneto.
They chose to have the first celebration at Marylake in King City
because of its Canneto-like natural setting. The committee still
sends money to Settefrate each year. (When devotees make a dona-
tion they indicate if they want a portion to go to Settefrate.) The
Settefrate church usually receives between $500 and $1,000 from
the Canneto Society in Toronto.

In future, supporters of the devotion would like to convince the
archdiocese to dedicate an older church to the Madonna di Canneto, and they have asked the local Catholic authorities about this
possibility. Others wish to build a cathedral-like church similar to
the basilica of Ste-Anne-de-Beaupré in Quebec, an expensive pros-
pect calling for proper marketing and advertising. Most have been

adamant, however, that they would not want to confuse the issue by using the secular world of advertising and commercialism to build their cathedral.

This ethnohistory of La Società di Canneto has featured three central elements that point to the relevance of religious societies in the construction of Italianness in Toronto. First, the history of the Madonna's pre-Christian origins underscores the limitations of the formal church teachings over popular religious beliefs. According to the ethnohistory, spirituality and mysticism were long associated with the area, from its site as a temple to a Roman goddess to the curative powers of its spring waters. The Madonna in turn was expected to cure ailments of all sorts.

The second issue raised by the story of the Società in Canada and in Lazio pertains to the latent anticlericalism of the people and the issue of ownership of a religious festival. La Società di Canneto maintains its own clubhouse for the Madonna and refuses to come under the direct control of the clergy. The Società will enter into a contractual agreement with the Church to hold a Mass with its festa celebration, but will not surrender its statue to a church unless it is consecrated in the name of their Madonna.

Anticlericalism does not mean that the people are not religious. The views of some of the participants reminds one of the views of the Italian miller Menocchio in Carlo Ginzburg's *The Cheese and the Worms* (1980), who believed the clergy and laity were equals before God and that the clergy was involved in the business of exploiting the poor for the church.

Finally, religious societies or clubs are another part of the organizational framework that constitutes the social field of Italianness for immigrants to help them establish a life in Canada. Although principally a club based on devotion to the Madonna di Canneto, the club also engages in social events that help reinforce communal solidarity. The nostalgia for the place of emigration in this case has created an ambition on the part of organizers to construct a cathedral in a geographic space similar to their land in Lazio. The recreation of the festa as an annual event draws people from Lazio, Campania, and Abruzzo together every year to maintain, renew, and reconstitute links with a community of believers.

Final Remarks

Sidney Mintz once properly defined *superstition* as 'the other man's [sic] religion.' It is unlikely that Mintz had Italian-Canadian Catholicism in mind when he asserted this point, but certainly the friction between the formal church rules and the popular religious practices leads to a misunderstanding over the meaning of religion. This chapter has attempted to illustrate that tension. Furthermore, through a discussion of a particular religious society I have emphasized the centrality of these societies to the religious meanings of popular Italian-Canadian Catholicism. In the summer months people sometimes make pilgrimages from as far away as New York State to attend these *feste*, but a closer and more frequent interaction occurs between people who emigrated to Canada from different parts of the Italian peninsula. Italians living in Toronto have begun to discover each other's popular religious festivals. These encounters have helped to encourage the proliferation of feste in the city over the last several years, thereby reinforcing the centrality of these religious practices in the creation and expression of Italianness and Italian-Canadian Catholicism in Toronto.

9. Italianità for the Canadian-Born

Fieldnote, 23 June 1995

The heavy bass of hip-hop and techno-dance music seeped through the partition in the Montecassino banquet hall. On one side of the barrier was a graduation dance of Chaminade high school. Its students, many of them of Italian heritage, were dressed in formal wear and were dancing and preening for each other. On the other side of the barrier a recognition dinner sponsored by Centro Scuola was honouring the Italian consul with a violin solo by a young Italian-Canadian student, and many were praising the consul for his efforts to bring the Italian language, arts, and culture to the Italian-Canadian community. A more discordant yet more telling juxtaposition could not have occurred during the evening. One speaker said he hoped the Italian-Canadian culture offered by Centro Scuola would prevail for children of Italian heritage, over the din that reverberated from next door.

This chapter explores the less obvious changes occurring through the generations in the Italian-Canadian settlement. It discusses some central themes that have transformed the meaning of Italian-ness in Toronto in recent years, and thus the relationship between Italian immigrants and their children. It also explores the changing conception of work that results in tensions and misreadings by the different generations. Finally, a brief look at the *Eyetalian* magazine will highlight some of the disjunctures between different age cohorts in the community.

Any reading of generational change must consider the larger

ways in which images of Italians have been transformed within Canadian society during the past fifteen years. These popular images influence the way people of Italian heritage, both young and old, construct and express their Italianness. I divide this period into two eras: pre- and post-1982. The championship year of Italy's national soccer team in the World Cup in Spain is useful as the symbolic transition event that signified a constellation of complex conditions leading to changing meanings associated with Italy and Italians in Toronto's public culture. In the pre-1982 period Italians often were portrayed either as *cafoni* (rural louts) or Mafiosi.

According to the list of 'intended occupations' declared by Italians who came to Canada in the postwar period, more than 75 per cent planned to work in low-skilled manufacturing, construction, and labourer positions. More than 70 per cent of Italian immigrants fifteen years old or older in 1971 had less than a ninth grade education (Jansen and La Cavera 1981). Concomitant with their socioeconomic status, the stereotype of the Italian man pictured him as a hardworking uneducated labourer who provided the brawn necessary to build Toronto's urban infrastructure. At the same time idyllic images of Italian peasants bringing their agricultural skills to urban Toronto and planting backyards full of tomatoes, grape vines, and beans nourished images of a people with, if not loutish qualities, at least peasant simplicity. Educators in Toronto's primary and secondary schools then contributed to this portrait by streaming the children of immigrants into vocational and technical schools. Italian schoolchildren whose home language was the paese dialect and school language was English were doubly challenged by the conflicting preconceptions held by educators and by supportive but inadequately equipped parents who had few English-language skills and limited formal education.

The relationship between Italians and organized crime is an equally important image that influences the manner in which Italians were, and are, perceived in Toronto's public culture. In some instances the two images, cafoni and mafiosi, have intertwined in the public view. For example, in the late 1960s and early 1970s protracted labour unrest and violence in the construction industry fuelled speculation about its connections to organized crime.

Since people of Italian heritage were associated with that industry, the problems encouraged conjecture. In 1974 a royal commission established to investigate these problems reported extensively on shootings, bombings, threats, and assaults within contracting businesses (Waisberg 1974). Later, in March of 1979, the CBC presented a series called *Connections*, replete with innuendo about the ties between Italian Canadians and organized crime. This television special received considerable attention within the Italian-Canadian community. In fact, Senator Peter Bosa, an appointee of Italian heritage, rose in the Senate to denounce the way Italians were portrayed in the production (Senate Debates 1979). He argued that the media's portrayal of Italians as criminals influenced the views Canadians held about them. That spring a Gallup poll that surveyed Canadian perceptions of Italians confirmed this fear. Despite federal statistics demonstrating that Italian Canadians are law-abiding, fully 47 per cent of the people who saw the television program believed Italians were associated with criminality and 37 per cent of those who had not seen it held a similar opinion (Bagnell 1989; R.F. Harney 1985).

The perception of criminality can develop when one community misinterprets the cultural use of public spaces by members of another community. In the 1960s and 1970s Italian Canadians, mostly male, would gather on College street in front of Italian bars and cafés to listen to soccer games on the radio and pass the time in camaraderie. In many instances this form of public culture, which combined the immigrants' need for a familiar gathering place similar to the public space of an Italian town's piazza, created conflict with conservative Anglo-Canadian notions of public space and culture. Numerous stories persist in the memories of older immigrants, of Toronto policemen telling groups of Italians to 'move along' or 'break it up' as they stood listening to the soccer games and chatting after Sunday morning Mass. Part of this aggressiveness on the part of Toronto's police force no doubt had to do with their preconceptions of immigrants in general, and Italians in particular, as associated with illicit and illegal activity.

If the images of pre-1982 made it difficult for Italian Canadians to feel a sense of belonging and acceptance in Toronto, the early 1980s

saw the insertion of new images into Toronto's public culture that
have had a significant impact on the attitudes of younger Italian
Canadians. Three pivotal changes occurred at this time. First, Italy
emerged as a major economic power, having been one of the poorest countries in the world following the Second World War. *The
Economist* in 1981 described Italy's both small- and medium-sized
industrial structure as the most dynamic in Europe. Fuelling this
economic boom were exports of clothing, textiles, and furniture as
well as robotics and machine tools (Spotts and Wieser 1986). Italian
fashion, food products, olive oil, ceramics, and cars also became
highly sought-after status commodities. Second, Italy's national soccer team's victory in the World Cup roused Italian Canadians to
gather on St Clair Avenue to celebrate following the game. In the
hundreds of thousands, Italian Canadians met on Corso Italia honk-
ing horns and waving Italian flags. The spontaneity of the event and
its general lack of problems suprised both Italian Canadians themselves and the general public. The event became an epiphanic
moment in which Toronto's Italian community claimed public
space it was once told by police to abandon.

Third, Italian Canadians had also achieved some economic success and stability by this period. In 1981 they still lagged behind the
national average wage income ($11,990 to $12,306); however, if
one used a more culturally sensitive indicator of mobility, home-
ownership, Italians showed significant economic advancement
(Sturino 1986). By the mid-1980s as many as 86 per cent of Italians
owned their homes, as compared to the 70 per cent national average. Furthermore, in Ontario 83 per cent of Italians owned homes
valued at more than $100,000, as compared to the provincial aver-
age of 24 per cent. Even in Toronto the proportion was still favour-
able: 50 per cent (Italian) to 53 per cent (city average). In the field
of education, as well, young Italian Canadians approached the
national average for post-secondary education, their numbers up
dramatically since 1971. Yet a more revealing statistic has shown that
for people of Italian heritage between the ages of fifteen and twenty-
four, a higher percentage remained in school when compared to
the total in Canada, Ontario, and Toronto (Jansen 1986; 1991).

In the early 1980s large Bay Street law and accounting firms that had turned away job applicants of Italian heritage now eagerly sought their younger brothers and sisters. In the mid-1980s even political rhetoric acknowledged the changes. In a compact turn of phrase, and not a touch of hyperbole, then Prime Minister Brian Mulroney (with a little help from his Italian-Canadian advisers) once noted that 'the first generation of Italian Canadians built the city of Toronto; the present generation owns it.' One of my informants commented on these changes in the community: 'Some time in the 1980s we got a little money, Italian products got trendy, and we got into conspicuous consumption.'

The Work of Different Cultural Fields

With the following words, one young Italian-Canadian man commented on his father and on work: 'My Dad didn't come here for freedom of speech. He could have yelled his fucking head off in the village square if he liked. He came here to work. [Canada] was a country, like the United States and Britain, that believed in full employment.'

One concept that exposes the different ways generations understand their lives is that of work. The 1980s may have seen some Italian Canadians begin to participate in the North American consumer market, but that picture offers only a partial and distorted depiction of the prevailing attitudes of the time. As the statement above underscores, immigrants came here with the intention of working hard to earn financial security for themselves and their families. Little attention was paid to the more ideational areas associated with a change in homeland and in economic stability. In general, especially for the immigrant generation that came between 1952 and 1962 and worked in the physically demanding construction and manufacturing sectors or in metal foundries and rural work camps, the concept of work had, and still has, specific meanings. Work is physical labour. Work is done to create financial certainty. Work is part of the sacrifice that life entails. Work is practical. Work is a necessary part of the family economy.

An informant who became active in local school-trustee politics, and was later a provincial member of parliament and cabinet minister, explained that his mother never quite understood that he worked. One of his brothers, a carpenter, *did* work, and as a reward would receive a tender maternal back massage after his long physical day. Despite the typically long hours of a politician's day, my informant's family still considers him to be free and available to run errands during the day. As his mother would say, 'Show me your hands and I'll tell you if you have worked.'

Education is important, but generally only in so far as it pertains to creating employment stability or greater economic opportunity. Learning in the sense that it means changing and challenging the preconceptions and tenets of your parents is not considered the appropriate result of education by many Italian-Canadian parents. Nevertheless education is highly prized by immigrant parents who may have been illiterate or had limited education themselves, but who feel great pride in seeing their children read a book, do their homework, and succeed in school. Parents see reading as the key to success. This is one reason immigrant parents see teaching as a good profession; the other is the perceived stability of the position. It is not inconsistent to discover this respect for education in conjunction with an inability of parents to easily or actively assist their children in the learning process. One informant, who is a writer/editor and was once a teacher, remarked that the only thing his parents ever asked him to read was the phone bill.

The disjunctures and fissures between parents and children as to the meanings they associate with work provides opportunity for plenty of playful exchanges. The idiosyncrasies of parents has become a common topic of discourse among immigrants' children. In 1994 the *Eyetalian* magazine received a JobsOntario Community Action grant through the provincial government's Ministry of Citizenship, which was to help them expand their work beyond publishing and into the network of business activities in the arts and in cultural initiatives among Italian Canadians. The celebratory launch and cheque-presentation ceremony by the Minister of Citizenship was held at the popular midtown Italian restaurant grano, whose owner has been a generous supporter of cultural activities and the magazine. After speeches by several ministers, the editor, and the publisher, the key participants gathered around an oversized styrofoam cheque made for the ceremonial transfer and publicity photographs. A few moments later the magazine's editor joked with friends about the way his father might react to the cheque. Imitating his father, he held the styrofoam cheque up as if to measure it for size and durability, then said the words he imagined his father would say: 'Son, this is perfect for some insulation. Where can I get more?'

Immigrant experiences are also gendered. Italian-Canadian immigrant children are confronted continually with conflicting and contradictory messages about the expectations of society. For example, the meanings associated with work and education operate in competing and differently gendered cultural fields. Southern Italian peasant cultural expectations have generally restricted women to activities within certain limits. The concept of *onore* (honour) that infused peasant rural society in Italy and much of Europe created two poles of gendered expectations. The Italian family's women were to be sexually pure. On the other hand, Italian men, through hard work and sacrifice, were to offer in return for this sexual fidelity a stable home for their women and children. The extension of this notion of male power and authority was the fear that female infidelity would bring shame to the family. As a result a pattern of male supervision of women in public spaces became established, and public space became male domain, and private space, female (Galt 1992; Brogger 1971; Davis 1973; Cronin 1970). It should be cautioned that this easy academic distinction ignores the activities and labour of women outside the home and lacks the subtlety to comprehend the blurring of social roles in everyday practices (see Iacovetta 1993; Gabaccia 1984; Bell 1979).

Nevertheless, the hegemony of patriarchal organization in the southern Italian family has severely restricted women's choices and chances. In migration the incompleteness in a hegemonic system becomes more pronounced (Gramsci 1971); thus more social space for women is created. The children of immigrants have negotiated between the expectations of their parents and those of a North American society that allows for more frequent exposure of women in public spaces, social movements that encourage equality, and mandatory schooling up to the age of sixteen (Colalillo 1981). Another newer ideology has emanated from relatives who remained in Italy. Several informants have spoken of the different, and generally more progressive, attitudes their uncles and aunts who remained in Italy had towards women's opportunities as compared to their parents.' After all, Italy had undergone massive social change in the twenty years since most Italians emigrated and since the subsequent return visits of their children in the summers. Referenda in the 1970s making abortion available and approving divorce occurred in a social atmosphere far more liberal than that from which the vast majority of Italians had emigrated (Spotts and Wieser 1986). It is in this competing field of public culture that young Italian-Canadian women find themselves.

Angela, a lawyer in her mid-twenties, summed up these competing strains well. She spoke of her mother's determination that her daughter not be denied the formal education she herself never had. In Italy the demands of the family economy prevented her mother from going to school; there was only enough money for her brothers to attend. As a result my informant's parents were determined to be very supportive of their daughter: 'They never, ever, said to me, "When are you getting married?" Most of my girlfriends faced that question. Hardly any of my girlfriends have university degrees. My experience is very different than theirs. Even [men] my age don't like what I stand for or what I have done ... [that I'm] a woman with a professional degree and career.'

A group of young women of Italian-Canadian heritage organized in the early 1990s into a group called Voce Alternativa (Alternative Voice) to act as a network and support group for one another. The wider public noticed the group for the first time when an op-ed piece appeared in the *Toronto Star* urging people of Italian heritage to evaluate their own historical oppression in southern Italy. With this in mind they were to challenge the value of celebrating Columbus's quincentenary, given the violence North America's Native population experienced following 1492 (Cafiso et al. 1992). A subsequent effort by Voce Alternativa, however, is what interests us here, because it had to do with the image of women in society and especially Italian-Canadian women.

A landmark event for Toronto's Italians since 1966 has been

Johnny Lombardi's CHIN picnic. At first it was held on Toronto's Centre Island, but more recently it has occurred every summer on the Canadian National Exhibition lands by the city's lakeshore. CHIN and Johnny Lombardi have become icons in the Italian-Canadian community, not least because of Lombardi's unabashed showmanship. In the early postwar years he owned one of the few grocery stores that sold Italian products. Through the 1950s and early 1960s he broadcast a brokered radio program through CHUM that offered Italian-language shows. By 1967 he won a licence for a new radio station (CHIN) that was initially Italian-language-based, but quickly broke into the multilingual market-place. Previously, people had had to listen to Italian-language radio from Buffalo and Niagara Falls, N.Y. Today, on Sundays, Lombardi also features a television variety program with music and performances from Italy's famous San Remo musical festival and RAI television. Pasta-eating contests, Italian singers and dancers, arcade games, and polyethnic performances by dancers and singers have been hallmarks of the CHIN picnic. One standard and much-followed event at the picnic has been the CHIN bikini contest.

In the summer of 1993 Voce Alternativa convinced Toronto's civic government, the Metro Toronto Council, to vote in favour of sending a recommendation to the board of governors of Exhibition Place, the site of the picnic and bikini pageant, to 'consider a policy which will see the discontinuance of beauty pageants at Exhibition Place before signing new contracts' (*Corriere Canadese*, 11 June 1993). In the end, after some debate in public and some bluster from Lombardi, who threatened to take his picnic and the revenue generated from it outside of Metro, the bikini contest continued. Nevertheless, Voce Alternativa's actions illustrate several important themes concerning the transition of expectations among Italian-Canadian women. Its members saw the bikini pageant as a degrading and superficial way to view women, and they urged Italian Canadians and others to re-examine how inadequately images of women are constructed in popular discourse in North America. And they chose this iconoclastic Italian-Canadian event as their platform.

One might speculate that part of the allure of the CHIN bikini

contest for young Italian-Canadian males is that the women in the
contest do not appear to represent the 'good Italian' girls their
parents expect them to marry. One of the ironies of the pageant is
that few of the participants are of Italian heritage, which may further distance them as exotic 'others' for the Italian-Canadian male.
In fact, a cursory look at a recent CHIN picnic media launch
revealed that the labourers at the event, waitresses and servers,
were Italian-Canadian women, but the pageant participants generally were not.[1] The challenge by Voce Alternativa, however, has represented a challenge to male authority in the community. In
contrast to the expected norms of behaviour in public discourse,
for southern-Italian women Voce Alternativa members have challenged male actions. The extensive press coverage surprised the
group, but it should not have. Voce Alternativa had disputed the
views of a significant male public persona, not only in the Italian-
Canadian community but also in Toronto's public culture.

The *Eyetalian* Magazine

In the fall of 1993 the first issue of the *Eyetalian* magazine
appeared. A product of a group of second-generation Italian Canadians in their late twenties, the magazine was intended to create a
forum for young Italian-Canadian writers, playwrights, artists, and
designers. At first the quarterly magazine's headquarters were in a
rented house in the Eglinton and Dufferin area. Now the *Eyetalian*
has established an office within Columbus Centre and has begun
to nurture its relationship with some of the established institutions
within the community. The name *Eyetalian* has caused some in the
older generation to wince with displeasure. It is too similar to the
derogatory pronunciation they often heard from other Canadians
when they wanted to belittle Italian immigrants in the difficult
years of the fifties, sixties, and seventies. But it is partly for this very
reason that the editors chose the term. Subaltern groups such as
immigrants often subvert the meanings of words used by dominant
groups and then transform the meanings of these words from deri-
sion to respect to reassert some power (Spivak 1993). Furthermore, the founders liked the play on the word *eye*, which suggests

an eye on and into the community. In the opening editorial the editors argued that little was known about Italian Canadians or Italian-Canadian artists, either within or outside the community. 'It is the magazine's aim to reveal to the community, and to the nation, the unique culture, history, sensibility, and viewpoints of North American Italians. However, it does not indulge in mere glorification. Rather, it takes in the achievements of the community with one eye, while the other is fixed on the many sources of conflict which flow from its cultural baggage' (Esposito 1993).

Topics covered have ranged from senior housing shortages, youth in the community, gender questions, restaurant profiles, and historical accounts to interviews with writers Nino Ricci and Mary Di Michele and actor Tony Nardi. Each issue of the magazine tries to define, illuminate, question, and understand what Italian Canadianness is. Initially the magazine had a more exclusive focus on the arts – poetry, fiction, and so on – in the Italian-Canadian community, but there has been a shift recently to a more inclusive view of culture that incorporates not just the fine arts but social issues, problems, and concerns. To expand their reach they then created, in late 1994–1995, the Avanti Arts and Business Association, with assistance from Ontario's JobsOntario Community Action Program. This was a $300-million, three-year program instituted by the Ontario NDP government to spur local community economic development as part of their overall JobsOntario economic strategy. Other Italian-Canadian organizations using this program included the ICBC, Centro Scuola, *Corriere Canadese*, Casa D'Abruzzo Benevolent Corporation, and the Canadian Italian Federation of Students. Avanti Arts acts as an organizing body for readings, film festivals, and other cultural activities. It also encourages links between business, publishing, and culture. Often these projects are done in association with other organizations such as the National Film Board, the Istituto, the Columbus Centre, or the Italian Canadian Federation of Students, to name just a few.

The *Eyetalian* publishes in English because it is the language of communication for second-generation Italian Canadians. Frequently, paese or local dialect is used as a marker of social inclusion, exclusion, and comparison. Second-generation Italian Canadians

compare their home dialects in casual, good-humoured, social conversations. For the editors and others in their age cohort multiple
languages are part of their cultural field. As a result snatches of Italian, paese dialect, or the distinctive ethnolect (ethnic dialect) of
Italiese created here in Canada from the experiences of Italian
immigrants, may be incorporated into conversations to emphasize a
point or to establish certain thresholds of belonging (Danesi 1985).
But as the editors insist, English is the base communicative medium
for Italian Canadians who have gone to school, to work, and who live
in Toronto.

The choice of language for the media clearly constitutes a significant shift in the imagining of the community. The Italian-
Canadian print, radio, and video media have been in Italian. At
times the major daily *Corriere Canadese* has published English-
language sections or columns, and recently CFMT (Channel 47)
has introduced a Sunday evening review of Italian A-league soccer
in English. A Toronto Italian-Canadian magazine called *Mosaico*,
which also published in English, existed for a few years in the
1970s. Nevertheless the *Eyetalian* is part of a group of new media
offered by the children of immigrants seeking to speak to a
younger generation. The radio program 'Red, Hot & Green,' on
CHRY, York University's campus station, and two television programs, 'jumpcut' (sic) on Channel 47 CFMT, which was just can-
celled in 1997, and 'Profili,' a short-lived program on the Shaw
Cable community station are three other recent media projects
that focus on Italian-Canadian youth. Many in the Italian-language
media are uncomfortable with the shift, not only because they
believe Italian culture cannot be understood without the Italian
language but also because they harbour a more visceral fear of losing their audience, and their jobs.

Interestingly, the Italian government representatives at the Istituto Italiano di Cultura in Toronto have fewer qualms about the
language issue (see Chapter 2). A cynical interpretation of their
attention to the *Eyetalian* might suggest that it started in response
to the changes in their mandate required by law 401, passed in
Rome in 1990, which urged the cultural institutes to take a greater
interest in the cultural activities of Italian diaspora communities.

The verve and vigour of the *Eyetalian*'s staff create a perfect enterprise for Istituto directors to harness and to claim some credit when they report to *i vertici* (senior management) in the Italian government bureaucracy. Class and status also have something to do with the relationship. The *Eyetalian*'s initiatives have more in common with the interests of the educated and cultivated European foreign service agents than with the practical and 'folkloric' world of immigrant parents. The relationship between the Istituto and the magazine is mutually sympathetic in the sense that the Italian foreign service employees, often from the north of Italy, find it easier to communicate with the university-educated children of immigrants than with their generally rural, southern parents.

Recently an issue of the *Eyetalian* provoked a controversy in a segment of the community that felt unfairly targeted and depicted. In a cover story examining the cultural interests and aspirations of students who live in the suburban community of Woodbridge, on the northern border of Toronto, the writer criticized the materialism, conservative gender expectations, and indifference to culture and learning of students that she perceived at two Catholic high schools in the area. According to the editors, Woodbridge was chosen because of its heavy Italian-heritage settlement and popularly identifiable image. But, they insist, the main concerns raised by the article, such as the materialism and minimal interest in intellectual and cultural pursuits by youth, signified meaningful social issues for the whole community.

Woodbridge is a township within the city of Vaughan that has experienced massive growth in the last twenty years as part of Toronto's suburban sprawl. Between 1976 and 1991 its overall population has grown from 7,571 to 44,350, of which 73.2 per cent are Italian. The median household income is $69,423, compared to Metropolitan Toronto's at $43,212 (Census 1991). The newness of the Woodbridge neighbourhoods, their wealth, and their residential concentration of Italians has led to the creation of an identifiable image, whether apocryphal or real. It is a place often referred to disparagingly by other Italian Canadians as the home of the *Ginos* and *Ginas* (stereotypically, young fashion-conscious Italian-Canadian males and females), whose focus is conspicuous consumption and who are neglectful of the values of hard work, community, and culture. In fact the criticisms in the article only echo what people have been saying and joking informally about the area for the past ten years. During fieldwork I even met Woodbridge residents who expressed some concern about the place. Carlo, an immigrant who had left Lazio in 1953 and was now a successful plumbing contractor, referred to his home as 'Wopbridge,' *Wop* being the derisive term used to describe Italian immigrants by the host society in North America.

The movement of people to suburban enclaves is the result of many choices and aspirations: more space, a larger house, an easier commute to work, and so on. However another, often-whispered, reason for some is that they wished to 'live with their own.' This is not always phrased as a desire to live away from others, but sometimes. People have mentioned the multiracial changes that have occurred in the St Clair Avenue area or in Downsview, where new settlements of South Asians, West Indians, and Latin Americans present new cultural challenges and opportunities for misunderstanding and social conflict. As one can see, some conditions were already evident in the collective consciousness of Woodbridge citizens in their reactions to criticism.

Suburbanization has unintended social consequences (Baumgartner 1988). The enlargement of dwellings and personal property in the spatially planned suburb leads to the reduction of familiar interactions with neighbours and friends. Whereas in the past people might have hung out on the front stoop or in the streets, now they spend more time in their homes with little contact with or knowledge of their neighbours. One young male informant spoke at length about life in Woodbridge:

> The thing that strikes me as different in Woodbridge is the concept of neighbourhood. If you grew up in the city in the St Clair and Dufferin area or in Downsview, kids in the streets were busy playing street hockey or kicking a ball. In Woodbridge the streets are deserted. You do not see your neighbours; You don't talk to all of your neighbours; you do not know all of them. This is partially due to the fact that this is a new community. Anything they do requires

driving. People don't walk to the park or the corner store. There is less interaction between people in the suburbs because people are driving everywhere. This sucks. I don't see anybody, ever. You see the people next door but you don't know the names of the people ten houses down or all along your street. You don't know the faces of the kids, and if you do you're not sure who the parents are. In Downsview or St Clair you knew everybody within ten houses of your own. When you're sixteen or seventeen if you wanted to go out for a coffee or to the donut shop you could walk to meet your friends. In Woodbridge it's not like you go outside and see three or four different friends playing football in the park.

Does this distance from neighbours and the lack of knowledge of who is around have an impact on us? Of course it does. There is less respect for the neighbours because you don't know them and they don't know you. There are no problems doing wheelies in your car because you are not afraid of a neighbour calling your parents to complain. They will not hunt you down and tell you to never do it again. In Downsview or St Clair you would drive cautiously along the side-street, then you could peel out around the corner as you got out of the neighbourhood.

The article, entitled 'The Armani Generation,' stirred debate and indignation on the part of Woodbridge residents. It was one of the rare occasions in which Italian-Canadian media have criticized the community. People responded through call-in shows on CHIN and CIAO radio and wrote letters (some in English) to the editor of the Italian-language newspaper *Lo Specchio*, which is distributed in the city of Vaughan and northern Metro Toronto. To the *Eyetalian*'s credit all inquiries were answered, and in fact many letters hostile to the magazine and the story were published in subsequent issues.

The intensity of some of the displeasure reverberating in Woodbridge is also underlined by the fact that people called to complain about the article even though they had never read it. At one point a group of parents considered suing the magazine for slander! A special program, 'A Voi La Scelta' (The Choice Is Yours), which discusses current issues relevant to the Italian-Canadian community on the predominantly Italian-language cable station Telelatino, devoted ninety minutes to a panel discussion about the issue. Participants included the publisher of the magazine, several professors, this anthropologist, a community priest involved in substance abuse social work, the writer Nino Ricci, and an audience of mostly high school students and a few teachers who offered questions and comments. The visceral reaction and the hostility to the article, aside from the quality of its reporting or its accuracy, reflected an uneasiness with communal self-criticism. Those who did not like the article interpreted it as questioning the sacrifice and hard work of immigrant parents whose long years of labour had finally born fruit, and who now were being criticized by their own, one who should know better. From the perspective of the magazine's staff, they were satisfied that they had managed to encourage some discussion about culture and learning within the community.

Final Remarks

At the beginning of the 1980s a transformation occurred in the way Italianness and the Italian community were imagined. New meanings entered the swirl of competing images to create further layers and greater complexity within the construction of Italianness. The images of Italians and Italianness were recast. A people that were once seen as peasant simpletons became entrepreneurs of rustic design and eternal wisdom or innovators in fashion and industrial design. The portrait of Italians as organized criminals changed to one of Italians as hard-working, prescient, and insightful business people. As a result the children of Italian immigrants confronted new meanings with which to construct their Italianness, and the altered generational meanings of work, education, and gender began to contribute to misunderstandings between age cohorts.

In the fall of 1994 the *Eyetalian* helped organize a career and culture day at the Columbus Centre in conjunction with the Canadian Italian Federation of Students. After a series of informative career sessions and artistic performances the day ended with a panel discussion of the question, 'Beyond Baggio: Do Italians have a reason to get excited about anything but World Cup soccer?' The 1982 spontaneous outpouring of communal pride had occurred again throughout the World Cup games in 1994, but hadn't happened on other occasions. Was there anything else? For some in the second generation of Italian Canadians there is an impatience with the caution of their parents. For many more, suburban life offers few opportunities to express themselves. Furthermore, stereotypes still linger. The charm of Mediterranean exotica in 'Little Italies' around the city creates opportunities for Italian Canadians to reap financial rewards by marketing their 'Italian' authenticity, their 'practical knowledge,' and their 'cultural vitality' to the Canadian public; but it also limits and restricts those who wish to break out into different fields and new directions.

Nevertheless, as members of the second generation talked to me about their ethnic identity, many seemed overtaken by an optimistic mood. They were confident of their numeric strength, as though they had absorbed Anderson's (1983) notion of an imagined community and were comfortable negotiating between Canadian cultural expectations and Italianità. Many felt strongly that the moment has arrived for Italian Canadians to assert themselves in the emerging transnational era.

Afterword

Whether I was driving, flying, or travelling on a bus, a trolley, or a subway, this book has kept me on the move. The mileage covered, I hoped, led to places that Italian Canadians went to mingle and make sense of their lives.

At first my agenda made for contrived meetings, and my questions ignored the obvious and could not uncover the more subtle contradictions and ambiguities of daily life. The anticipation of arrival at a place of encounter or a site of activity often made me a little anxious, and I rehearsed prepared questions and assessed agendas I needed to follow. There were perhaps points I wanted to clear up, a turn of phrase in local Calabrese or Abruzzese dialect that I needed explained. There was no complete perspective from which to stand back and survey the landscape. There was no high point in Toronto's west-end neighbourhoods or in the rapidly transforming greenbelt of Vaughan to observe the thousands of lives embedded in the circuits of Italianità. The more involved I became in the stories of one group, the less likely I was even to enter the lives of the neighbours a few doors down.

It seemed I was coming closer to the lives and experiences of Italian Canadians when I noticed that my travels between locations were no longer deliberate sojourns into spaces I thought I would find Italianità. Instead, the highways and suburban streets I travelled corresponded to the everyday places many Italian Canadians used in the urban landscape. Conversations would occur in places such as a tavola calda while seeking the best veal sandwich, a law

office between discussions about equity, and a new friend's back-
yard as we stacked used two-by-fours that had been thoroughly
cleared of nails by his aging immigrant father. I would drive north
after a mid-afternoon interview with a man from Molise. With the
seeds of fresh figs still stuck between my teeth I would stop for an
espresso and fresh bread at Il Dolce Sogno (The Sweet Dream)
Bakery. One day I would linger, after a long interview with a family,
in a Downsview cantina, a cool cellar storage room filled with
homemade wine, *mosto* (grape must) from California, cured
cheeses, and dried eggplant. In the evening I would be off to a
banquet hall in Rexdale for a gathering to raise funds for a
regional centre that was, at that moment, not much more than
blueprints and dreams. Some time later I hoped to join an Italian-
Canadian youth soccer team touring in Emilia-Romagna.

Telephones, television, and the internet link kith and kin
together, and help nourish common thoughts and sentiments by
stretching social space beyond backyards and work sites. But face-
to-face encounters, aided by the ordinary routes of cars and air-
planes, helped ground their communal connections, and mine.

The routes I travelled meant that I chose not to follow other
paths, missed other meeting sites. The choice of pursuing a certain
route or the serendipity of travelling one path meant that I
encountered only the people who intersected with my particular
journey. I did not participate in every festa, banquet, and dinner-
dance, nor did I find every Italian-owned bakery.

But it was in the travelling that I discovered Italianità. I picked
my routes by chance and circumstance. It is my hope that this book
will encourage others to do the same.

Appendix

TABLE 1
Proportional Distribution of Postwar Emigration from Italy

Year	Total	Europe %	U.S. %	Australia %	Canada Number	%T
1946	110,286	93	5	–	–	–
1947	254,144	76	9	–	58	–
1948	308,515	63	5	1	2,406	1
1949	254,469	37	5	4	5,991	2
1950	200,306	27	5	7	7,135	4
1951	293,057	51	4	6	21,467	7
1952	277,535	52	3	10	18,742	8
1953	224,671	50	4	6	22,610	10
1954	250,925	43	10	7	23,440	9
1955	296,826	50	12	9	19,282	7
1956	344,802	60	11	7	28,008	8
1957	341,733	69	5	5	24,536	7
1958	255,459	62	10	5	28,502	11
1959	268,490	81	4	5	23,734	9
1960	383,908	81	4	5	19,011	5
1961	387,123	85	4	4	13,461	4
1962	365,611	86	4	4	12,528	3
1963	277,711	85	5	4	12,912	5
1964	258,482	84	3	4	17,600	7
1965	282,643	82	4	4	24,213	9
1966	296,494	74	10	4	28,591	10
1967	229,264	73	8	6	12,102	5
1968	215,713	73	10	7	16,745	8
1969	182,199	76	9	5	9,441	5
1970	151,854	76	10	4	7,249	5

TABLE 1 (*concluded*)

Year	Total	Europe %	U.S. %	Australia %	Canada Number	%T
1971	167,721	79	9	4	6,128	4
1972	141,852	79	10	3	5,207	4
1973	123,802	80	9	3	4,078	3
1974	112,020	78	8	3	4,421	4
1975	92,666	78	7	3	3,662	4
1976	97,247	75	7	3	3,586	4
1977	87,655	74	7	2	2,677	3
Total:	7,535,183	69	7	5	429,523	6

Source: Adapted from Clifford Jansen and Lee La Cavera. 1981. *Fact-Book on Italians in Canada*. Toronto: Institute for Social Research, York University; and Roma: Istituto Centrale di Statistica. Annuario Statistico Italiano, 1946–1977.

TABLE 2
Italian Heritage Population by Canadian Cities

City	Total pop.	Total Italian	Italian single	Italian multiple
Toronto	3,893,046	387,380	311,215	76,165
Montreal	3,127,240	207,315	165,735	41,580
Vancouver	1,602,500	60,310	30,660	29,650
Hamilton	599,760	58,785	40,190	18,595
St Catharines/Niagara	364,550	41,570	26,535	15,035
Ottawa/Hull	920,855	32,645	17,885	14,760
Windsor	262,075	27,130	18,795	8,335
Calgary	754,035	23,900	10,725	13,175
Edmonton	839,925	21,590	10,455	11,135
London	381,520	15,425	7,300	8,125

Source: Census Canada 1991, cat. 93-315

TABLE 3
Italians in Metro Toronto (CMA), 1941–1991

Year	Total pop. Toronto	Italian heritage	Multiple ancestry	% of total	Foreign born Ital.	% of total
1941 T	900,000	17,887	NA	2.0	4,870	0.5
M	436,157	9,552	NA	2.2	2,926	0.7
F	464,334	8,335	NA	1.8	1,994	0.4
1951 T	1,117,470	27,962	NA	2.5	NA	
M	544,171	NA	NA	0.0	NA	
F	573,299	NA	NA	0.0	NA	
1961 T	1,824,481	140,378	NA	7.7	96,072	5.3
M	903,255	74,185	NA	8.2	51,981	5.8
F	921,226	66,193	NA	7.2	44,091	4.8
1971 T	2,628,130	271,755	NA	10.3	167,735	6.4
M	1,301,375	142,265	NA	10.9	89,145	6.9
F	1,326,755	129,490	NA	9.8	78,590	6.9
1981 T	2,998,945	323,340	26,140	10.7	NA	
M	1,465,165	166,605	12,935	11.4	NA	
F	1,533,780	156,735	13,205	10.2	NA	
1991 T	3,893,046	387,375	76,165	10.0	NA	
M	1,906,760	197,525	38,015	10.4	NA	
F	1,986,285	189,865	38,155	9.6	NA	

Sources: Canada. *Census*, 1941–1991; Iacovetta (1992: 210)

TABLE 4
Intended Occupations of Total and Italian Labour-Force Immigrants by
Period of Immigration

	Upper non-manual		Manual	
Years	T %	I %	T %	I %
1952–61	12.6	1.0	62.8	77.4
1962–71	29.0	4.0	39.3	77.7
1972–78	29.8	16.6	37.6	65.1

Source: Jansen 1988

TABLE 5
Italian Heritage Population by Province, 1991

	Total Italian population	Italian single origins	Italian multiple origins
Canada Total	1,147,775	750,055	397,720
Male	585,670	388,805	196,865
Female	562,105	361,250	200,855
British Columbia	111,985	49,260	62,725
Alberta	61,240	24,745	36,495
Saskatchewan	8,295	1,975	6,320
Manitoba	17,895	8,120	9,775
Ontario	701,430	486,760	214,670
Quebec	226,650	174,530	52,120
New Brunswick	5,000	1,320	3,680
Nova Scotia	11,915	2,715	9,200
Prince Edward Island	670	45	625
Newfoundland	1,740	290	1,450
Yukon	450	135	315
Northwest Territories	515	160	355

Source: Census Canada 1991, cat. 93-315.

Notes

1 For an interesting discussion of the concept diaspora coupled with examples, see Robin Cohen's (1997) introductory volume in which he develops a typology of five different forms of the phenomenon: victim, labour, trade, imperial, and cultural. He stresses that these are not mutually exclusive types. Italians in Canada conform most closely to the labour diaspora type because they have expanded the frontiers of their homeland to find work, maintained group ties and links to Italy and other places Italians have migrated, and at least initially, faced some exclusion from the host society (Canada).

Tölölyan (1996) also provides a very insightful exploration of changes in the concept. He enhances Connor's (1986) sense that a diaspora is 'that segment of a people that lives outside the homeland' by urging us to see these segments as collectivities or communities embedded and interconnected, with changes occurring in the homeland and other parts of the transnation. This process of change influences cultural practices, politics, economics, discourses and social life.

2 Anthony Cohen's (1985) discussion of community as a contextually contingent 'symbolic construction' has guided my approach to studying the collective life of Italians in Toronto.

3 Similarly, Hastrup and Olwig (1997:11) argue that we need to examine 'cultural sites' created by the people we study even if the creation and use of these sites seem to challenge the traditional anthropological effort to de-essentialize culture and the idea of bounded, homogeneous local cultural entities. They argue it is important for anthropologists to explore 'the "place" of culture in both the experiential and discursive spaces that people inhabit or invent.'

CHAPTER TWO   Italy, Migration, and Settlement in Canada

1 Robert F. Harney has written a brilliant account of the forms and manifesta-
tions of anti-Italian feeling in the English-speaking world. He connects these
themes with migration history to indicate why governments in North America
were reluctant to encourage Italian immigrants. See R.F. Harney, 'Italophobia:
An English-speaking Malady?' (1985).

2 The internment of people of Italian heritage by the Canadian state during the
Second World War because of their real or supposed involvement with Fascism
is a politically charged issue today. The National Congress of Italian Canadians
(NCIC) successfully lobbied and secured an apology for the internment on
behalf of the Canadian state by Prime Minister Brian Mulroney during his last
term. Subsequently the NCIC has urged the Liberal government to offer repa-
rations to those interned to offset losses incurred while they were at Camp
Petawawa. Other political parties occasionally use the issue to score short-term
political points. This issue is in need of serious academic attention, free from
the agendas of various interested parties. Most engaged in the debate agree
that the suspension of civil liberties and the internment of people based solely
on their surname or ethnic origin is unacceptable. Many of those interned
had only a patriotic link to the Italian state, which happened to be under the
control of the Fascist party. Further, the bigoted racialist attacks on Italian
Canadians during this period were reprehensible. Disagreement arises over
the degree of Fascist involvement and influence among people of Italian heritage in Canada during this period. To what extent were those interned actu-
ally pro-Fascist activists and threats to the Canadian state? More troubling for
the idea of community cohesion is another question some have raised: To
what extent did some people of Italian heritage, for personal or commercial
advantage, falsely accuse others of activities associated with Fascism? It should
be noted that during my fieldwork, among mostly postwar Italian immigrants,
the issue had no resonance.

3 From the 1986 census, Jansen (1991:161) analysed the occupational status of
people with different forms of Italian heritage: Italian single, Italian multiple,
and Canadian-educated Italian. These three categories, which he compared to
a fourth category of all persons in Canada, require some explanation. The
'Italian single' category comprised those who were claiming Italian origin
only. 'Italian multiple' people were those whose ethnic origin was Italian in
addition to another origin. Finally, 'Canadian-educated Italians' were all those
with some Italian ancestry who had been born in Canada, or who had immigrated to Canada before the age of fifteen and had therefore received some
primary and/or secondary education in Canada.

4 At the time of my initial research Al Palladini was known for his affable, gim-
micky radio ads and sales efforts, but today (1997) he is the minister of transportation in the Ontario government.

5 A *gettone* table, also known as a *foosball* table, is a game table that simulates
soccer. The table's surface is painted like a soccer field and there is a goal at
either end. Two to four players commonly compete, although part of the
excitement of the game is the verbal jousting that comes from observers. Each
team has three or four lines of players. Each line is connected to a metal rod
that stretches the width of the table; therefore the players cannot move inde-
pendently of the rod they are connected to.

6 I have calculated the percentages of Italians based on the combined numbers
of respondents who claimed single and multiple Italian ethnic origin by census tract (1991) in CMA Toronto (the Census Metropolitan area).

7 To find conclusive data on how Italians in CMA Toronto voted in the Charlottetown referendum is difficult, if not impossible. We might be able to see a
suggestion of their voting pattern if we look at the raw data of Yes and No votes
by electoral district, but any conclusions are highly tenuous. In the three electoral districts with the heaviest Italian-Canadian populations the Yes vote percentages in favour of the Charlottetown Accord were Eglinton-Lawrence (58
per cent), York-Centre (54 per cent), and York North (58 per cent). These
percentages compare with the less than 1 per cent margin of victory for the
Yes side in all of Ontario (*Referendum '92: official voting results*. Chief Electoral
Officer of Canada, 1992).

CHAPTER FOUR The Piazza of Corporate Unity

1 In 1995, after a legal and structural reorganization of the ICBC and in an
effort to increase the sophistication of fund-raising practices, the corporation's name was changed to Villa Charities (Ariemma 1997).

2 In the brief submitted to the Ontario Ministry of Culture, the ICBC outlined
the benefits of a cultural centre:

Leadership development: The inherent cooperative and competitive
atmosphere of the centre's activities will act as a catalyst and accelerate the
development of leaders. This objective is an extremely vital necessity in
order to assure the continuity of the work of the corporation as well as the
development of leaders in other areas of the life of the province.
Lifestyle: The preservation and development of traditional cultural traits,
with the addition of Canadian culture, can and does produce a lifestyle
enriched in form and substance by contributing cultures.
Positive intra-community communication: The Centre will provide a

forum where different groups within our community can communicate, express their aspirations, and implement their programs. This will encourage and promote mutual appreciation, respect, and cooperation. Community responsibility: Our community is learning the responsibility of self-help. The Centre will be another vehicle in which the Corporation can instill social and civic responsibilities towards the society at large. Integration: New immigrants gain a higher self-esteem in direct proportion to the achievements of their communities. This encourages the assertion of one's own identity and therefore contributes to the integration of newly arrived immigrants with those already established.

Promotion of citizenship: The respect earned through the efforts of people in our community working together can only be positive and take integration one step further ... good and responsible citizenship.

3 It is difficult to find reliable statistics on intermarriage between Italian and Portuguese Canadians, but at one parish in central Toronto, St Anthony's on Bloor Street, an analysis of weddings over the last five years offers some insight. Of the 244 weddings between 1992 and 1996, there were 33 weddings between Italian and Portuguese Canadians. The number of intermarriages between these groups has gradually risen in these five years, from five in 1992 to nine 1996.

CHAPTER SIX Culture, Calcio, and Centro Scuola

1 These last three authors, Pier Giorgio Di Cicco, Antonino Mazza, and Caterina Edwards are some of the many Italian-Canadian writers who have found encouragement and support from Centro Scuola.

2 The Istituto is a government agency of the Italian Ministry of Foreign Affairs. It was established in 1976 as a cultural wing of the Italian Consulate General in Toronto. It serves to promote Italian culture to the general Canadian public, but in 1990 Bill 401 from Rome encouraged the institute to offer language courses and to become more involved in Italian-Canadian community cultural activities.

3 Since the main body of this fieldwork was completed Centro Scuola has undergone a transformation and expansion. It has solidified its relationship as the cultural engine within Columbus Centre. The director has become both the head of Centro Scuola and the cultural director at Columbus Centre. Moreover, the Centre received a JOCA (JobsOntario Community Action Program) grant from the previous Ontario government, which has helped expand its publishing and cultural activities. It has started a program to teach summer courses in English for Italians. Because of Centro Scuola's reputation in Italy

for its educational activities and its linkages with Italian educational institutions, it hopes to attract people to the program. This program is seen as a potential source of revenue to augment the institution's grant funding from various governments.

CHAPTER NINE Italianità for the Canadian-Born

1 Not all Italian Canadians feel the same way about beauty pageants. In the last few years a Miss Italia nel Mondo pageant has been held in Italy. It invites young women of Italian heritage from around the world who have won in their local diaspora competitions. Preliminary rounds to choose a Canadian participant occur within the social field of the Italian-Canadian community and are broadcast on Telelatino. Here, all the participants are Italian Canadian. Perhaps because the winner competes in Italy and must express some interest in Italian art and culture, parents seem to be more accepting and enthusiastic about this event. Its style better reflects the images of modern Italy than the CHIN bikini contest.

AFTERWORD

1 James Clifford (1988, 1997) has been the most persuasive writer to urge anthropologists to see these routes, paths, and travels as central sites for researchers to pursue. Others (Rouse 1991; Glick-Schiller et al. 1992) have been more specific about calling our attention to the transnational links, circuits, and routes that migrants use. A thoughtful passage by Michael Gilsenan (1982: 269–73) led me to reflect on the journeys I made during my fieldwork.

Glossary

Words and Phrases

Amici, qui si fa la comunità o si muore. Friends, the community is made or it dies.

ambiente. Environment, surroundings.

americani (pl.), o (sing.). Americans.

anziani (pl.), o (sing.). Elderly.

apaesemento. Mondialization; globalization of the home-town village.

assessore. Assessor, councillor, minister.

azzurri. Sportsmen who play for the Italian national soccer team.

bella vita, la. The beautiful life.

caffè. Espressó coffee, espresso coffee bar.

cafone, i (pl.). Southern Italian peasant, boor, lout.

calcio. Soccer.

campanilismo. Parochialism, exaggerated local pride and loyalty to those from your own locality. It constitutes a cultural framework with a distinctive moral and social universe.

campanile. Bell tower.

Casa d'Italia. Italian consulate.

casa populare, una. Public housing.

casa di riposo per persone anziane, una. Rest-home for seniors.

chiacchera, le. Chatter or gossip.

Ciociaro, i (pl.). Person from Ciociara, a province of the Italian Region of Lazio. Refers to the traditional leather shoes peasants in the region wore.

comitato. Committee, board.

Comitato italiano all' estero. Committee of Italians overseas.

compaesano, i (pl.). Fellow villagers.

comparaggio. Ritual kinship.

compare, i (pl.). Godfather, sponsor; (pl.) godfathers or godparents.

comune. Municipality.

consigilio. (or **comitato**), i (pl.). Council.

consultore. Member of a council, councillor.

contadino, i (pl.). Peasant.

corno. Horn.

corso. Main street, avenue.

espresso, i (pl.). Coffee.

fare l'America. To take a journey to America.

Federazione. Federation, association.

festa. Holiday, festival.

Friulanità. Friulan spirit or ambience.

gettone table. Soccer table game.

gli italiani all' estero. Italians overseas.

istituto. Institute.

Italianità. Italian spirit or ambience.

Lazio. Central Italian region of Latium.

madrepatria. Motherland.

mal'occhio. Evil eye.

mangia-cake. Pejorative term for non-Italians. Literally cake-eater. Suggests that a lack of appreciation for real bread and food also indicates a lack of culture and social skills.

mezzogiorno (d'Italia). South of Italy.

mosto. Must; unfermented or fermenting juice used for making wine.

nonni. Grandparents.

onore. Honour.

padrone, i (pl.). Master, owner, employer, labour agent.

paese, i (pl.). Country, home town, native village.

parentela. Relatives, kinfolk.

patronato, i (pl.). Charitable institution, benevolent fund.

piazza, piazzetta. Town square, marketplace.

piazza dell' immaginazione, una. Imagined piazza.

piazzetta. Little town square.

presepii (pl.), o (sing.). Christmas cribs.

Risorgimento. Movement to reunite Italy.

scopa. Italian card game.

Tangentopoli. City of bribes; name given to corruption uncovered in early 1990s in Milan involving politicians, major businessmen, and kickbacks.

tavola calda. Licensed snack bar.

tressette. Italian card game.

tricolore (il Tricolore). Tricolour (Italian tricolour, or flag).

Veneto, i (pl.). Person from region of Veneto.

vertici, i (pl). Senior or top management personnel in Italian government bureaucracy.

vu torna. You who have returned (from migration).

zio, zia. Uncle, aunt.

Organizations

Calabro-Canadian Confederation. Organization of Calabrian-Canadian clubs in Toronto.

Casa D'Abruzzo. Cultural centre and senior's home built and operated by members of the Abruzzese-Canadian community.

Centro Canadese Scuola e Cultura Italiana: Canadian Centre for Italian Culture and Education.

CIPBA. Canadian Italian Professional and Business Association.

CMHC. Canadian Mortgage and Housing Corporation.

Columbus Centre. Cultural and recreational centre built and operated by the ICBC (Villa Charities).

Commissariato Generale dell 'Emigrazione. General Commission of Emigration (an Italian government agency).

CONI (Comitato Olimpico Nazionale Italiano): Italian National Olympic Committee.

COSTI (Centro Organizativo Servizio Tecnico Italiano): Social service agency created by Italian immigrants in 1963, to aid immigrant adjustment to the Canadian job market.

FACI (Federation of Canadian Italian Associations). Precursor to the NCIC (*see* below).

FIGC (Federazione Italiana Giuoco Calcio). Federation of Italian Soccer Clubs.

ICBC (Italian Canadian Benevolent Corporation). Incorporated in 1971; officially changed its name to Villa Charities Inc. in 1995.

IPC (Italian Pastoral Commission). Advisory group of priests ministering to Italian Canadians in Toronto.

Istituto Italiano di Cultura (Italian Cultural Institute). Cultural agency of the Italian government.

Ministero Degli Affari Esteri. Ministry of foreign affairs in Italy.

NCIC (National Congress of Italian Canadians). Federated umbrella organization of Italian clubs and associations, formed in 1974, which lobbies governments and the media.

Villa Charities. Name given in 1995 to the constellation of activities and centres run by the ICBC (Columbus Centre, Villa Colombo, Vita Community Living, etc.).

Villa Colombo. Home for the aged built and operated by the ICBC.

Voce Alternativa (Alternative Voice). Italian-Canadian women's group.

References

Primary Sources

Canada, *Census*. 1941–1991.

Centro Scuola Files, Annual Reports. 1977–1993.

Gianni Grohovaz (Italian Canadian journalist and social activist). Papers deposited at the Multicultural History Society of Ontario.

Italian Canadian Benevolent Corporation, Annual Reports (1975–1994) and archival papers.

Instituto Italiano di Cultura (1993).

Pitto, Cesare. 1994. Personal communication to the author (letter).

Newspapers

Corriere Canadese (also occasionally appearing as *Corriere Illustrato*). Toronto's oldest Italian-language newspaper.

The Liberal. English-language newspaper in Richmond Hill, north of Metropolitan Toronto.

Lo Specchio. Italian-language newspaper servicing northwest suburbs of the GTA.

Il Tevere. Italian-language newspaper in Toronto during the 1970s and early 1980s (now defunct).

Toronto Star. Canada's largest newspaper.

Secondary Sources

Anderson, Benedict. 1983. *Imagined Communities: Reflections on the Origins and Spread of Nationalism*. London: Verso.

Appadurai, Arjun. 1990. Disjuncture and Difference in the Global Cultural Economy. *Public Culture*. 2(2): 1–24.

– 1993. Patriotism and Its Futures. *Public Culture* 5(3): 411–29.

– 1996. *Modernity at Large: Cultural Dimensions of Globalization.* Minneapolis: University of Minnesota Press.

Archdiocese of Toronto, Chancery Office. 1981. Direttive per la Celebrazione delle Feste dei Santi.

Ariemma, Virginia. 1997. *The Story of Villa Charities.* Toronto: Villa Charities.

Artibise, Alan F.J. 1988. Canada as an Urban Nation. *Daedalus* 117(4): 237–64.

Badone, Ellen. 1990. Introduction. In Ellen Badone (ed.), *Religious Orthodoxy and Popular Religious Faith in European Society,* pp. 3–23. Princeton: Princeton University Press.

Bagnell, Kenneth. 1989. *Canadese: A Portrait of the Italian Canadians.* Toronto: Macmillan.

Bailey, F.G. 1971. *Gifts and Poison: The Politics of Reputation.* Toronto: Copp Clark.

Banfield, Edward C. 1958. *The Moral Basis of a Backward Society.* New York: Free Press.

Barth, Fredrik (ed). 1969. *Ethnic Groups and Boundaries.* London: George Allen and Unwin.

Barthes, Roland. 1982. *Mythologies.* Translated by Annette Levers. New York: Hill and Wang.

Bartole, Sergio. 1984. Il Caso Italiano. *Le Regioni* XII(3): 411–29.

Basch, Linda. 1987. The Vincentians and Grenadians: The Role of Voluntary Associations in Immigrant Adaptation to New York City. In Nancy Foner (ed.), *New Immigrants in New York,* pp. 159–94. New York: Columbia University Press.

Baumgartner, M.P. 1988. *The Moral Order of a Suburb.* New York: Oxford University Press.

Bayor, Ronald. 1978. *Neighbors in Conflict.* Baltimore: Johns Hopkins University Press.

Bell, Rudolph M. 1979. *Fate and Honor, Family and Village: Demographic and Cultural Change in Rural Italy since 1880.* Chicago: University of Chicago Press.

Bentley, G. Carter. 1987. Ethnicity and Practice. *Comparative Studies in Society and History* 29(1): 24–55.

Berryman, J. 1986. *Implementation of the OHLP: A Case Study of the Extended School Day Model.* PhD diss., University of Toronto.

Bhabha, Homi K. 1990. *Nation and Narration.* London: Routledge.

Blau, Peter M. 1964. *Exchange and Power in Social Life.* New York and London: John Wiley & Sons.

Bo, Vincenzo. 1984. *Feste, Riti, Magia.* Bologna: Edizioni Dehoniane.

Boissevain, Jeremy. 1970. *The Italians of Montreal: Social Adjustment in a Plural*

Society. Ottawa: Studies of the Royal Commission on Biligualism and Biculturalism. Ministry of Supply and Services Canada.

– 1977. When the Saints Go Marching Out: Reflections on the Decline of Patronage in Malta. In E. Gellner and J. Waterbury (eds.), *Patrons and Clients in Mediterranean Societies*, pp. 81–96. London: Duckworth.

Bourdieu, Pierre. 1977. *Outline of a Theory of Practice*. Cambridge: Cambridge University Press.

Breton, Raymond. 1964. Institutional Completeness of Ethnic Communities and
the Personal Relations of Immigrants. *The American Journal of Sociology* 70(2):
193–205.

– 1984. The Production and Allocation of Symbolic Resources: An Analysis of
the Linguistic and Ethnocultural Fields in Canada. *Canadian Review of Sociology
and Anthropology* 21:123–44.

– 1986. Multiculturalism and Canadian Nation-Building. In Alan Cairns and Cyn-
thia Williams (eds.), *The Politics of Gender, Ethnicity, and Language in Canada*. Toronto: University of Toronto Press.

Brettell, Caroline B. 1990. The Priest and His People: The Contractual Basis for
Religious Practice in Rural Portugal. In Ellen Badone (ed.), *Religious Orthodoxy
and Popular Religious Faith in European Society*. Princeton: Princeton University
Press.

Briggs, John W. 1978. *An Italian Passage: Immigrants to Three American Cities,
1890–1930*. New Haven: Yale University Press.

Brogger, Jan. 1971. *Montevarese: A Study of Peasant Society and Culture in Southern
Italy*. Oslo: Scandinavian University Books.

Brotz, Howard. 1980. Multiculturalism in Canada: A Muddle. *Canadian Public
Policy* 6:41–6.

Brown, Peter. 1981. *The Cult of the Saints. Its Rise and Function in Latin Christianity*.
Chicago: University of Chicago Press.

Buranello, Robert, and Michael Lettieri. 1993. Italian Regional Organizations. In
Julius Molinaro and Maddalena Kuitunen (eds.), *The Luminous Mosaic: Italian
Cultural Organizations in Ontario*. Welland: Editions Soleil.

Cafiso, Jenny, et al. 1992. Italian Canadians should confront cultural icon. *Toronto
Star*, 19 Oct., 25A.

Calzavara, Liviana. 1982. *Social Networks and Access to Job Opportunities*. PhD diss.,
University of Toronto.

Cannistraro, Philip V., and Gianfausto Rosoli. 1979. Fascist Emigration Policy in
the 1920s: An Interpretive Framework. *International Migration Review* 13(4):
673–92.

Carella, Anthony, and Joanne Chianello. 1990. *Directory of Italian Canadian
Resources in Ontario*. Toronto: NCIC.

Carstens, Peter. In Defence of Community Paradigms in Sociology and Social
    Anthropology: Paper presented at the annual meeting of the Canadian Sociol-
    ogy and Anthropological Association, Calgary, Alta., June 1994.
Chapman, Charlotte Gower. 1971. *Milocca: A Sicilian Village.* Cambridge, Mass.
    Schenkman.
Clifford, James. 1988. *The Predicament of Culture.* Cambridge: Harvard University
    Press.
− 1994. Diasporas. *Cultural Anthropology.* 9(3): 302–38.
− 1997. *Routes: Travel and Translation in the Late Twentieth Century.* Cambridge: Har-
    vard University Press.
Clivio, Gianrenzo P. 1985. Su alcune caracteristiche dell'Italiese di Toronto.
    Il Veltro 3–4:anno XXIX:483–93.
Cohen, Abner. 1969. *Custom and Politics in Urban Africa.* Berkeley: University of
    California Press.
Cohen, Anthony P. 1985. *The Symbolic Construction of Community.* London:
    Tavistock.
Cohen, Robin. 1997. *Global Diasporas: An Introduction.* London: UCL Press.
Colalillo, Giuliana. 1981. *Value Structures Within Italian Immigrant Families: Continu-
    ity or Conflict?* PhD diss., University of Toronto.
Connor, Walter. 1986. The Impact of Homelands upon Diasporas. In Gabriel
    Sheffer (ed.), *Modern Diasporas in International Politics,* pp. 16–45. London:
    Croom Helm.
Conzen, Kathleen, et al. 1990. The Invention of Ethnicity: A Perspective From the
    USA. In *AltreItalie.* Turino: Agnelli.
Cronin, Constance. 1970. *The Sting of Change: Sicilians in Sicily and Australia.*
    Chicago: University of Chicago Press.
Cumbo, Enrico Carlson. 1993. Impediments to the Harvest: The Limitations of
    Methodist Proselytization of Toronto's Italian Immigrants, 1905–1925. In Mark
    George McGowan and Brian Clarke (eds.), *Catholics at the 'Gathering Place,'*
    pp. 155–76. Toronto: Dundurn Press.
Cummins, Jim, and Marcel Danesi. 1990. *Heritage Languages: The Development and
    Denial of Canada's Linguistic Resources.* Toronto: Our Schools/Ourselves Foun-
    dation.
Danesi, Marcel, and Alberto Di Giovanni. 1985. Ethnic Languages and Accultura-
    tion: The Case of Canadians. *Canadian Ethnic Studies* 17(1): 98–103.
− 1989. Italian as a Heritage Language in Ontario: An Historical Sketch. *Polyphony*
    2:89–94.
Davis, John. 1973. *Land and Family in Pisticci.* London: London School of
    Economics.
de Certeau, Michel. 1984. *The Practice of the Everyday Life.* Translated by Steven
    Randall. Berkeley: University of California Press.

Del Giudice, Luisa. 1992. Italian Traditional Song in Toronto: From Autobiography to Advocacy. *Journal of Canadian Studies*, 74–80.

Despres, Leo. 1967. *Cultural Pluralism and Nationalist Politics in British Guiana.* Chicago: Rand McNally.

Di Iulio, Palmacchio. 1991. From ICBC: This Is the Italian Canadian Contribution to the Spirit of Multiculturalism. *Lifestyle* (6):iii (June):11.

Di Tota, Mia. 1981. Saint Cults and Political Alignments in Southern Italy. *Dialectical Anthropology* 5:317–29.

Douglas, Mary. 1966. *Purity and Danger: An Analysis of Concepts of Pollution and Taboo.* London: Routledge and Kegan Paul.

– 1990. Foreword to *The Gift:* The form and reason for exchange in archaic societies, by Marcel Mauss. Translated by W.D. Halls. New York: W.W. Norton, 1950.

Douglass, William. 1984. *Emigration in a South Italian Town.* New Brunswick, N.J.: Rutgers University Press.

Eidheim, Harald. 1963. Entrepreneurship in Politics. In Fredrik Barth (ed.), *The role of the entrepreneur in social change in Northern Norway.* Bergen: Scandinavian University Books.

Eriksen, Thomas H. 1991. The Cultural Contexts of Ethnic Differences. *Man* (N.S.) 26: 127–44.

– 1993. *Ethnicity and Nationalism: Anthropological Perspectives.* London: Pluto Press.

Esposito, Pino. 1993. From the Editor. *Eyetalian* 1:1.

Favero, Luigi, and Graziano Tassello. 1978. Cent'anni di emigrazione italiana (1876–1976). In Gianfausto Rosoli (ed.), *Un secolo di emigrazione italiana: 1876–1976*, pp. 9–64. Rome: Centro Studi Emigrazione.

Fleras, Augie, and Jean Leonard Elliott. 1991. *Multiculturalism in Canada.* Scarborough, Ont.: Nelson.

Foerster, Robert F. 1919. *The Italian Emigration of Our Times.* Cambridge: Harvard University Press.

Fortunato, Giustino. 1911. *Il mezzagiorno e lo stato italiano.* Vol. 2: *Discorsi politici, 1890–1910.* Bari: Giuseppe Laterza e figli.

Gabaccia, Donna R. 1984. *From Sicily to Elizabeth Street: Housing and Social Change Among Italian Immigrants, 1880–1930.* Albany: State University of New York Press.

Galt, Anthony H. 1974. Rethinking Patron Client Relationships: the Real System and the Official System in Southern Italy. *Anthropological Quarterly* 47:182–202.

– 1992. *Town and Country in Locorotondo.* Toronto: Harcourt Brace Jovanovich.

Geertz, Clifford. 1963. The Integrative Revolution: Primordial Sentiments and Civil Politics in the New States. In *Old Societies and New States*, pp. 105–57. New York: Free Press.

– 1973. In *The Interpretation of Cultures*, pp. 360–411. New York: Basic Books.

– 1973. In *The Interpretation of Cultures*, pp. 3–30. New York: Basic Books.

– 1983. *Local Knowledge: Further Essays in Interpretive Anthropology.* New York: Basic Books.

Gellner, Ernest. 1964. *Thought and Change.* London: Wiedenfeld & Nicholson.

– 1983. *Nations and Nationalism.* Oxford: Basil Blackwell.

Giddens, Anthony. 1990. *The Consequences of Modernity.* Cambridge: Polity Press.

– 1984. *The Constitution of Society.* Cambridge: Polity Press.

Gilsenan, Michael. 1982. *Recognizing Islam. An Anthropologist's Introduction.* London: Croom Helm.

Ginzburg, Carlo. 1980. *The Cheese and the Worms.* Translated by John and Anne Tedeschi. Baltimore: Johns Hopkins University Press.

Glazer, Nathan, and Daniel P. Moynihan. 1963. *Beyond the Melting Pot.* Cambridge: MIT Press.

Glick-Schiller, Nina, et al. 1992. *Towards a Transnational Perspective on Migration: Race, Class, Ethnicity and Nationalism Reconsidered.* New York: New York Academy of Sciences.

Gold, Gerry L. (ed.). 1984. *Minorities and Mother Country Imagery.* St John's: Memorial University.

Graburn, Nelson H.H. (ed.). 1976. *Ethnic and Tourist Arts: Cultural expressions from the Fourth World.* Berkeley: University of California Press.

Gramsci, Antonio. 1966. *La questione meridionale.* Roma: Editori Riuniti.

– 1971. *Selections from the Prison Notebooks.* New York: International Publishers.

Grohovaz, Gianni. 1985. See You at Brandon Hall. Oh! ... I Mean the Italo-Canadian Recreation Club. *Polyphony* (7): ii (fall/winter): 98–103.

Guardiani, Francesco. 1982. From the Editor. In *25th Anniversary Club Abruzzi.* Toronto: Club Abruzzi.

Gupta, Akhil, and James Ferguson. 1992. Beyond 'Culture': Space, Identity, and the Politics of Difference. *Cultural Anthropology* 7(1): 6–23.

Handler, Richard. 1988. *Nationalism and the Politics of Culture in Quebec.* Madison: University of Wisconsin Press.

Hannerz, Ulf. 1989. Notes on a Global Ecumene. *Public Culture.* 1(2): 66–75.

– 1992. *Cultural Complexity. Studies in the Social Organization of Meaning.* New York: Columbia University Press.

Harney, Nicholas DeMaria. 1992. *Buste, Bomboniere* and Banquet Halls: The Economy of Italian Canadian Weddings. *Studi Emigrazione* 106: 263–75.

Harney, Robert F. 1981. Toronto's Little Italy. In Robert F. Harney and J. Vincenza Scarpaci (eds.), *Little Italies in North America, 1885–1945,* pp. 41–62. Toronto: MHSO.

– 1985. Italophobia: An English-speaking Malady? *Studi Emigrazione* 22(77): 6–44.

– 1988. 'So Great a Heritage as Ours': Immigration and the Survival of the Canadian Polity. *Daedalus* (117)iv(fall): 51–97.

– 1989. Caboto and Other Parentela: The Uses of the Italian-Canadian Past. In Roberto Perin and Franc Sturino (eds.), *Arrangiarsi: The Italian Immigration Experience in Canada*. Montreal: Guernica.

– 1991. If One Were to Write a History of Postwar Italia. In B. Ramirez and P. Anctil (eds.), *If One Were to Write a History of Postwar Italia: Selected Writings by Robert F. Harney*. Toronto: MHSO.

– 1993. Undoing the Risorgimento: Emigrants from Italy and the Politics of Regionalism. In Nicholas DeMaria Harney (ed.), *From the Shores of Hardship: Italians in Canada*. Welland, Ont.: Editions Soleil.

Harney, Robert, and Harold Troper. 1975. *Immigrants: A Portrait of the Urban Experience*. Toronto: Van Nostrand Reinhold.

Harvey, David. 1989. *The Condition of Postmodernity.* Oxford: Blackwell.

Hastrup, Kirsten, and Karen Fog Olwig. 1997. Introduction. In *Siting Culture: The Shifting Anthropological Object*, pp. 1–14. London: Routledge.

Herzfeld, Michael. 1992. *The Social Production of Indifference*. Chicago: University of Chicago Press.

Hine, David. 1996. Federalism, Regionalism and the Unitary State: Contemporary Regional Pressures in Historical Perspective. In Carl Levy (ed.), *Italian Regionalism: History, Identity and Politics*, pp. 109–130. Oxford: Berg.

Iacovetta, Franca. 1988. Working-Class Immigrants: Southern Italians in Post-War Toronto. Doctoral dissertation. York University.

– 1992. *Such Hardworking People: Italians in Postwar Toronto*. Montreal: McGill-Queen's University Press.

– 1993. Writing Women into Immigration History: The Italian Canadian Case. *Altreitalie* 9: 1–25.

Isaacs, Harold R. 1975. *Idols of the Tribe: Group Identity and Political Change*. New York: Harper & Row.

Istituto Centrale di Statistica. *Annurario Statistico Italiano*. 1947–1981. Roma.

Jansen, Clifford. 1987. *Fact-Book on Italians in Canada*. 2d ed. Toronto: Institute for Social Research, York University.

– 1988. *Italians in a Multicultural Canada*. Queenston: Edwin Mellon Press.

– 1991. Educational Accomplishments of Italian Canadians in the Eighties. *Studi Emigrazione/Etudes Migrations* 102: 159–79.

Jansen, Clifford, and Lee La Cavera. 1981. *Fact-Book on Italians in Canada*. Toronto: Institute for Social Research, York University.

– 1986. Italians in the Multicultural Society of the Eighties. *Polyphony* 7(2): 128–31.

Kenny, Michael, and David I. Kertzer. 1983. *Urban Life in Mediterranean Europe:/ Anthropological Perspectives*. Urbana: University of Illinois Press.

Keyes, Charles F. 1976. Towards a new formulation of the concept of ethnic group. *Ethnicity* 3(2): 202–13.

King, R., and Strachan A. 1980. The Effects of Return Migration on a Gozitan Village (Malta). *Human Organization* 37(2): 175–9.

Kuitunen, Maddalena. 1993. Centro Canadese Scuola e Cultura Italiana. In Julius Molinaro and Maddalena Kuitunen (eds.), *The Luminous Mosaic: Italian Cultural Organizations in Ontario.* Welland: Editions Soleil.

Lee, Benjamin. 1993. Going Public. *Public Culture* 5(2): 165–78.

Levin, Michael. 1993. Ethnicity and Aboriginality: Conclusions. In *Ethnicity and Aboriginality: Case Studies in Ethnonationalism.* Toronto: University of Toronto Press.

– 1995. Understanding Ethnicity. *Queen's Quarterly* 102(1): 71–84.

Levy, Carl (ed.). 1996. *Italian Regionalism: History, Identity and Politics.* Oxford: Berg.

Lopreato, Joseph. 1967. *Peasants No More.* San Francisco: Chandler Publishing Company.

MacCannell, Dean. 1984. Reconstructed Ethnicity: Tourism and Cultural Identity in Third World Communities. *Annals of Tourism Research* 11:375–91.

MacDonald, J.S. 1963. Agricultural Organization, Migration and Labour Militancy in Rural Italy. *Economic History Review* 16 (1–3): 61–75.

Marchetto, Fr. Ezio. 1985. The Catholic Church and Italian Immigration to Toronto: An Overview. *Polyphony* 7(2): 106–9.

Mauss, Marcel. 1967. *The Gift: Forms and Functions of Exchange in Archaic Societies.* Translated by Ian Cunnison. New York: Norton.

Migliore, Sam. 1997. *Mal'uocchiu. Ambiguity, Evil Eye, and the Language of Distress.* Toronto: University of Toronto Press.

Ministero degli affari esteri. 1984. *Associazioni Italiane nel Mondo 1984.* Rome: Istituto Poligra Fico e Zecca Dello Stato.

Mitchell, Clyde. 1966. Theoretical Orientations in African Urban Studies. In Michael Banton (ed.), *The Social Anthropology of Complex Societies.* ASA Monograph, 4:37–68. London: Tavistock.

Moss, Leonard W., and Stephen C. Cappannari. 1962. Estate and Class in a Southern Italian Hill Village. *American Anthropologist* 64(2): 287–300.

Nagata, Judith. 1969. Adaptation and Integration of Greek Working Class Immigrants in the City of Toronto. *The International Migration Review.* 4(1): 44–69.

Nelli, Humbert S. 1970. *The Italians in Chicago, 1880–1930: A Study in Ethnic Mobility.* New York: Oxford University Press.

Nitti, Francesco. 1958. *Scritti sulla questione meridionale.* Vol. 1: *Saggi sulla storia del emigrazione, emigrazione e lavoro (1888–1908).* Bari: Editori Laterza.

O'Bryan, K.G., J. Reitz, and O. Kuplowska. 1976. *The Non-official Languages Study.* Ottawa: Supply and Services Canada.

Ontario Debates. 1979. *Official Report (Hansard).* 17/04/79: S-4: 112–14; 20/04/79: 27, 1161–8.

Orsi, Robert Anthony. 1985. *The Madonna of 115th Street: Faith and Community in Italian Harlem, 1880–1950*. New Haven: Yale University Press.

Pennacchio, Luigi. 1993. The Torrid Trinity: Catholicism, Fascism and Toronto's Italians, 1929–1943. In Mark George McGowan and Brian Clarke (eds.), *Catholics at the 'Gathering Place,'* pp. 233–54. Toronto: Dundurn Press.

Peter, Karl. 1981. The Myth of Multiculturalism and Other Fables. In Jorgen Dahlie and Tissa Fernando (eds.), *Ethnicity, Power and Politics in Canada*, pp. 56–67. Toronto: Methuen.

Philpott, Stuart. 1973. *West Indian Migration: The Monserrat Case*. London: Althone Press.

Pitto, Cesare (ed.). 1990. *La Calabria dei "Paesi." Per una antropologia della memoria del popolo migrante*. Pisa: ETS Editrice.

Porter, John. 1972. Dilemmas and Contradictions of a Multi-Ethnic Society. *Proceedings and Transactions of the Royal Society of Canada* 10:4.

Rami, Lucilla. 1972. Religiosità a Magia nel Sud. *Sociologia Revista di Studi Sociali* 6:95–145.

Ramirez, Bruno. 1988. Ethnicity on Trial: The Italians of Montreal and the Second World War. In Norman Hillmer et al. (eds.), *On Guard for Thee: War, Ethnicity and the Canadian State, 1939–1945*. Ottawa: Canadian Committee for the History of the Second World War.

– 1989. *The Italians in Canada*. Canada's Ethnic Groups Series, no. 14. Ottawa: Canadian Historical Association.

Referendum '92: Official Voting Results. 1992. Chief Electoral Officer of Canada.

Richmond, Anthony, and Warren Kalbach. 1980. *Factors in the Adjustment of Immigrants and Their Descendants*. Ottawa:

Rosati, Gioconda (Jackie). 1994 (19 July). Minister of Supply and Services. Interview *'Our Lives.'*

Rossi, Egisto. 1903. Delle condizioni del Canada rispetto all'immagrazione italiana. *Bollettino dell'emigrazione*. 4: 3–28.

Rouse, Roger. 1991. Mexican Migration and the Social Space of Postmodernism. *Diaspora* (1)1: 8–23.

Royal Commission on Bilingualism and Biculturalism. 1966. *Preliminary Report*. Ottawa: Ministry of Supply and Services Canada.

Sahlins, Marshall D. 1965. On the Sociology of Primitive Exchange. In Michael Banton (ed.), *The Relevance of Models for Social Anthropology*. London: Tavistock Publications.

Saifullah Khan, Verity. 1976. Pakistanis in Britain: Perceptions of a Population. *New Community* 5:222–30.

Scardellato, Gabriele. 1995. *Within Our Temple: A History of the Order Sons of Italy of Ontario*. Toronto: Order Sons of Italy of Canada.

Schachter, Gustav. 1965. *The Italian South: Economic Development in Mediterranean Europe.* New York: Random House.

Schneider, David M. 1984. *A Critique of the Study of Kinship.* Ann Arbor: University of Michigan Press.

Senate Debates. 17 October 1979 (Senator Peter Bosa).

Sidlofsky, Samuel. 1969. Post-War Immigrants in the Changing Metropolis – With Special Reference to Toronto's Italian Population. 2 vols. PhD diss., University of Toronto.

Silone, Ignazio. 1934. *Fontamara.* New York: H. Smith and R. Haas.

Spivak, Gayatri Chakravorty. 1993. *Outside in the Teaching Machine.* New York: Routledge.

Spotts, Frederic, and Theodor Wieser. 1986. *Italy: A Difficult Democracy.* Cambridge: Cambridge University Press.

Steiner, Christopher B. 1994. *African Art in Transit.* Cambridge: Cambridge University Press.

Stokes, Martin. 1992. *The Arabesk Debate: Music and Musicians in Modern Turkey.* Oxford: Clarendon Press.

Sturino, Franc. 1978. Family and Kin Cohesion among South Italian Immigrants in Toronto. In Betty Boyd Caroli et al. (eds.), *The Italian Immigrant Woman in North America.* Toronto: MHSO.

– 1986. The Social Mobility of Italian Canadians: 'Outside' and 'Inside' Concepts of Mobility. *Polyphony* 7(2): 123–7.

– 1990a. *Forging the Chain: Italian Migration to North America, 1880–1930.* Toronto: MHSO.

– 1990b. La 'Mondializzazione' del Paesanismo tra i Rendesi del nuovo mondo. In Cesare Pitto (ed.), *La calabria dei 'paesi.' Per una antropologia della memoria del popolo migrante.* Pisa: ETS Editrice.

Talai, Vered. 1989. *Armenians in London: The Management of Social Boundaries.* Manchester: Manchester University Press.

Tarrow, Sidney. 1967. *Peasant Communism in Southern Italy.* New Haven: Yale University Press.

Tepper, Eliot. 1994. Immigration Policy and Multiculturalism. In J.W. Berry and J.A. Ponce (eds.), *Ethnicity and Culture in Canada.* Toronto: University of Toronto Press.

Thomas, William I., and F. Znaniecki. 1958. *The Polish Community in America.* 2 vols. New York: Dover Publications.

Tölölyan, Khachig. 1996. Rethinking Diaspora(s): Stateless Power in the Transnational Moment. *Diaspora* 5(1): 3–36

Tomasi, Lydio. 1975. *The Other Catholics: A Preliminary Partial Report on the Italian Apostolate in Toronto's Archdiocese; 11: Priest's Survey.* New York: Center for Migration Studies.

Tosi, Arturo. 1991. *L'Italiano D'Oltremare*. Firenze: Giunti.

Trudeau, Pierre E. 1971. Statement by the Prime Minister, House of Commons, 8 October 1971. In *Multiculturalism and the Government of Canada*. Ottawa: Minister of State, Multiculturalism.

Turner, Victor. 1969. *The Ritual Process*. Chicago: Aldie.

Van Gennep, Arnold. 1961 [1910]. *The Rites of Passage*. Translated by M.B. Vizedom and G.L. Caffee. Chicago: University of Chicago Press.

Vecoli, Rudolph J. 1964. Contadini in Chicago: A Critique of the Uprooted. *Journal of American History* 51:404–17.

– 1969. Prelates and Peasants: Italian Immigrants and the Catholic Church. *Journal of Social History* 3:217–68.

Waisberg, Judge Harry. 1974. *Report of the Royal Commission on Certain Sectors of the Building Industry*. Toronto: Queen's Printer for Ontario. Vols. 1,2.

Warner, M. 1992. The Mass Public and the Mass Subject. In C. Calhoun (ed.), *Habermas and the Public Sphere*. Cambridge, MA: MIT Press.

Watson, James L. 1977. *Between Two Cultures. Migrants and Minorities in Britain*. Oxford: Basil Blackwell.

Werbner, Pnina. 1985. The Organization of Giving and Ethnic Elites: Voluntary Associations amongst Manchester Pakistanis. *Ethnic and Racial Studies* (8)3: 368–88.

– 1990. *The Migration Process: Capital, Gifts and Offerings among British Pakistanis*. New York: St Martin's Press.

– 1991. 'The Fiction of Unity in Ethnic politics.' In Pnina Werbner and Muhammad Anwar (eds.), *Black and Ethnic Leaderships in Britain*, pp. 113–45. London: Routledge.

Werbner, Pnina, and Muhammad Anwar (ed.) 1991. *Black and Ethnic Leaderships in Britain*. London: Routledge.

Yans-McLaughlin, Virginia. 1977. *Family and Community. Italian Immigrants in Buffalo, 1880–1930*. Ithaca: Cornell University Press.

Young, Crawford. 1976. *The Politics of Cultural Pluralism*. Madison: University of Wisconsin Press.

Zucchi, John. 1985. Italian Hometown Settlements and the Development of an Italian Community in Toronto, 1875–1935. In Robert F. Harney (ed.), *Gathering Place*. Toronto: MHSO.

– 1988. *Italians in Toronto: Development of a National Identity, 1875–1935*. Kingston: McGill-Queen's University Press.

Index

Abruzzese, 50, 81–2, 85, 98–9. *See also* Casa D'Abruzzo
amoral familism, 14
Anderson, Benedict, 4–6, 8, 89, 96, 173
Anishinabe First Nation, 76
anticlericalism, 149, 155
Anwar, Muhammad, 69–70, 94, 97, 107
apaesemento, 141. *See also* diaspora
Appadurai, Arjun, 6, 89, 93
Archdiocese of Toronto, 150
Artibise, Alan, 22
associations. *See* clubs and voluntary associations

Badone, Ellen, 145–6
Bagnell, Kenneth, 159
Bailey, F.G., 40, 50
Banfield, Edward, 14, 129
Barth, Fredrik, 49–50, 72
Barthes, Roland, 72
Bartole, Sergio, 85
Basch, Linda, 54
Baumgartner, M.P., 170
Bayor, Ronald, 54
Bell, Leland, 76

Bell, Rudolph, 13, 163
Bellantone, Ben, 138
Bentley, G. Carter, 5, 72
Berlusconi, Silvio, 84, 121
Berryman, J., 110
Bhabha, Homi, viii, 70, 89
Blau, Peter, 46
Bo, Vincenzo, 145
Boissevain, Jeremy, 14, 129, 145
Bosa, Peter, 159
Bourdieu, Pierre, 5
Breton, Raymond, 28, 105, 112
Brettell, Caroline, 152
Briggs, John, 130
Brogger, Jan, 14, 163
Brotz, Howard, 105
Brown, Peter, 145
Buranello, Robert, 29, 87, 127

Caboto, Giovanni, 15, 75
Cafiso, Jenny, 164
Calzavara, Liviana, 24
Camp Petawawa, 55
campanilismo: 126–7, 142; language and, 128; popular religion and, 145
Canadianization and education, 108, 113

Cannistraro, Philip V., 13
Cappannari, Stephen C., 129
Carella, Anthony, 87
Carrier, Joseph, 48
Carstens, Peter, 102, 141
Casa D'Abruzzo, 50, 80–2, 96–9, funding of, 167
Casa D'Italia, 32
Castrilli, Annamarie, 116
Catholic Church: Italian immigrants and, 147–52; reaction by, to popular religion, 153–6; religious orders, 147
Centro Canadese Scuola e Cultura Italiana, 102–23 passim; funding of, 167; origins of, 105–7
Chapman, Charlotte Gower, 145
chiacchera, la, 131
Chianello, Joanne, 87
CHIN: 61, 134, 154, 171, 185n1; women and picnic, 164–6
Ciociari, 43
CIPBA, 58
class: 4–5; in Italy, 11–12; status and, 46, 169
Clifford, James, 141, 185n1
Clivio, Gianrenzo, 103
clubs and voluntary associations: gender and, 131–2; post-war, 32–3, 37, 78, 127, 130–42; pre-First World War, 19–20; variety of, 29, 31, 54 See also regional clubs
CMHC, 63, 80, 97–8
Cohen, Abner, 5
Cohen, A.P., 4, 82–3, 89, 141, 181n2
Cohen, Robin, 181n1
CONI, 114, 118, 120
Colalillo, Giuliana, 163–4
Colombo, Cristoforo, 75–6
Columbus Centre. See Villa Charities

COMITES, 87
community: as fictive unity, 54, 79; Calabrese, 50, 101; communicative, 140–1, competition within, 50, 67–70; ethnic, 9, 29, 31, 123; imagined 8; thresholds of, 102, 141. See also Anderson, Benedict; Cohen, A.P.
Connor, Walter, 181
consultore, 85–7
Conzen, Kathleen, 5
Corriere Canadese (Illustrato), 9, 29, 63, 68, 87, 127, 138, 165, 168; funding of, 167
COSTI, 33, 56
Cronin, Constance, 14, 129, 163
culture: content of, 64–5, 71–4, 157, 173; language and, 103, 108–9, 122; sites of 3, 8, 181n3 (See also place); sport and, 103, 117–23; Veneto Centre as site of, 91–2. See also ethnicity; ethnocultural entrepreneur; Heritage Language Program
Cumbo, Enrico, 147
Cummins Jim, 108

Danesi, Marcel, 103, 106–8, 168
Davis, John, 14, 163
Davis, William, 61
de Certeau, Michel, 141
Del Giudice, Luisa, 134
Despres, Leo, 5
Di Giovanni, Alberto, 106–7, 112–13
Di Iulio, Pal, 52
Di Michele, Mary, 167
Di Santo, Odoardo, 80–1
Di Tota, Mia, 145
diaspora: consumption and, 6–7; forms of, 181n.1; governments and, 7, 168; links in the, 134–5; regional

identities and, 85, 89, 93, 101; sport and, 103, 117–23; transnationalism and, 6. *See also* Italian government; place; transnationalism
Douglas, Mary, 38, 40, 77
Douglass, William, 127, 141

Economist, The, 160
Eidheim, Harald, 104
Elliott, Jean Leonard, 105
Eriksen, Thomas H., 5, 6, 72
Esposito, Pino, 167
ethnic brokers, 4–5, 10. *See also consultore*; ethnocultural entrepreneur
ethnicity: 3, 5–6; content of, 74; ethnic group interaction, 48, 73, 74–8, 148; multiple layers of, 4, 10, 50, 82, 96, 98. *See also* community; culture; place
ethnocultural entrepreneur: 104–5, 112–16; imagining communities and, 107, 123; nexus of transnational fields, 119, 123
ethnolect, 168
evil eye, 145–6
Eyetalian: 157, 162; 166–73 passim; on culture and suburbs, 169–72; on language, 167–8; origins of, 166–7

FACI, 33, 58
Famee Furlane, 70, 90, 95
Favero, Luigi, 16
Ferguson, James, 8
Fleras, Augie, 105
Foerster, Robert F., 16
Fog Olwig, Karen, 181n3
Fortunato, Giustino, 12

Gabaccia, Donna, 129, 163
Galt, Anthony, 116, 163

Geertz, Clifford, 5, 52, 115, 117
Gellner, Ernest, 8
gender, 131–2, 163–6. *See also* women
Giddens, Anthony, 100
gifts: 39–51 passim; communal giving, 37–8; and ethnicity, 49–50; elite giving of, 47–50; fund-raising and, 46–8, 63, 73; La Società Canneto 43–4, 154–5; status and, 42–9, 52; trust in authority and, 40–1, 45, 49
Gilsenan, Michael, 185n1
Ginzburg, Carlo, 155
Giochi della Gioventù, 117–23
Glazer, Nathan, 54
Glick-Schiller, Nina, 185n1
globalization of culture: ethnicity and, 6. *See also* diaspora; transnationalism
Gold, Gerry, 7
Graburn, Nelson, 72
Gramsci, Antonio, 12, 163
Grohovaz, Gianni, 56
Guardiani, Francesco, 98
Gupta, Akhil, 8

Handler, Richard, 72
Hannerz, Ulf, 6
Harney, Nicholas, 41
Harney, Robert F., 16, 19, 56, 74–5, 86, 105, 159, 182n1
Harney, Robert, 108
Harvey, David 6, 100
Hastrup, Kirsten, 181n3
hegemony, 4, 67, 69, 88, 96, 105, 163
Heritage Language Program: politics of, 107–15 passim
Herzfeld, Michael, 77
Hine, David, 85

Iacovetta, Franca, 28–9, 56, 66, 146, 148–9, 163

Iannuzzi, Dan, 138
ICBC. *See* Villa Charities
internment, 20, 55, 182n2
International Languages Program. *See*
Heritage Language Program
Isaacs, Harold, 5
Istituto Italiano di Cultura, 115–17,
168–9, 184n2
Italian Canadian Recreational Club, 56
Italian government: institutions for
immigrants, 34; interest in immigrants, 54–5, 84, 87, 114; Ministry of
Foreign Affairs, 106, 114, 120,
184n2; Ministry of Public Education, 120. *See also* CONI; Giochi
della Gioventù; Istituto Italiano di
Cultura
Italian immigrants: children of, 7,
24–5, 37; early settlementof, 17–20,
125; generational differences, 22,
133; kinship and, 17, 21, 66, 130–1;
nature and, 27; restrictions on, 12,
19; second generation and, 161–73;
sources of, 21–2; state preferences
against, 16
Italian Immigrant Aid Society, 32, 56
Italian language: use of, 28; teaching
of, 108–14 passim
Italian-language media: 31, 51, 67,
168; Telelatino, 171–2, 185n1. *See
also* CHIN; *Corriere Canadese*;
ethnocultural entrepreneur;
Specchio, Lo
Italian Pastoral Commission: language and, 107; religious feste and,
149–51
Italy: agro-towns, 14, 127; Christian
Democrats, 84; economy in 1980s,
160; emigration from, 12–13; family
and kinship in, 14, 129; land tenure
in southern, 12–13; political cul-

ture, 4, 84; southern Catholicism in,
15. *See also* regions in Italy

Jansen, Clifford, 21–5, 160, 182n3
Jansen, Clifford, 158
Jewish community, 48, 73
JobsOntario Community Action Pro-
gram, 99, 162, 167, 184n3

Kalbach, Warren, 28
Kenny, Michael, 141
Kertzer, David I., 141
Keyes, Charles, 6
King, R., 139
kinship: 66, 129, 135; fictive, 88. *See
also* community; Italian immigrants
Kuitunen, Maddalena, 107, 110
Kuplowska, O., 109–10

La Cavera, Lee, 158
labour leaders, 138
Lee, Benjamin, 89
Lettieri, Michael, 29, 87, 127
Levin, Michael, 4–5
Levy, Carl, 84
Liberal party, 34, 111, 182n2
local identities. *See campanilismo*
Lombardi, Johnny, 165
Lopreato, Joseph, 15, 86

MacCannell, Dean, 72
MacDonald, J.S., 13, 129
Madonna di Canneto: booklet of,
43–4; feste, 144, 146; origins of,
152–5; procession of, 143–4
mafia: as stereotype, 60, 158–9; in
Italy, 84
Marchetto, Ezio, 148
Marchi, Sergio, 121
Marylake monastery, saints' feasts at,
136, 143–4, 154

mangia-cake, 39
Mauss, Marcel, 39–40, 42–3
Meech Lake and Charlottetown
    Accord, 36, 183n7
Mezzogiorno, 12
Migliore, Sam, 146
migration: costs of return, 139; expec-
    tations for, 138; postwar, 21; process
    of, 126; to America, 15–17
Ministero degli Affari Esteri, 29, 35,
    127
Mintz, Sidney, 156
Mitchell, Clyde, 82, 88
Molise, 79, 83, 90–1
Moss, Leonard W., 129
Moynihan, Daniel P., 54
multiculturalism, 36, 55, 57; as prac-
    tised by ethnic communities,
    75–8
Mulroney, Brian, 161, 182n2
Mussolini, Benito, 20

Nagata, Judith, 130
Nardi, Tony, 71, 167
nation-space: viii, 89–90; multicultur-
    alism and, 4, 105
national identity: Canadian, 35, 82;
    Italian regional identity and, 83
Native peoples, 75–6
NCIC, 31, 107, 182n2
neighbourhoods, Italian-Canadian,
    8–9, 27–8, 57, 126–7, 140–1; in
    Downsview, 135, 141, 170–1, 175;
    ethnic succession, 77–8; in Wood-
    bridge, 69, 82, 135, 141, 169, 170–1
Nelli, Humbert S., 130
New Democratic Party (NDP), 67, 138,
    167
Nitti, Francesco, 12

O'Bryan, K.G., 109–10

onore, 163
Ontario Ministry of Culture, 66
Orsi, Robert Anthony, 145

padroni, 17
Palladini, Al, 27 183n4
patron-client relations, 15; religion
    and, 145–6; state resources and, 41.
    See also ethnic brokers
pan-Italian institutions, 89, 103, 119,
    138; religion and identity as, 147;
    role of media and, 56
Pennacchio, Luigi, 20, 147
Peter, Karl, 105
Philpott, Stuart, 86
Pitto, Cesare, 141
place: ethnicity and, 139–41; music
    and, 133–4. *See also* culture,
    sites of
Porter, John, 105
Portuguese, 76–8; Italian intermar-
    riage with, 184n3
Progressive Conservative party, 111

Rae, Bob, 80–1, 138
Rami, Lucilla, 145
Ramirez, Bruno, 16, 55
regions in Italy: Calabria, 92, 101, 124;
    loyalties to, 70, 92–3; powers of,
    84–5; programs for immigrants, 85,
    89
regional clubs, 87–101 passim
Reitz, J., 109–10
religion, popular, 144–7, 155
reterritorialization, 8
Ricci, Nino, 167, 172
Richmond, Anthony, 28
Risorgimento, 12
Rosati, Gioconda, 58
Rosoli, Gianfausto, 13
Rossi, Egisto, 34

Rouse, Roger, 185n1
Royal Commission on Bilingualism and Biculturalism, 36

Sahlins, Marshall, 41
Saifullah Khan, Verity, 69
San Giorgio Morgeto: fieldnote about, 124–6; social club of, 29, 135–9
Scalabrini, Giovanni, 147
Scardellato, Gabriele, 20
Schachter, Gustav, 12
Schneider, David, 77
Sidlofsky, Samuel, 127
Silipo, Tony, 80, 115, 138
Silone, Ignazio, 128
Società Canneto, La. *See* gifts and religion; Madonna di Canneto
space: culture and, 159; ethnic identity and, 8, 140; social, 3, 46, 82, 87, 100, 103, 133, 163; Sora club as sociocultural, 139–42; time and, 6, 100, 141. *See also* clubs and voluntary associations
Specchio, Lo, 86, 93, 171
Spivak, Gayatri, 166
sport: generational communication and, 118. *See also* culture; Giochi della Gioventù
Spotts, Frederic, 85, 160, 164
Steiner, Christopher, 72
stereotypes of Italians, 16, 169, 173; local identities and, 128–9
Stokes, Martin, 133
Strachan, A., 139
Sturino, Franc, 14, 17, 22, 28, 66, 129, 134, 160
suburbs, 8–9, 170–3
Swarbrick, Anne, 115

Talai, Vered, 69

Tarrow, Sidney, 12
Tassello, Graziano, 16
Tepper, Eliot, 57
Tevere, Il, 63
Thomas, William I., 31
Tölölyan, Khachig, 181n1
Tomasi, Lydio, 149
Tosi, Arturo, 28
transnation. *See* diaspora
transnationalism: content of 7–8, 135; ethnic identity and, vii, 81, 100. *See also* diaspora; ethnocultural entrepreneur
Troper, Harold, 108
Trudeau, Pierre, 36, 57, 105
Turner, Victor, 102

United Steelworkers, 136–7
urban fieldwork, vii–ix; process of, 8–10, 27

Van Gannep, Arnold, 102
Vecoli, Rudolph J., 149
Veneto Centre, origins of 91–2, 94–6
Ventresca, Gino, 80–81
Villa Charities (ICBC), 52–79 passim; Columbus Centre, 52, 58, 62–4; gifts to projects at, 42–5; funding for, 167; name change, 183n1; Villa Colombo, 58–61, 137
Villa Colombo. *See* Villa Charities
Voce Alternativa, 164–6

Waisberg, Harry, 159
Warner, M., 89
Watson, James, 86
Wieser, Theodor, 85, 160, 164
Werbner, Pnina, 6, 46, 54, 69–70, 94, 97, 107

women: associations of, 33; family economies and, 28–9. *See also* gender
Woodbridge. *See Eyetalian*; neighbourhoods; stereotypes
work: changes in, for Italian Canadians, 160–1; gender and 163–4; and generational views, 161–4; profile of occupations, 24

World Cup, 76–7, 78, 118, 158, 160, 172–3

Yans-McLaughlin, Virginia, 66, 129
Young, Crawford, 104

Znaniecki, F., 31
Zucchi, John, 17, 20, 127, 147